THE BEST
AMERICAN
RECIPES
2003–2004

The Year's Top Picks

from Books, Magazines,

Newspapers, and the Internet

THE BEST AMERICAN RECIPES

2003–2004

Fran McCullough

and

Molly Stevens

SERIES EDITORS

With a foreword by

Alan Richman

Houghton Mifflin Company
Boston   New York
2003

Copyright © 2003 by Houghton Mifflin Company
Introduction copyright © 2003 by Fran McCullough and Molly Stevens
Foreword copyright © 2003 by Alan Richman

For information about permission to reproduce selections from this
book, write to Permissions, Houghton Mifflin Company,
215 Park Avenue South, New York, New York 10003.

Visit our Web site: www.houghtonmifflinbooks.com.

Library of Congress Cataloging-in-Publication Data is available.

ISSN: 1525-1101
ISBN: 0-618-27384-0

Designed by Anne Chalmers
Cover photograph by Beatriz DeCosta: Grilled Shrimp with
Prosciutto, Rosemary, and Garlic (page 142)
Food styling by Anne Disrude
Prop styling by Betty Alfenito

Printed in the United States of America

contents

foreword

I AM BY TRADE A RESTAURANT critic, which means I know how to eat. You can test me. I know a soufflé from a soubise, providing somebody sets them down before me and offers appropriate flatware.

Because of my work, I have accumulated some knowledge of food preparation. I know that cooks wait for pots to boil and quiches to firm. I have read that braising is not done in a brazier, although I have no idea why. I appreciate that French chefs are venerated because they blanch. I have never understood what blanching does, but as far as I can tell it is an essential and expensive step that accounts for the great difference in cost between French and American restaurants.

I almost never cook. Those who do are required to position themselves for hours in front of a stove, a device I have always considered uncomfortably hot. I certainly admire those who cook. I love the sounds that emerge from a French kitchen, the rage that explodes like a neglected pressure cooker. I long to work inside an Italian kitchen, next to a frail grandmother who hand-makes each and every tortellini, hour after hour, year after year, motivated by threats to move her to an assisted living facility if she lets up. I adore the lusty Greeks, forever overcooking their roasts, and our fun-loving Canadian neighbors, whose recipes all have something in common with party dips. Who cannot look in awe upon a Chinese kitchen in a frenzy of stir-frying and wonder how it does not explode in flames from all the peanut oil flying through the air?

Not only do I envy those who cook, I realized after reading this wonderfully accessible book that I might actually become one of them. For the first time, I came upon recipes that are not only comprehensible but also within the realm of possibility. The very first one is for Cheese Snips. I admit I'd never before encountered a foodstuff called a "snip." I always thought snips were small birds that nested in the drainpipes of Tudor houses.

I believe I am perfectly capable of making Cheese Snips, which are based on Rice Krispies, a ready-to-eat foodstuff brought to perfection by the employees of the estimable Kellogg Company of Battle Creek, Michigan. (By the way, there's a recipe farther along for Scotch-a-Roos, which also utilizes Rice Krispies, making this an extraordinarily user-friendly cookbook.) I had the same good feelings about Lorna Wing's Garlicky Potato Chips. She begins the cooking process with a bag of potato chips, which sell for 99 cents a bag at my local food emporium. The recipe promises that guests in your home will fight over these chips, which would be a welcome relief. Usually, when I prepare something, the only person my guests want to pound on is me.

Crabby Cheese Puffs are even easier. The directions call for the cook to melt cheese, well within my capabilities. Even the famous French chef Madeleine Kamman has a pretty simple recipe, and the French love to turn the obvious into the laborious. (That's why we eat Hellmann's and they make their own mayonnaise.) Her French Bread and Shallot Soup, as you can tell, calls for one troublesome ingredient: shallots. This isn't a suburban-level foodstuff. I found them by driving to a town fancier than the one where I live and double-parking outside a specialty shop filled with Mercedes drivers. Most of them had been running around looking for shallots, too.

A few of the recipes are too challenging for me. I'm a little afraid of anchovies, which means Sal Scognamillo's Antipasto Roasted Red Peppers with Anchovies and Bread Crumbs isn't going to come to fruition in my kitchen. I can make my pal Michele Scicolone's Escarole and Little Meatball Soup because it reminds me of the very first dish I ever cooked, a Cub Scout dish called campfire stew. Here's the recipe: make tiny meatballs from ground beef. Drop them into a pot. Add several cans of Campbell's Vegetable Soup. Heat until no longer soupy. Don't laugh. Angela Pontual uses exactly the same simmer-till-thick cooking technique for her Instant

Black Beans. I'll bet she was a Girl Scout back in Brazil.

I'm not one to complain, but I have issues with recipes from two famous chefs, Bobby Flay and Mario Batali. Flay's Roasted Turkey with Herbs includes a suggestion to save the neck and gizzards for future use in preparing stock. Chefs know how to save stuff for stock. Real people don't. When I unexpectedly encounter gizzards, I get them out of my house as quickly as possible. Batali's Pork Chops Milanese requires the cook to pound one-inch pork chops into one-quarter-inch pork chops. If I tried that at home, I'd reduce my kitchen counter to dust. Personally, I leave pounding to the pros.

I genuinely liked Mollie Katzen's recipe for Amazing Overnight Waffles, because, as the editors say, "There's fifteen minutes of work here." The recipe calls for yeast, and I barely know what yeast does, except that in the hands of the right winery it is capable of transforming grapes into Château Latour. Brooke Williamson's Olive Butter is a first-rate recipe because it's really short and the hardest part is chopping parsley. I do not own very good kitchen knives, but the ones I have go right through parsley.

Almost all the dessert recipes are fabulous. A lot of them call for heavy cream, which is one of the world's two foolproof ingredients. The other is butter. The only dessert recipe beyond my capabilities is the Skillet Blueberry Cobbler, which calls for a cast-iron skillet. I'm intimidated by cast iron because it's never supposed to be washed, so I'd be afraid my cobbler would taste like the bacon that was cooked in the pan in 1947. I like to conclude my cooking with Brillo, the only product capable of cleaning up the mess I make.

Allow me to digress. *Saveur* magazine, the source of the recipe for Pasta with Citrus Zest and Cream, made by Giuliano Gargani at his Trattoria Il Garga in Florence, is an admirable publication, but I want credit for discovering this dish. I wrote about Garga's Pasta Magnifico for *GQ* years ago, and this was it. Unfortunately for me, I wasn't clever enough to ask for the recipe, so I'm grateful to *Saveur* for making it a part of recorded culinary history. It isn't like any other pasta you'll ever taste. It doesn't taste Italian. It doesn't taste American. It tastes like a celebration. It's so outrageous you will want to have it as a main course and then you will want to have it again for dessert. Learn to cook it and you will be applauded at your dinner parties for the rest of your days.

If you make every recipe in this book — and I intend to try — by the time you have finished, you will know how to cook. If you read the Cook's Notes at the end of each recipe, you will know more about food preparation than you would if you went to cooking school. (I know, because I once went to cooking school in Lyon, and what I remember is that fish must be wrapped in bacon, a fundamental key to Lyonnaise cooking.) The Cook's Notes are surprisingly accessible. There's one below a recipe from Emily Luchetti, who is a big-time pastry chef, that reads, "Don't be skimpy with the frosting. A good cupcake has plenty of frosting."

You're really going to like this book. Because I am in the business of writing about food, people send me cookbooks every day. I throw out most of these books, knowing that they lead only to humiliation and despair. This one is different. I see myself not far in the future confidently crumbling up Bulgarian feta cheese for David Rosengarten's Shepherd's Salad, and I never even knew Bulgarians made feta cheese until I read it here. I know people are always talking about books they've read that have changed their lives, but those are usually about shaping personal strategies or making life matter again. This cookbook will not only show you the path to happiness, it will ensure that you don't go hungry along the way.

—ALAN RICHMAN

introduction

THIS YEAR WE WERE VERY MUCH taken by surprise when one of our most basic assumptions seemed to have a stake driven through its heart. All at once, around Thanksgiving, America decided it didn't want to cook anymore. From upscale food magazines to newspaper food sections and even news magazines, publications were loaded with bright ideas on how not to cook and get away with it. This 180-degree turnaround goes by several names: faking it, semi-homemade (that's TV cook Sandra Lee), can-opener gourmet. We shuddered at the very idea of giving up cooking for Thanksgiving, which struck us as positively un-American.

But once we thought about it, we concluded that breaking all the rules and making creative use of what's available is a completely American thing to do — at Thanksgiving or any other time of the year. And then we realized that in making the selections for this series, we ourselves have always been devoted to the smart shortcut recipe, not to mention using high-quality convenience foods to speed things along.

Few recipes in this book delight us as much as Garlicky Potato Chips (doctored commercial chips) or Instant Black Beans, a fast take on the Brazilian classic. Quick-cooking grits turn out to be just great in the right hands, much to our amazement. Bobby Flay's no-fuss turkey is a winner, as is Nigella Lawson's nearly instant Bitter Orange Ice Cream (and no, you don't need an ice cream machine). As long as the results are worth it, we're all in favor of the quick fix, and we've got plenty of quick fixes in this book.

In America, there's usually a diametrically opposite trend for everything, and food is no exception. If we don't want Grandma's Thanksgiving anymore, we do want her recipes. This year we were inundated with great hand-me-downs, from aunts and dads as well as grandmothers. Among our favorites are a terrific French creamy chocolate cake, a fabulous spaghettini with tuna and raisins, and a blueberry cobbler that's the best we've ever tasted. These heirloom recipes fall into the category of dishes we can't stop making, an occupational hazard of putting this book together.

Instead of keeping these passions to ourselves, we've decided to share them. We're adding a new category to our list of top ten this year: our own favorite recipes from the book. The fact is, though, whether the source is a tag on a gadget, a radio station's Web site, a chef's cookbook, a food magazine, or a regional newspaper, we love every recipe in this book and will make them all again, our test of something really good. And we think you too will find dozens of doable recipes that you'll return to, some of them so insanely simple that you'll want to share them with your non-cooking friends.

—FRAN MCCULLOUGH
and MOLLY STEVENS

our top ten recipes

BLB'S MINI BLTS (page 14)

The great American classic goes bite-size in these elegant, delectable canapés.

EGGS WITH CRUNCHY BREAD CRUMBS (page 72)

Silky eggs with slightly garlicky bread crumbs — what could be simpler or better for supper as well as breakfast?

CORN BREAD SALAD WITH GRILLED SAUSAGE AND SPICY CHIPOTLE DRESSING (page 68)

Served for supper or as a hearty first course, this bold Latin-flavored salad of grilled sausage, toasted corn bread, tomato, avocado, and fiery dressing is a runaway winner.

TORTILLA SOUP WITH CHICKEN AND AVOCADO (page 36)

A starter or a light meal, this easy-to-assemble soup gets great flavor and texture from a combination of a restorative chili-flavored chicken broth and crisp tortilla strips.

MUSSELS WITH SMOKY BACON, LIME, AND CILANTRO (page 148)

The best thing to happen to mussels in a long time. They're spicy, smoky, limey, buttery, and so tasty that you may never want to eat these shellfish any other way ever again.

SPAGHETTINI WITH TUNA SAUCE (page 92)

Everything you need to make this knockout savory-sweet-hot pasta is probably already in your kitchen. If not, it soon will be, because we guarantee this recipe is going to be a favorite.

GREENS WITH GARLICKY TOASTED BREAD CRUMBS (page 160)

Italians always have great ideas about cooking greens, but this one is new (to us) and so satisfying that it regularly turns up on our table.

BUTTERMILK SCONES (page 82)

Every time we serve these, someone demands the recipe. One longtime owner of a bed-and-breakfast says they beat any she's tasted.

LEMON POSSET (page 218)

Dress it up with raspberries and mint or eat it plain, this made-in-moments, mousselike dessert tastes ethereal. It's hard to imagine that something so elegant could be made from just lemons, cream, and sugar.

STICKY TOFFEE PUDDING (page 228)

A gooey, dense, coffee-flavored cake studded with chocolate chunks and oozing with buttery caramel sauce — what's not to love?

the year in food

TREND OF THE YEAR
Retro Food, Definitely

For several years now, we've been in the grip of comfort food, but this year it goes even further, all the way back to diner food and kitsch food from the Fifties. Eagle-eyed readers will notice that there are two recipes in this book featuring Rice Krispies, one to begin and one to end the meal. We love them both for their airy crunch.

VEGETABLE OF THE YEAR
Pumpkin

This big, fat, cheery vegetable stole the hearts of chefs this year — and everyone else too. Pumpkin works in both sweet and savory dishes. Check out the Southwestern Pumpkin Chowder and the Slow-Rising Pumpkin-Thyme Dinner Rolls. Our favorite is Martin Sheen's Favorite Cheesecake, the trademark dessert of the Sheen family, made with canned pumpkin.

TECHNIQUE OF THE YEAR
Slow Food

Besides being a way of cooking, this is an official movement that began in Italy to protect regionally diverse food. Slow food recently found a warm welcome in America; in fact, the society already has over 10,000 members. For depth of flavor, you can't beat slow-cooked food, such as the superb Roasted Fresh Ham with Salsa Verde, from Corby Kummer's *The Pleasures of Slow Food*.

INGREDIENT OF THE YEAR
Bacon

This year it's all but hanging from the sky in big strips, bringing its special flavor to fish stew, mussels, and even breakfast bread pudding. Bacon even got its own book this year, Sara Perry's *Everything Tastes Better with Bacon*. (She's right.)

TOOL OF THE YEAR
Oxo Angled Liquid Measuring Cup

We think this dishwasher-safe measuring cup belongs in everyone's kitchen. Careful cooks learned a long time ago that liquid ingredients are measured in a glass cup with a spout and dry ones in graduated metal or plastic measuring cups. This new plastic measuring cup for liquids has an ingenious marker built right into it (with metric measurements on one side), so you can measure accurately just by looking down from above, with no hoisting, squinting, or bending.

DRINK OF THE YEAR
Bourbon

It's about time we acquired a proper appreciation of our superlative native spirit. Warming, smoky bourbon is not only great to sip on its own, it has a magical effect on food. It's the secret ingredient in Regina Schrambling's terrific Bourbon Pecans, a holiday classic if we've ever seen one.

FRUIT OF THE YEAR
Kumquats

These little charmers turn up in everything from cranberry sauce to grilled kebabs. Once we had them in the kitchen, we started slicing them into salads and just eating them out of hand. Right behind kumquats in the lineup are plain old oranges, including their flesh, juice, and zest; their sweet freshness suddenly seems new and interesting. Nipping at citrus's heels is coconut, which appears in all kinds of recipes and in several forms, from coconut milk to freshly grated.

NUT OF THE YEAR
All of Them

This year it's all nuts, all the time: pistachios, pecans, cashews, walnuts, hazelnuts. Nuts also clambered onto the "good-for-you" list, getting a big boost from health-conscious cooks.

BACKLASH OF THE YEAR
Poor Food

After a long decade of luxurious treats, everything from caviar to lobster to Champagne, there's a new interest in frugal cooking (timely, given the state of the economy). Stale bread is the star of terrific dishes like Eggs with Crunchy Bread Crumbs or Greens with Garlicky Toasted Bread Crumbs. Eggs themselves have a new appeal, and they're just as likely to be served for dinner as for breakfast. Even leftover rice is to be wished for, since you can transform it into the lovely Minted Fried Rice or Chili Shrimp and Coconut Rice.

EXOTIC CUISINE OF THE YEAR
British

For several years now, we've watched breezy Brits such as Jamie Oliver, Nigella Lawson, Nigel Slater, and Delia Smith cook their way into our living rooms, so it seems entirely natural that classic English food should get some of the much-deserved limelight too. We're especially pleased to have that most brilliant British invention of all — gin and tonic — in a new, intensely limey version we find irresistible.

starters

Cheese Snips 2

Garlicky Potato Chips 4

Curried Chili Cashews 6

Bourbon Pecans 8

Olive Butter 9

Chopped Olive Spread 10

Salsa-Baked Goat Cheese 11

Crabby Cheese Puffs 12

BLB's Mini BLTs 14

Smoked Salmon Rolls with Arugula,
Mascarpone, Chives, and Capers 16

Antipasto Roasted Red Peppers
with Anchovies and Bread Crumbs 18

Italian Leek Tart (Porrata) 20

Seared Scallops with Crème Fraîche and Caviar 22

SOURCE: *Potluck at Midnight Farm* by Tamara Weiss
COOK: Nina Bramhall

cheese snips

THAT BREAKFAST CEREAL WITH THE SNAP, crackle, and pop makes these so interesting. They crunch and crumble deliciously, and they're also hot-hot-hot. We found them in a cookbook devoted to potlucks, food events that turn a neighborhood into a community — in this case, Martha's Vineyard.

Like all good breakfast cereal–based recipes, the snips go together in a flash in the food processor (though they're in the oven for 2 hours) and are made from kitchen staples, which is another big part of their appeal.

serves 16

16 tablespoons (2 sticks) unsalted butter, at room temperature

8 ounces sharp white cheddar cheese, grated

2 cups all-purpose flour

2 cups Rice Krispies

1 tablespoon Tabasco sauce (or less to taste; see note)

1 teaspoon cayenne pepper (or less)

1/2 teaspoon salt, or to taste

Preheat the oven to 325 degrees. Pulse the butter and cheese in a food processor until well combined. Add the flour and Rice Krispies and pulse again until well combined. Add the Tabasco, cayenne, and salt and pulse to blend.

Drop the dough by teaspoons onto an ungreased baking sheet. If you want, you can leave them as is, or flatten them with your hand for smoother snips. Bake the snips for 15 minutes (see note).

Turn off the oven and leave them in the oven for at least 2 hours and up to overnight to crisp them before serving.

cook's notes

- Although we think of ourselves as chile heads, we suggest starting out with half the heat listed — you can add more next time if these are too tame.

- The snips don't actually get brown; it may take them a little longer than 15 minutes to turn golden.

- Freeze leftover dough in a roll wrapped in plastic wrap — just thaw, slice, and bake when you're ready for another batch.

SOURCE: Renee Schettler in the *Washington Post*
COOK: Lorna Wing

garlicky potato chips

WE WERE READING AN ARTICLE about flavored butters when suddenly this idea for using garlic butter leaped out at us: hot potato chips with garlic butter! Potato chips seem to be in no need of enrichment, but on the other hand, we had to try them. So far, they've been the hit of every party where they've been served, sometimes so much so that eager fans end up fighting over them.

Even if you don't want to put it on the potato chips, the garlic butter is the best we've ever tasted. It's a two-step (but very easy) process. You mellow the garlic first in a little butter, then whip it into a fluffy mound. Put it on bread, pasta, vegetables, or even on steak (see tip).

serves about 10

4 tablespoons ($^1/_2$ stick) butter
4–7 teaspoons minced garlic

10-ounce bag potato chips, preferably thick-cut
Salt and freshly ground black pepper, to taste

Preheat the oven to 350 degrees. Melt the butter in a small skillet over medium heat. Add the garlic and cook, stirring frequently, just until it has softened but not browned, about 5 minutes.

Gently toss the garlic butter with the potato chips in a large bowl, coating each chip as best you can. Add salt — be careful, many chips are quite salty already — and pepper and toss again.

Arrange the chips in a single layer on a baking sheet. Bake until fragrant and golden, 4 to 7 minutes. Serve hot.

cook's notes

- You can make the garlic butter and toss it with the chips several hours ahead of serving; just bake and serve at the last minute.
- You can add spices: chili powder comes immediately to mind.

tips

- To make Lorna Wing's excellent garlic butter for bread, pasta, vegetables, or steak, soften the butter and whip it until fluffy. Melt an additional tablespoon of butter in the skillet for cooking the garlic. When the garlic is softened, remove the skillet from the heat and cool slightly. Mix the garlic mixture into the whipped butter and add salt and pepper to taste.
- Another over-the-top addition to hot potato chips: crumble Gorgonzola cheese over chips (ridged ones are best) and bake at 350 degrees for about 5 minutes, or until the cheese is melted. (From *Italian Comfort Food*, by the Scotto family.)

SOURCE: *Party Nuts!* by Sally Sampson
COOK: Sally Sampson

curried chili cashews

REMEMBER BEER NUTS? Crunchy, salty, sweet, and a bit spicy, they strengthen the thirst and forestall the appetite. These mildly spicy nuts do that too, but are a whole lot dressier — and better tasting. Serve them in a pretty bowl with drinks when guests come to dinner, or nibble on them in front of the TV. We also like to give them as gifts, since they keep so well.

As an accompaniment, offer small glasses of oloroso sherry or ice-cold India pale ale.

makes 4 cups

1 large egg white
1 teaspoon frozen orange juice
    concentrate
4 cups raw cashews
1/4 cup sugar

1 teaspoon kosher salt
1 teaspoon chili powder
1/2 teaspoon ground cinnamon
1/2 teaspoon curry powder

Preheat the oven to 225 degrees. Line a baking sheet with parchment paper. Whip the egg white in a large stainless steel bowl until it forms stiff peaks. Add the orange juice concentrate and whip again. Add the cashews and toss until well coated. Add the sugar, salt, and spices and toss until all the nuts are well coated.

Spread the nuts in a single layer on the prepared baking sheet. Bake, stirring every 10 minutes, until browned, 40 to 50 minutes.

Remove from the oven, immediately loosen the nuts with a metal spatula, and set aside to cool for at least 1 hour, preferably overnight, before serving.

cook's notes

❧ Be sure the mixing bowl is very clean. Any oily residue will make it impossible to whip the egg white.

❧ It's easiest to measure and mix the orange juice concentrate if you let it sit at room temperature a bit to soften.

❧ Find raw cashews in the bulk section at the grocery store or health food market.

❧ If you like things spicier, go ahead and up the ante with another shake of curry or chili powder or even a pinch of cayenne.

❧ The full flavor of the spices doesn't really come through until the cashews have cooled completely — at least an hour and preferably overnight. For longer storage, which is rarely an issue for us, keep them in an airtight tin.

SOURCE: *Los Angeles Times*
COOK: **Regina Schrambling**

bourbon pecans

THESE NUTS NEVER STAY AROUND FOR LONG. The bourbon-bitters-Worcestershire combo gives them a complex, mysterious flavor, so that you find yourself tasting one after another to figure out what's going on. Blanching the pecans in boiling water is an old Chinese trick that makes them especially crisp.

Although the nuts are not limited to any particular season and are a great prelude to a barbecue, they seem especially right for the holidays. They're even good after dinner, with a little Wild Turkey.

makes about 4 1/2 cups

1/2 cup top-quality bourbon
1 pound pecan halves
1 tablespoon corn oil
1 tablespoon Worcestershire sauce
1/2 teaspoon angostura bitters
1/2 cup sugar

1 teaspoon ground cumin
1/2 teaspoon cayenne pepper, or more to taste
1/2 teaspoon salt
1/4 teaspoon freshly ground black pepper

Preheat the oven to 325 degrees. Simmer the bourbon in a small saucepan over medium heat until it's reduced by a quarter, just a few minutes. Blanch the pecans in boiling water for 1 minute, then drain.

Combine the bourbon, oil, Worcestershire, bitters, and sugar in a large bowl. Add the hot pecans and toss. Let stand for 10 minutes.

Spread the pecans in a single layer on a large baking sheet. Bake until the nuts are crisp and the liquid has evaporated, 30 to 40 minutes, stirring every 10 minutes. Turn the nuts into a clean large bowl.

Combine the cumin, cayenne, salt, and pepper in a small bowl. Toss with the nuts and serve.

cook's note

By top-quality bourbon, we mean the cook should be guided by personal taste. That could be Maker's Mark (which we used) or pricey Knob Creek — or it could be good, cheap Rebel Yell.

SOURCE: *Saveur*
COOK: **Brooke Williamson**

olive butter

COMPOUND, OR FLAVORED, butters have always been the rage with chefs, and home cooks can make great use of them too. This olive butter is our favorite of the year. It's full of kalamata olives and has a touch of garlic. At Zax, a restaurant in Brentwood, California, it arrives at the table before dinner, along with a crusty baguette.

makes 1 1/2 cups

16 tablespoons (2 sticks) unsalted butter, softened

1/2 cup chopped pitted kalamata olives

Chopped leaves from 2 fresh parsley sprigs

1 garlic clove, minced

Coarse salt, to taste

Beat the butter in a medium bowl with a wooden spoon until smooth. Add the olives, parsley, and garlic and mix well. Season to taste with salt. Serve at room temperature.

cook's notes

- The flavored butter will keep for several days, tightly covered, in the refrigerator.
- Leftovers can be smeared over a grilled lamb chop or stirred into warm rice.

SOURCE: *The Jimtown Store Cookbook* by Carrie Brown, John Werner, and Michael McLaughlin
COOKS: Carrie Brown and John Werner

chopped olive spread

THE JIMTOWN STORE IS A DESTINATION MARKET FOR SONOMA food and wine mavens. Its most famous product is this amazing olive spread (called Chopped Olive Salad at the store). It's very wine-friendly, not to mention food-friendly, and it can be used in any number of ways (see note).

For about 3 minutes of actual work time, you get a superb condiment that will keep for days and make your guests very happy indeed. It's hard to imagine a more useful party trick.

makes 3 cups

12 ounces (3 cups) pimiento-stuffed green olives, halved if large

8 ounces (2 cups) pitted kalamata olives

1/4 cup drained capers

1 tablespoon finely chopped fresh oregano

4 oil-packed anchovy fillets, chopped (optional, but see note)

2 garlic cloves, smashed with the blade of a knife and finely chopped

1/4 teaspoon crushed red pepper flakes

3 tablespoons extra-virgin olive oil

1 teaspoon fresh lemon juice

Combine all the ingredients in a food processor and process with short pulses until evenly chopped. Do not overprocess — some texture should remain. Adjust the seasoning and serve.

cook's notes

❧ The spread is salty; if you'd like it less so, rinse the capers and anchovies well before using.

❧ We think the anchovies make a big difference here, so be sure to use them.

❧ You can refrigerate this spread for up to 10 days or freeze it for up to 2 months. Return almost to room temperature before using.

❧ Olive spread is great on sandwiches, especially Brie or goat cheese sandwiches; it's also delicious on crostini spread with goat cheese. It's a good secret ingredient in marinades, vinaigrettes, and pasta dressings.

SOURCE: *El Mundo de Frontera* newsletter
COOK: Rick Bayless

salsa-baked goat cheese

HERE'S A GREAT NEW IDEA for Super Bowl Sunday, from the newsletter of Chicago's terrific Mexican restaurant twins, Frontera Grill and Topolobampo. This spread/dip fulfills all possible requirements: it's quick, it's easy, it's delectable, you eat it with tortilla chips, and it goes with guacamole — and beer or margaritas or whatever else you're serving. It's one of those vanishing dishes — no leftovers.

It's not just a snack, though; it works very well as a first course to serve with drinks. The chips can be Frontera's new flavored chips, available at gourmet markets, or pita crisps, or just crisp toasts. You can spread it or dip it, as you like.

serves 4 to 6

$^{1}/_{4}$ cup pine nuts or coarsely chopped walnuts or pecans

1 3-ounce package cream cheese, softened

1 4-ounce log plain goat cheese (or you can just use more cream cheese)

1 cup salsa, such as Topolo Classic Salsa Veracruzana

1 tablespoon chopped fresh cilantro, for garnish

Tortilla chips or pita crisps, for serving

Preheat the oven to 350 degrees. Spread the nuts on a baking sheet and toast them in the oven until lightly browned and very fragrant, 7 to 8 minutes. Transfer to a medium bowl.

Add the cheeses to the bowl and combine thoroughly with the nuts. Scoop the cheese mixture into the center of a baking dish, such a decorative 9-inch pie plate, and form into a 5-inch disk. Spoon the salsa over and around the cheese.

Bake until heated through, 10 to 15 minutes. Sprinkle with the cilantro and serve as a dip or a spread with tortilla chips or pita crisps.

cook's notes

 If the salsa is very chunky, you might want to strain it or chop it in a food processor so the pieces won't fall off the chips.

 We like to heat the chips too — just a few minutes in the hot oven.

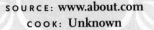

SOURCE: www.about.com
COOK: Unknown

crabby cheese puffs

ALL WE HAD TO HEAR WAS HOT CRAB, cheese, and pastry puffs, and we had to taste these rich little morsels. They're made with beer instead of water — the beer adds to the flavor and to the rise in the oven. After the puffs cool, the centers are filled with a mix of crabmeat and grated cheese, then heated until the cheese melts. They make the perfect mouthful with a cocktail, a glass of wine, or even a beer.

Besides being elegant and fun, these puffs can be made ahead. They're good for potlucks, since they travel well when filled but not yet baked. Just pop them into the oven before serving to melt the cheese.

makes 3 to 4 dozen

PUFFS

1 cup beer (preferably lager)
8 tablespoons (1 stick) butter, cut into pieces
1/2 teaspoon salt
1 cup all-purpose flour
4 large eggs

FILLING

1 cup fresh or pasteurized fresh crabmeat (see note)
1 cup grated cheddar cheese

Preheat the oven to 450 degrees. Grease two baking sheets.

TO MAKE THE PUFFS

Heat the beer, butter, and salt in a large saucepan over medium heat. As soon as the butter melts and the liquid boils, add the flour all at once and beat with a wooden spoon until the mixture forms a smooth ball. Remove from the heat and add the eggs 1 at a time, beating until smooth between each addition.

Drop the mixture by spoonfuls (a tablespoon works well) onto the prepared baking sheets. Bake for 10 minutes, then reduce the oven temperature to 350 degrees and bake for 5 to 10 minutes more, or until puffed and lightly browned. Let cool.

TO MAKE THE FILLING

Toss together the crabmeat and cheese in a medium bowl.

TO ASSEMBLE

Slice the top off each puff. Gently pull the moist dough out of the center and discard. Fill each puff with a generous portion of the crab mixture. If the tops are still intact, set them on top of the filling. (The puffs are fine topless, too.) Bake until the cheese has melted, 5 to 10 minutes. Serve immediately.

cook's notes

- A 6-ounce tub of fresh crabmeat will give you the 1 cup you need for this recipe. Be sure to pick over the crabmeat for any bits of shell or cartilage.
- The recipe calls for cheddar, but we like a mix of Swiss and cheddar just as much.
- Be sure not to let the beer mixture boil for too long, or you'll throw off the proportions of the recipe. As soon as the butter melts and the beer boils, proceed.
- If you make the (unfilled) puffs ahead, keep them at room temperature in an airtight container for up to 1 day. Once they're filled, they can sit for a few hours in the refrigerator before baking.

SOURCE: Jeffrey Steingarten
COOK: Bonnie Lee Black

blb's mini blts

THE STORY OF THIS RECIPE IS A TALE OF OBSESSION. We read a review of Jeffrey Steingarten's book at the hairdresser's and were immediately entranced with the idea of tiny BLT canapés, over which the reviewer waxed rhapsodic. We raced to the bookstore, eagerly looking for the recipe, but no such recipe was to be found.

As it turned out, the entire chapter containing this staggeringly wonderful recipe had been cut from the book at the last moment, after the review appeared. But Steingarten kindly provided the goods, and here they are.

He first tasted them at a party where Bonnie Lee Black, a Manhattan caterer, appeared, canapés in hand, just before leaving to join the Peace Corps in Gabon. They were quickly devoured, many of them by Steingarten, who managed to get the recipe days before the cook disappeared into West Africa. Steingarten says it best: "With every bite and every chew, you have the sensation of consuming the most ideal and epiphanic bacon, lettuce, and tomato sandwich you have ever tasted!" Just so.

makes 64 canapés

16 slices Pepperidge Farm or Arnold white sandwich bread
1/2 head iceberg lettuce
1 pound sliced bacon
1 1/4 pounds ripe yet firm tomatoes (about 3-inch-wide tomatoes)

3–4 tablespoons Hellmann's (or, in western states, Best Foods) Real Mayonnaise
Salt and freshly ground black pepper

Preheat the oven to 450 degrees. With a rolling pin, flatten each slice of bread to cardboard thinness. Cut 4 rounds from each slice of bread with a 2-inch cookie cutter. Press the rounds into mini-muffin pans to form shallow cups and bake until colored, about 6 minutes. (If you have no mini-muffin pans, just bake the circles of bread on a baking sheet.) Cool for 1 to 2 minutes, then invert onto a rack. Let cool to room temperature. These can be stored in an airtight container for several days. Their texture should remind you of toast: crisp yet slightly soft on the inside, without being tough or brittle.

Choose the largest and most perfect lettuce leaves. Cut out the toughest ribs and cut the leaves into strips $3/4$ inch wide. Piling up a few strips at a time, cut them crosswise into fine shreds about $1/16$ inch wide. Stop when you have $1^1/4$ cups.

Fry the bacon until very crisp and drain; crumble it into pieces the size of peppercorns. Core the tomatoes, squeeze out the seeds and juice, and cut the flesh into $1/8$-inch cubes. You should have $1^1/4$ cups.

Combine the bacon, lettuce, and tomato cubes in a large bowl. Stir in 3 tablespoons mayonnaise, adding a little more if needed to bind the mixture; too much makes the filling soggy and unbalances the tastes. Season with salt and 8 to 12 turns of the pepper mill. Fill each bread cup with a generous teaspoon of the BLT mixture and serve immediately.

cook's notes

- Pepperidge Farm makes a white toasting bread, which is *not* what you want for this recipe — it's much too thick.
- You'll need mini-muffin pans to make these into cupped canapés, but you can also make flat ones — they'll still taste great but they won't look as pretty.
- Cherry tomatoes are great in this recipe, and definitely extend the season for these delicious morsels.
- Although this recipe seems like simplicity itself, its success depends on finesse: cut the tomatoes really finely, don't upgrade the lettuce to romaine or you'll lose the crunch, and be very careful not to add too much mayo.

SOURCE: *In the Hands of a Chef*
by Jody Adams and Ken Rivard
COOK: Jody Adams

smoked salmon rolls with arugula, mascarpone, chives, and capers

THIS IS ONE OF THOSE DIVINE COMBINATIONS that Adams, a prominent Boston chef, credits to Peck, the Milanese gourmet emporium. It was at Peck that Adams saw a display of torta cheeses. One of them, featuring stripes of mascarpone and smoked salmon, struck her as an inspired idea. Indeed it is. The sweet, fresh, rich mascarpone doesn't take over the delicacy of smoked salmon the way other cheeses do; it's the perfect partner. Adams has contributed a few other key flavor elements: capers, lemon, and chives are classic, but the arugula is a nice, biting contrast.

The smoked salmon rolls can be charming little hors d'oeuvres or a more substantial appetizer, with several rolls placed over an arugula salad. We think this makes a pretty great breakfast or lunch too.

serves 6 as an appetizer, 12 as an hors d'oeuvre

5 ounces mascarpone (about $^2/_3$ cup)

2 tablespoons capers, rinsed and drained

2 tablespoons minced fresh chives

1 teaspoon fresh lemon juice

Kosher salt and freshly ground black pepper, to taste

$^3/_4$ pound smoked salmon, cut into 24 thin slices, 2–3 inches on the short side (presliced salmon is fine)

48 small, tender arugula leaves

Mix the mascarpone with 1 tablespoon of the capers, 1 tablespoon of the chives, and the lemon juice in a small bowl. Season with salt and pepper.

Lay the salmon slices out on a cutting board with one of their short sides facing you, with plenty of space above and below each slice. (You can do this in batches.)

Put a spoonful of the mascarpone mixture on the narrow end of a slice. Lay 2 arugula leaves, fanned slightly, across the mascarpone, so that the leaves will extend several inches from one end of the roll. Roll up the salmon slice and stand it upright, leaves pointed up, on a serving platter. Repeat with the remaining slices. Cover with plastic wrap and refrigerate until ready to serve.

Remove from the refrigerator, sprinkle with the remaining 1 tablespoon chives and 1 tablespoon capers, and serve.

cook's notes

- Presliced smoked salmon doesn't always neatly fall into slices that can be cut for the rolls. Sometimes it's very raggedy. In that case, just spread the salmon slices thinly with the mascarpone mixture (chop the capers before you mix them in), roll, and trim them into shapes you can spear with a toothpick. Serve on a bed of baby arugula.
- We beg you to make these with Jeremiah Tower's marinated capers (chop them first) on page 52 — sensational!

SOURCE: *Patsy's Cookbook* by Sal J. Scognamillo
COOK: Sal J. Scognamillo

antipasto roasted red peppers with anchovies and bread crumbs

SURE, STRIPS OF ROASTED RED PEPPERS make a great addition to any antipasto platter, but when you gussy them up and give them a quick pass under the broiler, they come out altogether special and irresistible. If you have anchovy haters in the house, don't even tell them what the ingredients are. They won't guess; they'll just love the piquancy of these peppers.

This colorful dish can be set out as an antipasto or served as a first course or even as a side dish with a roast or chops. We like to make extra, since leftovers are great on sandwiches, with eggs, on salads, or just as snacks.

serves 4 to 6

$1/4$ cup olive oil, plus 2 tablespoons for drizzling

4 garlic cloves, minced

4 roasted red bell peppers, peeled and seeded, each cut into 4–6 pieces (see note)

3 tablespoons chopped pitted gaeta or kalamata olives (about 18 olives)

2 tablespoons capers, rinsed and drained

2 tablespoons chopped fresh basil

1 tablespoon chopped oil-packed anchovies

Pinch of dried oregano

$1/3$ cup chicken stock or water

$1/4$ cup dry white wine

Salt and freshly ground black pepper

$1/4$ cup homemade seasoned bread crumbs (see note)

Preheat the broiler. Heat the $1/4$ cup oil in a large ovenproof skillet over medium heat. Add the garlic and sauté until golden, about 1 minute. Add the roasted peppers and sauté for 2 minutes. Add the olives, capers, basil, anchovies, oregano, stock or water, and wine and cook, stirring occasionally, until heated through, 3 to 4 minutes. Add salt and pepper to taste.

Sprinkle the bread crumbs over the pepper mixture and drizzle with the remaining 2 tablespoons oil. Broil for 2 to 3 minutes, or until lightly browned. Serve warm or at room temperature.

cook's notes

🌿 Roast the peppers on the racks of stovetop gas burners over high heat, turning with tongs, until the skins are blackened, 10 to 12 minutes. Or broil the peppers on a broiler pan about 5 inches from the heat, turning occasionally, about 15 minutes. Transfer to a bowl, cover tightly with plastic wrap, and let stand for 20 minutes. When cool enough to handle, peel the peppers, discarding the stems and seeds.

🌿 We've made this dish with plain bread crumbs and it's equally good, just as long as you use homemade bread crumbs and not the superfine, superdry ones that come in a can. Here's how to make seasoned bread crumbs alla Patsy's: for 1 cup of bread crumbs, mix in 2 tablespoons grated Parmigiano-Reggiano, $1/4$ cup minced parsley, a pinch of oregano, 1 minced garlic clove, 3 tablespoons olive oil, and salt and pepper to taste.

tip

Blend good-quality feta cheese with sautéed red peppers for an easy and tasty dip, called *ktipiti* in Greek. Remove the seeds and membranes from 1 red bell pepper and 2 hot red peppers. Cut all the peppers into strips and sauté them in 3 tablespoons olive oil over medium heat until softened, 10 to 15 minutes. Let cool slightly. Scrape the peppers into a food processor along with any oil left in the pan. Add 1 pound crumbled feta and 3 to 4 tablespoons yogurt and process until smooth. Add more yogurt as needed to achieve the right consistency. Cover and chill until ready to serve. Makes about 2 cups. (From *Modern Greek* by Andy Harris.)

SOURCE: James Beard Foundation calendar
COOK: Cesare Casella

italian leek tart (porrata)

THIS HANDSOME TART COMES FROM CESARE CASELLA, the chef-owner of Beppe restaurant in New York City, who specializes in Tuscan farmhouse cooking. It's not a quiche, despite its eggs and milk. It's more of a cross between a quiche and a rustic leek pie. There's just enough custard to hold together the chopped pancetta, the soft-cooked leeks, and the small bit of cheese.

Chef Casella serves it as a first course, which is how we first encountered it. We have since learned to love it for lunch or a light supper. While it's best served soon after baking, it holds well and makes a fine room-temperature addition to a buffet table.

serves 6

1 9-inch all-butter piecrust, unbaked (see note)
1/4 cup extra-virgin olive oil
2 pounds leeks, white parts only, washed well and thinly sliced crosswise
Salt and freshly ground black pepper

3 large eggs
1 cup milk
2 tablespoons freshly grated Pecorino Romano cheese
2 tablespoons freshly grated Parmigiano-Reggiano cheese
3 1/2 ounces pancetta, finely chopped

Preheat the oven to 375 degrees. Line a 9-inch pie plate with the piecrust. Prick the bottom, cover with aluminum foil, fill with pie weights or dried beans, and bake until the dough has set, 8 to 10 minutes. Remove the foil and the weights and bake until light golden brown, 5 to 7 minutes more. Set aside to cool. Turn the oven down to 350 degrees.

Heat the olive oil in a large skillet over medium-high heat. Add the leeks, season with salt and pepper, and cook until soft, about 8 minutes. Remove from the heat and cool.

Beat together the eggs, milk, and cheeses in a medium bowl. Stir in the cooled leeks. Sprinkle the chopped pancetta on the bottom of the baked piecrust. Pour in the leek mixture. Bake until the filling is set, nicely browned, and slightly risen, about 1 hour. Let the tart sit for 15 minutes before serving (the center will sink).

cook's notes

❧ To make a butter piecrust, combine 1 cup all-purpose flour and a pinch of salt in a medium bowl. Add 1 stick of cold unsalted butter, divided into ½-inch cubes, and cut in with a pastry cutter, two knives, or your fingers until the butter is in pea-sized lumps. Sprinkle 2 to 3 tablespoons icewater over the flour, mix with a fork, and gather into a ball. Wrap in plastic and let rest for at least 30 minutes. Roll out on a lightly floured surface into a 12-inch round.

❧ Be sure to use a 9-inch pie pan and not a shallower straight-sided tart pan. If you want a flatter tart, you'll have to go to a 10-inch tart pan to accommodate the filling.

❧ For the best flavor, grate the cheeses yourself right before using.

SOURCE: Bellwether Farms crème fraîche package
COOK: Cynthia Callahan

seared scallops
with crème fraîche and caviar

HERE'S A LUXURIOUS APPETIZER FOR AN OCCASION when you want to pull out all the stops but don't feel like working too hard: luscious sea scallops, lightly seared and topped with a dollop of crème fraîche and a bit of caviar.

Don't substitute sour cream for the crème fraîche. Its richness works perfectly with the other elements. And since it's such a tiny amount of caviar, we recommend going for the good stuff.

makes 24

- 1 teaspoon vegetable oil
- 12 large sea scallops, each cut horizontally into 2 rounds
  Salt and freshly ground black pepper
- 1/4 cup crème fraîche
- 1/2 ounce caviar
- 4 fresh chives, cut into 1-inch lengths

Heat the oil in a large nonstick skillet over medium-high heat. Season the scallop halves with salt and pepper. Cook the scallops until golden on the bottom, about 2 minutes. Turn and sauté until just cooked through, about 1 minute more. Drain on paper towels. Let cool to room temperature.

Top each scallop with 1/2 teaspoon crème fraîche. Divide the caviar evenly among the scallops. Garnish each with a piece of chive and serve.

cook's notes

- Ask for "dry" sea scallops at the market for the best taste and texture. "Wet" scallops have been soaked in a sodium solution that compromises their quality.
- Remove and discard the rubbery little side muscles that you often find still attached to the scallops.
- If you have a 12-inch nonstick skillet, 24 scallop halves should all fit at once. Otherwise, you'll have to sear them in batches.
- The scallops may be seared up to 3 hours ahead and kept on a plate in the refrigerator until you need them. Bring to room temperature before assembling the canapés.

soups

Escarole and Little Meatball Soup (Minestra) 24

Garlic Soup with Ham and Sage Butter 26

Elwood's Ham Chowder 27

Pumpkin Chowder 28

Lentil and Swiss Chard Soup 30

Broccoli-Leek Soup with Lemon-Chive Cream 32

Quick Asian Noodle Soup with Lemongrass and Mushrooms 34

Tortilla Soup with Chicken and Avocado 36

French Bread and Shallot Soup 39

Cream of Grilled Tomato Soup 40

Tomato-Bread Soup (Pappa al Pomodoro) 42

Blender Gazpacho 44

Lime-Cucumber Soup with a Kick 46

SOURCE: *The Sopranos Family Cookbook*
by Allen Rucker and Michele Scicolone
COOK: Michele Scicolone

escarole and little meatball soup (minestra)

YOU JUST KNOW THE SOPRANO FAMILY IS EATING the kind of Italian food that's getting harder and harder to find in our increasingly upscale Italian restaurants. This dish has that real-thing feeling; surely this is someone's grandmother's famous soup recipe.

The soup is delicate but filling at the same time, with its pasta and baby meatballs. Unless you have Soprano-size appetites, this is a main-dish soup. We've cut the recipe in half so it will fit in your soup pot.

serves 6

½ head escarole (about ½ pound)

1½ large carrots, chopped

12 cups chicken stock, preferably homemade

MEATBALLS

½ pound ground veal or beef

½ cup plain bread crumbs

½ cup freshly grated Parmigiano-Reggiano cheese

¼ cup very finely minced onion

1 large egg

½ teaspoon salt

Freshly ground pepper, to taste

4 ounces ditalini or tubetti, or spaghetti broken into bite-size pieces

Freshly grated Parmigiano-Reggiano cheese

Trim the escarole and discard any bruised leaves. Cut off the stem ends. Separate the leaves and wash well in cool water, especially the center of the leaves where soil collects. Stack the leaves and cut them crosswise into 1-inch strips. You should have about 4 cups.

Combine the escarole, carrots, and stock in a large pot. Bring to a simmer and cook until the escarole is almost tender, about 30 minutes.

TO MAKE THE MEATBALLS

Meanwhile, combine the ground meat, bread crumbs, cheese, onion, egg, salt, and pepper in a medium bowl. Shape the mixture into tiny balls, less than 1 inch in diameter.

TO ASSEMBLE

When the escarole is almost tender, stir in the pasta and return the soup to the simmer. Drop the meatballs into the soup. Cook over low heat, stirring gently, until the meatballs and pasta are cooked, about 20 minutes. Taste for seasoning. Serve hot with grated Parmigiano-Reggiano.

cook's notes

- If you can't find escarole, use chard with a little radicchio to contribute the same element of slight bitterness.
- Try hard to find one of the first two pasta suggestions; broken spaghetti isn't the pasta of choice here.

tip

Don't toss out the rind from the chunk of Parmigiano-Reggiano. Instead, collect spent rinds in a zip-top plastic bag in the refrigerator or freezer. The next time you make an Italian stew or soup, add the rinds; they'll thicken the stew as it cooks, and once they soften, they're very tasty.

SOURCE: *Between Bites* by James Villas
COOK: Jeremiah Tower

garlic soup with ham and sage butter

FOR SOME REASON, GARLIC SOUPS ABOUNDED this year, and we tried several before we discovered this knockout. It has a deep garlic flavor and a satiny quality. We especially like the ham-sage butter that's swirled into the soup just before serving. Country ham is best, but prosciutto is fine.

serves 6

- 15 garlic cloves, unpeeled (see note)
- 3 cups chicken stock
- 1/4 cup diced cured country ham or prosciutto
- 5 fresh sage leaves

- 3 tablespoons butter, at room temperature
- Salt and freshly ground black pepper, to taste
- 1/2 cup heavy cream
- 3 large egg yolks

Combine the garlic cloves and stock in a large, heavy saucepan and simmer over low heat until the garlic is soft, about 30 minutes. Let the mixture cool slightly, then puree it, using the fine-mesh disk of a food mill or a food processor. Press the mixture through a sieve back into the saucepan and set aside.

Meanwhile, chop the ham and sage together very finely and place in a bowl. Add the butter and salt and pepper and mix until well blended. Set aside.

Whisk together the cream and egg yolks in a small bowl. Set aside.

Bring the garlic soup to a boil. Remove it from the heat and gradually whisk in the cream mixture until the soup is thickened slightly. (If the soup doesn't thicken, return it to the heat for 1 minute, whisking constantly; do not let it boil.) Ladle the soup into warm soup plates and spoon an equal amount of the ham-sage butter onto the center of each serving.

cook's note

℘ If you have big, fat garlic cloves, they won't soften in the 30 minutes of cooking time, so peel them first. One whole head of garlic is about the right amount.

SOURCE: *Martha Stewart Living*
COOKS: Elwood and Donald Barickman

elwood's ham chowder

THIS ISN'T A CREAMY CHOWDER but a light broth with pretty bits of collards and red potatoes. It's a family recipe in the best sense, not handed down but lovingly created by a father-and-son team. The Barickmans took the chowder idea and applied it to Southern ingredients — ham and collard greens — with fine results. Although the soup is filling, it's not at all heavy.

serves 8

1 tablespoon vegetable oil
1 pound Virginia ham, cut into 1/2-inch pieces
2 large onions, cut into 1/2-inch pieces (about 3 cups)
4 garlic cloves, thinly sliced
2 bunches collard greens (about 1 pound), stemmed and coarsely chopped
7 cups chicken stock or low-sodium canned chicken broth
2 cups beef stock or low-sodium canned beef broth

8 medium red potatoes, cut into 1/2-inch cubes (about 6 cups)
1 28-ounce can whole tomatoes with juice, coarsely chopped
1 1/2 tablespoons chopped fresh thyme leaves
1 1/2 tablespoons chopped fresh flat-leaf parsley
Salt and freshly ground black pepper to taste
Hot pepper sauce (optional)

Heat the oil in a large stockpot over medium-low heat. Add the ham and cook until it starts to release its juices, about 2 minutes; do not brown. Add the onions and garlic. Cook, stirring occasionally, until soft, about 10 minutes.

Working in batches if necessary so as not to overcrowd the pot, add the collard greens, tossing frequently with tongs until they are thoroughly wilted. Add the chicken and beef broth, potatoes, tomatoes and their juice, thyme, and parsley. Bring to a boil, then reduce the heat to a gentle simmer. Cook, stirring and skimming any foam from the surface occasionally, until the potatoes are easily pierced with a paring knife, 30 to 40 minutes. Remove from the heat and season with salt, pepper, and hot sauce. Serve hot.

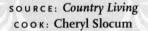

SOURCE: *Country Living*
COOK: Cheryl Slocum

pumpkin chowder

PUMPKIN IS THE CENTERPIECE of this slightly spicy, slightly sweet fall soup with a Southwestern accent. In small portions, it makes a fine beginning to a Thanksgiving dinner. (You may want to cut the recipe in half.)

Once the peppers are roasted (which can be done a day ahead), making the rest of the soup is a snap. You can also leave the chicken out. If you do, it's a good idea to use the trick on page 39 to enrich the broth.

serves 16 as an appetizer or 6 as a main course

2 red bell peppers

2 jalapeño peppers

2 tablespoons olive oil

1¹/2 pounds boneless, skinless chicken breasts, diced

1 small pumpkin (about 2 pounds), peeled, seeded, and cut into 1-inch chunks

3 leeks, white and light green parts only, chopped

3 tablespoons all-purpose flour

2 teaspoons ground cumin

1 teaspoon chili powder

1 teaspoon salt

¹/2 teaspoon freshly ground black pepper

1 ear corn, kernels removed (about 1 cup)

1 tablespoon minced fresh oregano leaves

3 14-ounce cans low-sodium chicken broth

¹/2 cup sour cream (optional)

Preheat the broiler. Place the bell peppers and jalapeños on a baking sheet and broil, turning occasionally, until the skins blacken, about 10 minutes. Seal the charred peppers in a plastic bag for 10 to 12 minutes. Peel, stem, seed, and cut the peppers into ¹/2-inch pieces. Set aside.

Heat the olive oil in a large Dutch oven over medium-high heat. Add the chicken and sauté, stirring, until browned. Remove the chicken and keep warm.

Add the pumpkin and leeks to the Dutch oven and sauté for 5 minutes. Add the flour, cumin, chili powder, salt, and pepper and cook for 1 to 2 minutes. Add the roasted peppers, chicken, corn, oregano, and broth and bring to a boil.

Reduce the heat to low and simmer for 30 minutes, or until the pumpkin is tender. Garnish with sour cream, if desired, and serve hot.

cook's notes

- You can substitute butternut squash for the pumpkin if you wish.
- Defrosted frozen corn kernels will work just fine in the soup.

SOURCE: *Food & Wine*
COOK: Tasha Prysi

lentil and swiss chard soup

WE DON'T ALWAYS THINK OF LENTIL SOUP as bright and fresh-tasting. But that's exactly what this one is and why we love it so much. The flavor comes from a good dose of fresh lemon juice added to the soup just before serving. It's a sure antidote to the winter doldrums, and it's even good for you — lemon juice is an excellent source of vitamin C and powerful antioxidants. Don't even think about making this soup with anything but the real thing.

This soup has another big advantage over most lentil soups. Because it's made with only 1 cup of lentils, it's not gloppy but brothy and elegant in a homey sort of way. Serve it in small cups at the start of a meal or in wide bowls with crusty bread for a light supper.

serves 6

4 cups water
4 cups chicken stock or canned low-sodium chicken broth
1 cup brown lentils, rinsed
Salt
3 tablespoons olive oil, plus more for serving (optional)
1 large onion, finely chopped
Pinch of crushed red pepper flakes

$1/2$ cup coarsely chopped fresh cilantro
4 garlic cloves, finely chopped
1 bunch green Swiss chard ($1^1/4$ pounds), ribs removed and reserved for another use, leaves coarsely chopped
$1/3$ cup fresh lemon juice
Freshly ground black pepper

Combine the water, stock, lentils, and $1^1/2$ teaspoons salt in a medium saucepan and bring to a boil. Cover partially and cook over medium-low heat until the lentils are barely tender, about 25 minutes.

Meanwhile, heat the 3 tablespoons oil in a large skillet over medium-high heat. Add the onion, red pepper flakes, and a pinch of salt and cook, stirring occasionally, until the onion is lightly browned, 7 to 8 minutes. Add the cilantro and garlic and cook for 1 minute more. Gradually add the chard leaves and cook, stirring occasionally, until wilted, about 3 minutes.

Add the chard mixture to the lentils, cover partially, and simmer until thickened, about 15 minutes. Stir in the lemon juice and season with salt and pepper. Ladle the soup into bowls, season with more pepper and olive oil, if desired, and serve.

cook's notes

- One use for the leftover chard stems is to make them into a gratin. Chop them into long pieces and sauté them in a bit of olive oil with garlic until browned and softened. Transfer to a gratin dish or shallow baking dish and add a few tablespoons of heavy cream and some grated cheese. Bake at 400 degrees until bubbly and browned.

- If you've got a top-shelf extra-virgin olive oil, drizzle a thread of it onto each bowl just before serving. It will make this soup sing.

SOURCE: *Food & Wine*
COOK: Diane Rossen Worthington

broccoli-leek soup with lemon-chive cream

THIS SOUP IS EASY TO MAKE but deeply flavored, thanks to its three oniony elements — leeks, garlic, and chives — and the delectable lemony sour cream mixture that goes both into and on top of the finished soup. Broccoli is rarely the star of anything, but here it shines.

Working time is about 30 minutes start to finish, so this is a great weekend lunch or weekday dinner soup, served with good bread and a salad.

serves 4

1 tablespoon unsalted butter

1 tablespoon extra-virgin olive oil

2 medium leeks, white and tender green parts only, finely chopped

1 1/2 pounds broccoli, stems peeled and sliced 1/2 inch thick, florets cut into 1-inch pieces

3 garlic cloves, thinly sliced

5 cups chicken stock or canned low-sodium chicken broth

Salt and freshly ground white pepper, to taste

1/2 cup sour cream

1/4 cup freshly grated Parmesan cheese

1/4 cup snipped fresh chives

Finely grated zest of 1 lemon

2 tablespoons fresh lemon juice

Melt the butter with the olive oil in a medium saucepan over medium-high heat. Add the leeks and cook, stirring, until softened, about 3 minutes. Stir in the broccoli, garlic, and stock, season with salt and white pepper, and bring to a boil. Cover partially and simmer until the broccoli is tender, about 20 minutes.

Meanwhile, combine the sour cream, Parmesan, chives, lemon zest, and lemon juice in a small bowl. Season with salt and white pepper.

Transfer the soup to a blender in batches and puree until smooth. Return to the saucepan and briefly reheat. Stir in half of the lemon-chive cream. Ladle the soup into shallow bowls and pass the remaining lemon-chive cream at the table.

cook's note

- You'll need to cool the soup a bit before pureeing it in the blender; otherwise it may spurt out of the container.

- If you need to puree the soup while it's hot, either use an immersion blender right in the pot or fill the blender jar only two thirds full and remove the little plug in the lid so the pressure won't build up and make the soup explode.

SOURCE: *Appetite* by Nigel Slater
COOK: Nigel Slater

quick asian noodle soup with lemongrass and mushrooms

THE SUBTITLE FOR THE BRILLIANTLY IRREVERENT BOOK by British cookbook author Nigel Slater is *So What Do You Want to Eat Today?* This soup is just the kind of answer we might give most days. It's light, soothing, and quick as anything. Indeed, if you've got a well-stocked kitchen, you'll probably be able to toss it together in a matter of minutes. The lemongrass might be the one thing you have to shop for, but it's getting easier to find, and it gives the broth such a sharp, clean edge that you won't want to omit it.

You'll see that the proportions here are for one serving, which makes sense because this is the kind of warming bowl to make when you're alone for lunch and want something besides cold leftovers. It's great for supper, too, or late at night when you need a little something to revive your soul. If you do want to share, it's easy enough to multiply the ingredients.

serves 1

1–2 tablespoons peanut oil
1 stem lemongrass, tough outer leaves discarded, inner heart finely sliced
1 shallot, finely chopped
1 medium garlic clove, crushed
A large handful of button or cremini mushrooms, sliced or quartered
Chicken or vegetable stock, enough to fill a large soup bowl

1 star anise pod
Sugar, to taste
Salt and freshly ground black pepper, to taste
Thai fish sauce (nam pla), to taste
A handful of Asian noodles, depending on your appetite
Fresh basil and mint leaves
Lime wedges

Bring a large saucepan of water to a boil.

Heat a wok or large skillet over high heat. When it is hot, add the oil and let it shimmer for a second or two before adding the lemongrass, shallot, and garlic. Let them sizzle briefly — you don't want them to color too much — then add the mushrooms and stir-fry for a few minutes until tender, juicy, and appetizingly golden in patches.

Add the stock to the wok or skillet and bring to a boil. Simmer for 2 minutes, then add the star anise, a big pinch of sugar, a pinch of salt, some black pepper, and a few shakes of fish sauce. Go easy on the fish sauce. Keep tasting until you have something you really like.

Meanwhile, drop the noodles into the boiling water (see note). Whip them out as soon as they're tender and put them into a large, deep soup bowl. Add the basil and mint to the bowl and a good, big squeeze of lime. Remove the star anise and ladle the soup into the bowl and serve.

cook's notes

- It's a good idea to check the directions on the noodle package to determine how to cook them. Some Asian noodles, like rice noodles, are best soaked briefly in hot water and not boiled.
- If you're doubling or tripling the recipe, 1 star anise pod will do. Not until you start making enough to feed 5 or 6 will you need a second pod.
- While we love the combination of fresh basil and mint, you can use only one or the other. Fresh cilantro is fine too.
- Shallow Chinese soup spoons work well for eating this soup.

SOURCE: *Fine Cooking*
COOK: Martha Holmberg

tortilla soup with chicken and avocado

WE LOVE THE COMPLEXITY AND COMFORT of a bowl of real tortilla soup, but we aren't always up for the toasting, soaking, and grinding of chiles required. So we were excited to find this recipe for a streamlined version made from ordinary ingredients that delivers extraordinary results. Sure, our traditionalist friends will turn up their noses, but we can't get over how well this recipe works. In place of dried chili peppers, Martha Holmberg, the editor in chief at *Fine Cooking* magazine, has devised a mix of finely chopped onion, tomato paste, and supermarket chili powder that serves as the flavor base. To this, she adds skinless chicken thighs and canned chicken broth (although you certainly could use homemade) and gently simmers the chicken until it's tender and juicy and the broth is flavorful.

Finishing each bowl with a few spoonfuls of canned black beans, corn kernels (canned or frozen work well), and fresh tomato turns this soup into a substantial meal.

serves 2

1 tablespoon vegetable or olive oil

1/4 cup finely chopped onion (about 1/2 small onion)

1 tablespoon chili powder, or more to taste

1 tablespoon tomato paste

2 skinless chicken thighs (bone-in or boneless)
Salt

4 cups canned low-sodium chicken broth or homemade chicken stock

6 2-inch stems fresh cilantro

3/4 cup diced fresh tomato

1/2 cup corn kernels (fresh, canned, or frozen)

1/2 cup canned black beans, rinsed and drained
Crispy tortilla strips (recipe follows)

GARNISH

1 ripe avocado, diced and tossed with a squeeze of lime juice

1/4 cup crumbled queso fresco, feta, or ricotta salata cheese

2 dollops sour cream

1/4 cup coarsely chopped fresh cilantro leaves
Lime wedges, for serving

Heat the oil in a large saucepan over medium heat. Add the onion and cook until softened but not browned, about 3 minutes. Add the chili powder and tomato paste and stir with a wooden spoon to mix and cook briefly; take care not to let the chili powder scorch.

Season the chicken thighs lightly with salt and nestle them in the tomato-chili paste, turning them once so they're entirely coated. Add about $^1/_2$ cup of the stock and adjust the heat to a simmer. Cover and cook the chicken, turning once, until it's extremely tender when pierced with a knife, 30 to 40 minutes. Add a little more broth if the pan is drying out. When the chicken is done, remove it from the pan, let it cool a bit, and then cut or shred it into bite-size pieces, discarding any bones or bits of fat or gristle. Set the shredded meat aside.

If there is any visible grease in the pan, spoon it off. Add the remaining stock and the cilantro stems, stir, and simmer, uncovered, until the broth has reduced by about one third, 20 to 30 minutes.

Meanwhile, fry the tortilla strips as directed.

Divide the shredded chicken, tomato, corn, black beans, and tortilla strips between two large soup bowls. Reheat the broth if necessary so it's piping hot and pour it into the bowls. Serve immediately. Add the avocado, cheese, sour cream, chopped cilantro, and a big squeeze of lime to each bowl at the table.

cook's notes

꾜 While the soup is best with all the ingredients, you can eliminate either the corn or the beans — but not both. Whatever you do, don't forget the squeeze of lime.

꾜 The soup can be made ahead and kept overnight in the refrigerator. The garnishes of avocado and chopped cilantro are best prepared right before serving.

tip

Real homemade chicken stock is better than canned, of course, but sometimes there's just no time. That's where Michael Chiarello's Cheater's Chicken Stock comes in handy. Combine two 14-ounce cans low-sodium chicken broth with 1$^1/_2$ cans water in a large saucepan. Add 1 small celery rib, chopped; 1 small carrot, chopped; $^1/_2$ cup coarsely chopped mushrooms; 1 bay leaf, crumbled; $^1/_4$ teaspoon whole black peppercorns, and a few stems flat-leaf parsley. Bring to a simmer over medium heat, adjust the heat to maintain a gentle simmer, and cook for 30 minutes. Cool briefly, then strain. (From *Michael Chiarello's Casual Cooking*.)

soups

crispy tortilla strips

4 6-inch fresh corn tortillas $^1/_2$–1 cup vegetable oil, for frying

Cut the tortillas into $^1/_4$-inch-wide strips. Line a plate or tray with two layers of paper towels. In a small, high-sided saucepan, heat about 1 inch of oil over medium heat. When it reaches 375 degrees or when a strip of tortilla sizzles immediately when dipped in the oil, add 6 to 8 tortilla strips. With tongs or a long fork, "scrunch" the strips for a second or two so they take on a wavy shape. Fry until the strips aren't bubbling much and have become pale brown, about 1 minute. Transfer to the paper towels to drain. Repeat with the remaining tortilla strips.

cook's note

The crispy tortilla strips can be made up to a day ahead and kept in a dry spot. If you're in a jam and don't have time to fry the strips, go ahead and use broken store-bought tortilla chips. The chips won't be quite the same, but the soup will still be plenty good.

SOURCE: *When French Women Cook*
by Madeleine Kamman
COOK: Henriette

french bread and shallot soup

IN HER WONDERFUL GASTRONOMIC MEMOIR of the old days in France, Madeleine Kamman devotes whole chapters to home cooks. Henriette (the women aren't given last names) lived in Normandy at the edge of the English Channel and used her native ingredients in a frugal but exuberant way. This soup is an exemplary example. A twist on French onion soup, it's laden with cream rather than cheese, and the bread is pureed and mixed into the soup instead of floating on top. The result is so thick it could pass as a sauce.

This is rib-sticking winter food, just the thing after skiing or other brisk exertions. It's easy to make and easy to love.

serves 4 to 6

4 tablespoons ($^1/_2$ stick) butter
$^2/_3$ cup chopped shallots or leeks
6 $^1/_2$-inch-thick slices day-old
French bread, crusts removed
$^2/_3$ cup whole milk
2 cups heavy veal or chicken stock
(see note)

Salt and freshly ground black
pepper
$^2/_3$ cup heavy cream
$^1/_3$ cup sour cream
$^1/_3$ cup chopped fresh parsley

Heat the butter in a medium saucepan. Add the shallots or leeks and toss briefly in the hot butter without letting the vegetables color at all.

Meanwhile, soak the bread slices in the milk for 10 minutes. Puree the bread and milk in a blender.

Mix the bread puree with the stock in the blender and add it to the saucepan with the shallots. Simmer for 15 to 20 minutes. Add salt and pepper to taste. Mix together the heavy cream and sour cream in a small bowl and add it to the soup. Add the parsley and reheat well. Serve the soup very hot.

cook's note

"Heavy veal or chicken stock" may stop you in your tracks. In Henriette's kitchen, of course, the stock would be homemade and heavy (or rich) by definition. You can approximate that by simmering some chicken parts in low-sodium canned chicken broth for about 30 minutes to enrich the broth.

SOUPS

SOURCE: www.restaurantvillegas.com
COOK: Eric Villegas

cream of grilled tomato soup

A READER TIPPED US OFF to this magical soup, the brainchild of a chef in Okemos, Michigan.

There are just a few secrets here: using the best vine-ripened tomatoes (preferably heirlooms) you can find, grilling the tomatoes until they char a bit, seasoning them all the way through the cooking, and using real cream. How much cream? The less you use, the more defined and intense the tomato flavor will be. Don't cheat and substitute milk — if you taste the soup before you add the cream, you'll think it's nothing special, but the cream takes it right over the top.

serves 4 to 6

5 pounds tomatoes, cored (red or yellow beefsteaks, heirlooms, or romas)

About 1 tablespoon French sea salt

About 1 tablespoon coarsely ground black pepper

Hot sauce to taste, preferably Clancy's Fancy

1–3 cups heavy cream, to taste

Preheat the grill (see note). Put the tomatoes on the grill rack cut side up, not touching each other. Grill them for 10 to 20 minutes, or until their skins start to turn black. Turn with tongs and grill the other sides.

Using tongs, transfer the grilled tomatoes to a large saucepan and break them up a bit. Add some of the salt and pepper and a jolt of hot sauce. Cook over medium heat for 10 to 20 minutes, stirring very frequently, until reduced to a sauce consistency. Be careful not to let the tomatoes scorch. You should have 4 to 5 cups.

Add the remaining salt and pepper and more hot sauce. The tomatoes will be chunky at this point (too chunky, we think); if you want the soup to be smooth, puree it in a blender or put it through a food mill. Taste and adjust the seasonings.

Add 1 cup of the cream and simmer until heated through, 3 to 5 minutes. Taste again for seasoning and to see if you'd like more cream. As soon as the soup tastes exactly right, serve it immediately.

cook's notes

- If you have no grill, you can broil the tomatoes. Put the oven rack in the highest position and watch carefully.

- You can grill the tomatoes in advance. Store them in the refrigerator or even the freezer until you're ready to make the soup.

- Shortcut: use canned organic fire-roasted tomatoes. Drain the tomatoes (enough for 5 cups) and heat them in a saucepan before seasoning and adding the cream. They won't be as delicious, of course, but they'll still be good.

SOURCE: Janet Fletcher in the *San Francisco Chronicle*
COOK: Matt Colgan

tomato-bread soup
(pappa al pomodoro)

AT À CÔTÉ RESTAURANT IN OAKLAND, CALIFORNIA, Matt Colgan knows just what to do with end-of-the-season tomatoes: he puts them in this simple bread-and-water Italian soup. Colgan makes it in a surprising way, baking it in the oven for hours with a little white wine. The soup is so good that it should become an annual treat to close the tomato season.

You don't have to peel or seed the tomatoes, because the soup base gets pureed and strained. The base goes together quickly, and once you've got it, the soup's ready in just a few minutes.

serves 6

3/4 pound day-old country-style bread, cut into 2-inch chunks

5 pounds slicing tomatoes (not romas), cored and quartered

1 1/2 red onions, thinly sliced

1/2 cup whole peeled garlic cloves

1/2 cup extra-virgin olive oil, plus more for garnish

1/2 cup dry white wine

Salt and freshly ground black pepper, to taste

3–4 large fresh basil sprigs

Chicken stock, low-sodium canned chicken broth, or water, as needed

Freshly grated Parmesan cheese, for garnish

Preheat the oven to 350 degrees. Put the bread chunks in a large nonreactive roasting pan. Cover the bread with the tomatoes, onions, garlic, 1/2 cup olive oil, wine, and salt and pepper. Cover and bake for 2 hours. Remove from the oven, bury the basil sprigs in the hot mixture, cover, and let steep for 30 minutes (see note). Remove the basil and puree the mixture in a food processor, in batches if necessary. Press through a coarse sieve to remove the tomato skins and seeds. Taste and adjust the seasonings.

Add stock or water to thin the base as you like it, then heat through. Serve the soup warm with olive oil to trickle over and a little Parmesan to pass at the table.

You can skip the steeping step and add a few torn basil leaves as a garnish at the last minute.

Among our favorite bread-tomato recipes is Catalan tomato toasts, the Spanish version of bruschetta, from the employee newsletter of the famous Ann Arbor delicatessen, Zingerman's. To make them, toast some good country bread until it's light brown, slide a cut clove of garlic across its face, and press a very ripe tomato half into the toast. When you take the tomato away, its juice will have run right into the bread. Add an enthusiastic drizzle of extra-virgin olive oil and a sprinkle of sea salt, and serve warm. This is not only no work at all, it's just unimaginably good (from co-owner Ari Weinzweig).

In his book *Bread and Oil,* Tomás Graves (son of the celebrated poet Robert Graves) describes a similar treat from the Balearic islands called *pa amb oli:* toast 2 slices of bread lightly, rub them with the split tomato, place 2 thin slices of cured ham between the bread slices, and serve with black olives. This sandwich could easily be a meal, with cheese, omelets or scrambled eggs, and a fresh salad.

SOURCE: *My Kitchen in Spain* by Janet Mendel
COOK: Janet Mendel

blender gazpacho

THERE ARE NO FEWER THAN SEVEN GAZPACHO RECIPES in Janet Mendel's Spanish cookbook. We went straight for the simplest one. Unlike the endless parade of boring gazpachos we're used to, this one has authentic flavor that's the result of achieving perfect balance and using really ripe tomatoes. You can garnish it with minced fresh vegetables or not, as you like.

Instead of requiring you to finely chop copious amounts of vegetables and mix them together, this soup takes advantage of the blender. But not just any blender: to make the recipe work properly and to avoid having to peel the tomatoes, you need at least 300 watts and a sharp blade. Most current blenders can do the job, especially ice-chopping ones or bar blenders.

serves 6

4 slices stale country bread, crusts removed

2 garlic cloves

2 pounds ripe tomatoes (about 5), seeded (see note)

2 teaspoons salt

1/4 teaspoon ground cumin

1/3 cup extra-virgin olive oil

1 1/2 cups cold water

2 tablespoons white wine vinegar

1/3 cup chopped green bell pepper, for garnish (optional)

1/3 cup chopped cucumber, for garnish (optional)

1/3 cup chopped onion, for garnish (optional)

1/2 cup croutons or diced bread, toasted crisp, for garnish (optional)

Break the bread into big chunks and soak it in water to cover until softened, about 15 minutes. Squeeze out the water and place the bread along with the garlic in a blender. Blend until smooth.

Add the tomatoes and puree. Add the salt and cumin. With the motor running, slowly add the olive oil in a stream — the soup will turn orange as the oil is incorporated. Blend in 1/2 cup of the water and the vinegar.

Place the gazpacho in a tureen, pitcher, or bowl and stir in the remaining 1 cup of water. Chill until ready to serve.

If you're using the garnishes, serve them in separate bowls or in separate piles on a platter, to be passed at the table.

cook's notes

- If you don't take the seeds out of the tomatoes, they'll add bitterness to the soup. To seed the tomatoes, core them and cut them in half crosswise. Spoon out the seeds or squeeze the tomatoes over a sieve into a bowl; the sieve will catch the seeds. Put the juice into the gazpacho.
- Andalusians like their gazpacho a little creamier and paler. For that style, add 2 extra slices of bread and use $\frac{1}{2}$ cup olive oil instead of $\frac{1}{3}$ cup.
- If you want more vegetables in the soup, add a 2-inch square of green bell pepper and a 2-inch chunk of cucumber to the blender along with the tomatoes.
- You can also turn this soup into a drink by adding cold water and serving it in tall glasses, minus the garnishes.

SOURCE: Candy Sagon in the *Washington Post*
COOK: Patricia Solley

lime-cucumber soup with a kick

ON A HOT DAY, IT'S HARD TO IMAGINE anything more refreshing and naughtier than this zesty cold soup. Think margarita meets gazpacho. The secret ingredient is tequila, paired here with cooling cucumbers and green grapes, and with lime, jalapeño, and cilantro upping the voltage. The soup inspires amazed expressions on the faces of those who taste it for the first time.

Patricia Solley is the creator of www.soupsong.com, a Web site devoted to soup, and she's completely obsessed with the subject. We're sticking with this one, not only because it's so unusual but also because it's made in just a few minutes.

serves 4

2 limes
1/2 jalapeño pepper, seeded and coarsely chopped, or to taste
2 large cucumbers, peeled and coarsely chopped
2 cups seedless green grapes
4 scallions, white and tender green parts, coarsely chopped

1/4 cup coarsely chopped fresh cilantro, or to taste
1/2 cup coarsely chopped green or yellow bell pepper
1/4 cup tequila, or to taste
Lime zest, scallions, and cucumbers, for garnish (optional)

Grate the zest from the limes and squeeze the juice. Add the zest and juice to a food processor or blender with all of the remaining ingredients except the tequila and the garnish, if using. Blend until smooth. Strain the mixture into a bowl, pressing on the solids to release as much liquid as possible. If desired, strain the mixture again. Cover and refrigerate until chilled through, at least 30 minutes.

Just before serving, add the tequila and mix well. Ladle into individual bowls and serve immediately, garnished if you like.

salads

The Wedge 48

Grilled Onion Salad 50

St. John's Parsley and Onion Salad 52

Salade Russe 54

Raspberry, Avocado, and Watercress Platter 56

Moroccan Carrot Salad with Cumin 58

Shepherd's Salad with Bulgarian Feta 59

Green Bean Salad with Olives, Goat Cheese, and Basil Vinaigrette 60

Zucchini, Corn, and Tomato Salad 62

Zucchini Salad with Lemon and Mint 64

Italian-Style Tuna Salad with Green Beans, Potatoes, and Red Onion 66

Corn Bread Salad with Grilled Sausage and Spicy Chipotle Dressing 68

The Easiest, Sexiest Salad in the World 70

SOURCE: *Desperation Entertaining!*
by Beverly Mills and Alicia Ross
COOKS: Beverly Mills and Alicia Ross

the wedge

REMEMBER WHEN LETTUCE MEANT ICEBERG? We've come a long way since then, but there are still times when we crave that crisp, refreshing, watery crunch. Happily, lots of trendy restaurants — most notably, steak houses — are right there with us, and they've resurrected the wedge. A perfect wedge is nothing more than a single chunk of iceberg draped with your favorite dressing. Blue cheese is probably the most popular, but vinaigrette, Russian, French, or just about anything else goes. Some cooks even add a crumble of bacon — something we would never argue with. Whatever its clothing, the wedge is all about the contrast of the clean crunch of iceberg with the richness of a good salad dressing.

Serve wedge salads on cold plates as a first course — none of that froofy European after-dinner stuff here. The most obvious dish to follow would be a good steak.

serves 8

DRESSING

1/2 cup mayonnaise
1/2 cup sour cream
 1 teaspoon Worcestershire sauce
1/2 cup crumbled blue cheese

SALAD

2 heads iceberg lettuce (see note)

TO MAKE THE DRESSING

Stir together the mayonnaise and sour cream in a small bowl. Stir in the Worcestershire and blue cheese. Mash the chunks of cheese against the side of the bowl to break them up some. The dressing can be refrigerated, covered, for up to 1 week.

TO MAKE THE SALAD

Remove and discard the core of each head of lettuce. Rinse, shake off excess water, and dry with paper towels. Cut each head into quarters, so you end up with 8 wedges.

Arrange each lettuce wedge on a salad plate. Spoon over about 2 tablespoons dressing, or more to taste. Serve immediately, passing extra dressing at the table.

cook's notes

- Look for small to medium-size heads of iceberg. If they're very large, cut each head into 6 wedges, not quarters.
- Iceberg tastes best if it's crisp and cold, so don't let it sit out too long before making the salad.
- If the dressing seems too thick, add a tablespoon or so of red or white wine vinegar. In addition to making the dressing a bit easier to spoon, we really like the way the extra zing from the vinegar helps cut the richness.

tip

In place of creamy blue cheese dressing, we're also very fond of a version that Steve Schimoler, the chef at the Mist Grill in Waterbury, Vermont, included in his cookbook, simply titled *The Mist Grill*. Arrange 6 to 8 thinly sliced red onion rings over each lettuce wedge, crumble on a generous dose of blue cheese, then drizzle over 2 tablespoons of a sharp vinaigrette dressing.

SOURCE: Jonathan Reynolds in
the *New York Times Magazine*
COOK: Vincent Scotto

grilled onion salad

IS THIS AN APPETIZER, A SIDE, OR A SALAD? It works for all three purposes, but however you serve it, everyone at the table will be overjoyed. Scotto, chef-owner of Gonzo, a friendly neighborhood Italian restaurant in Manhattan's West Village, just can't seem to take this dish off the menu, and for good reason.

The tower of charred onions is bathed in olive oil, sprinkled with Parmesan and croutons, and anointed with a final drizzle of lemon and olive oil to bring it all together.

serves 4

4 large yellow onions, unpeeled
10 tablespoons olive oil
   Kosher salt
2 ³/4-inch-thick slices Tuscan bread

1 garlic clove, unpeeled, halved lengthwise
¹/4 cup fresh parsley leaves
¹/4 cup shaved Parmesan cheese
3 tablespoons fresh lemon juice

Preheat a griddle over medium-low heat. Cut off the end of each onion so that you can see the rings. Cut the onions crosswise into ³/4- to 1-inch-thick slices, keeping the rings intact and the skins on as much as possible. Brush the cut sides of the onions with 4 tablespoons of the oil and sprinkle with salt. Grill the onion slices in the pan until tender and caramelized, about 20 minutes per side. If they burn, scrape off the charred portion. (A little tastes okay.) Let cool.

Meanwhile, grill the bread until toasted, rub both sides with the cut sides of the garlic, and sprinkle with 2 tablespoons of the oil and salt to taste. Cut into croutons.

When the onions are cool, remove the remaining skins and separate the onions into rings — they will resemble small bottomless bowls. Divide half of the onions among 4 plates and sprinkle with half the parsley, half the Parmesan, and half the croutons. Repeat the layers with the remaining ingredients on top. Drizzle with the lemon juice and the remaining 4 tablespoons oil and serve.

cook's notes

❦ If it's summer and sweet onions such as Vidalias are around, you can cook the onions on an outdoor grill in very little time — just watch them carefully to make sure they don't burn.

❦ Can't find Tuscan bread (which traditionally has no salt)? Use any good rustic-style bread made without added fat.

salads

51

SOURCE: *Jeremiah Tower Cooks* by Jeremiah Tower
COOK: Fergus Henderson

st. john's parsley and onion salad

WE'RE PARTIAL TO PARSLEY SALADS, which are the ultimate in fresh herbal taste. This one, from a London restaurant, is like no other. What makes it such a standout is mellowed big salted capers, which must be prepared ahead. These fashionable capers are often unbearably salty, but California chef Tower rinses them thoroughly and gives them some time in a bath of white wine and olive oil with herbs. They're as startlingly good on smoked salmon, deviled eggs, or a sandwich as they are in this salad. Once we made them, we vowed to have a jar always at the ready in the fridge.

serves 4

MARINATED CAPERS
Large capers, packed in salt
1 part dry white wine
2 parts olive oil
Fresh thyme or fresh basil sprig
or both

SALAD
1/4 cup Marinated Capers, drained
1/4 cup extra-virgin olive oil
1 tablespoon freshly grated
lemon zest
2 tablespoons fresh lemon juice
1 large red onion
2 tablespoons chopped fresh mint
1/2 teaspoon sea salt
2 cups fresh flat-leaf parsley leaves
(see note)
Freshly ground black pepper

TO MAKE THE MARINATED CAPERS

Rinse the capers very well and let them soak in cold water for 20 minutes. Repeat two more times. Drain them and put them in a jar to cover with the wine, oil, and herb(s). Cover and store in the refrigerator for up to 2 weeks.

TO MAKE THE SALAD

Combine the oil, capers, lemon zest, and juice in a small bowl.

Cut the onion crosswise into 1/16-inch-thick slices and put them in a bowl, dividing them into rings. Add the mint and salt and toss. Cover and let stand for 10 minutes.

Add the parsley and the caper mixture to the onions. Season with pepper and toss briefly.

- Jars of salted capers are available in gourmet stores.
- You may want to chop the parsley leaves, since they can be hard to chew.
- You can prepare all the elements ahead and mix them at the last minute. The salad stays perky on a potluck table or a buffet.
- Serve with slabs of hot grilled country bread.

SOURCE: *San Francisco Chronicle*
COOK: Michael Wild, after his mother

salade russe

THIS IS ONE OF THOSE CLASSIC RECIPES that tastes entirely up-to-date and exciting every time we serve it. The salad comes from Michael Wild, the owner of Bay Wolf restaurant in Oakland, California. Born in Paris at the beginning of World War II, Wild says he learned much of what he knows about food from his mother. This salad, which she called "summer salad," was one of her father's favorites. It's assembled from dependable ingredients like radishes, cucumber, and hard-cooked eggs, and so can be served year-round.

This salad is ideal for entertaining, since its staged preparation requires you to start it ahead of time. Salting the cucumber and radishes up to 4 hours ahead revives them so they taste fresh-picked. It can be dressed and garnished up to an hour before serving, meaning less fussing around at the last minute.

serves 6

1 bunch radishes
1¹/₂ teaspoons kosher salt
1 English cucumber
1 cup sour cream or crème fraîche
¹/₂ teaspoon Dijon mustard
A few steamed potatoes, peeled and cut into small cubes, or cubed pickled beets (optional)

3 hard-cooked eggs, peeled and coarsely chopped
2 teaspoons chopped fresh dill
¹/₄ teaspoon freshly ground black pepper

At least 1 hour (and up to 4) before serving, thinly slice the radishes and sprinkle them with ¹/₂ teaspoon of the salt. Peel the cucumber, halve it lengthwise, then thinly slice or chop and sprinkle with the remaining 1 teaspoon salt. Set the radishes and cucumber aside.

About 1 hour before serving, stir together the sour cream or crème fraîche and the mustard in a small bowl. Pat the radishes and cucumber dry or gently squeeze them to rid them of excess moisture. Combine the radishes, cucumber, potatoes or beets (if using), three fourths of the hard-cooked eggs, three fourths of the chopped dill, the mustard mixture, and the pepper. Toss well.

Just before serving, garnish with the remaining egg and dill.

cook's notes

- English cucumbers are the long, skinny ones, sometimes called hothouse cucumbers. They're usually sold shrink-wrapped.
- To hard-cook eggs, set them in a saucepan just big enough to hold them and cover with water. Slowly bring the water to a boil. Cover and remove from the heat. Let the eggs sit in the pan for 15 minutes. Rinse under cold running water, then crack the shells gently all over and peel under the running water.

tip

For an insanely simple version of a creamy cucumber salad, try the one in the re-released *The French Menu Cookbook,* by Richard Olney. Peel and rinse 2 medium cucumbers. Cut the cucumbers in half lengthwise, remove the seeds, slice crosswise, and spread the slices out in layers on a plate, generously sprinkling each layer with salt. Let sit for 1 to 2 hours. Drain well, pressing firmly, and pat dry. Whisk together the juice of $1/2$ lemon (or more to taste), $1/2$ cup heavy cream, and freshly ground black pepper to taste. Add to the cucumbers and sprinkle with chopped fresh chervil or dill. Serves 2 to 4. This same dressing is delicious on thinly sliced raw button mushrooms. Marinate the mushrooms for a while in fresh lemon juice, salt, and pepper. Then add the cream (without any additional lemon) and taste for seasoning.

SOURCE: *Complete Vegetarian Cookbook*
by Charmaine Solomon
COOK: Charmaine Solomon

raspberry, avocado, and watercress platter

THE FIRST VERSION OF THIS UNUSUAL SALAD was a throw-it-to-gether effort based on what happened to be on hand, and it featured strawberries and avocado — a classic, if somewhat unlikely, combination. Charmaine Solomon liked it so much she wanted to make it again, but alas, no strawberries at the market. But there were some raspberries, and this stellar salad is the result.

We probably don't need to point out that this salad features red and green, but you may want to note that it keeps well on a buffet table and looks gorgeous, with the jewel-like raspberries twinkling among all the different shades of green. All these qualities make it a good holiday choice.

serves 6

DRESSING
2 tablespoons light fruity olive oil
1 tablespoon walnut oil
1 tablespoon raspberry vinegar
1 teaspoon honey
1/2 teaspoon sea salt
Good grinding of black pepper

SALAD
2 ripe but firm avocados
4 cups lightly packed tender watercress sprigs
1 basket raspberries (about 8 ounces), rinsed and drained

TO MAKE THE DRESSING

Whisk together all the ingredients in a small bowl; the dressing will be thick.

TO MAKE THE SALAD

Quarter the avocados, remove the skin, and cut the flesh crosswise into slices, dropping them into a bowl.

Spoon the dressing over the avocado, being sure to cover all of the slices. Toss very gently; avocados are fragile.

Line a platter with the watercress sprigs and arrange the avocado on top. Tumble the raspberries over the avocados.

cook's note

❦ Walnut oil, delicious as it is, is both pricey and very perishable. Buy a small bottle, preferably European, and keep it refrigerated. Use it or lose it; rancid oil is a very bad bargain, both in taste and health.

SOURCE: *Saffron Shores* by Joyce Goldstein
COOK: Simy Danana

moroccan carrot salad with cumin

STALWART CARROTS TO THE RESCUE! This salad comes in very handy during those months of the year when the produce department is looking a bit tired. It's also useful when you need a salad in a flash. As long as you have a bag of carrots, a lemon, and some basic spices in the cabinet, you're good to go.

The flavors are bright and sharp, and the salad adds a great splash of color to any plate or buffet. It can be served warm or left to sit for a few hours at room temperature.

serves 4 to 6

1 pound carrots, peeled and cut into thin slices or strips
1 garlic clove, smashed
Salt
1/4 cup fresh lemon juice

1 teaspoon ground cumin
1 teaspoon sweet paprika
1/8 teaspoon cayenne pepper (optional)
2 tablespoons olive oil

Cook the carrots and garlic in boiling salted water until tender, 5 to 8 minutes. Drain. While still warm, toss with the lemon juice and spices in a large bowl. Stir in the olive oil and season to taste with salt. Serve at room temperature.

cook's notes

ᘓ Unless you're diligent about buying fresh spices every few months, you'll get the best cumin flavor if you grind your own cumin seeds. Toast them first for maximum flavor.

ᘓ Use a good-quality extra-virgin olive oil if you have one on hand.

tip

Joyce Goldstein also offers an Algerian version of this carrot salad: increase the garlic to 3 cloves, add a pinch of ground caraway seeds, and replace the lemon juice with vinegar. This treatment is good with beets, too.

SOURCE: *The Rosengarten Report*
COOK: David Rosengarten

shepherd's salad with bulgarian feta

THE ROSENGARTEN REPORT IS A NEWSLETTER TREAT jammed with eating adventures and wild enthusiasms from master eater David Rosengarten, who travels the globe, fork in hand, in search of the best, the unsung, and the mildly sensational. Although the Bulgarian version of Greek salad is famous, we'd never heard of it before Rosengarten offered his adaptation. There's no wet lettuce to drag the salad down, no olives to make it too salty — just a perfect balance of the simplest ingredients.

serves 4

2 cups diced tomatoes (about 4 small)

2 cups fresh flat-leaf parsley leaves

1 cup seeded and diced green bell pepper (about 1 large)

1 cup diced cucumber (about 1 small one or 1/2 large English cucumber)

1 cup coarsely chopped red onion

1 cup Bulgarian feta chunks (see note)

1 teaspoon very finely minced garlic

3 tablespoons fruity olive oil

3 tablespoons fresh lemon juice
Salt and freshly ground black pepper

Combine all the ingredients except the salt and pepper in a large bowl and mix thoroughly. Just before serving, season to taste with salt and pepper.

cook's notes

❧ Bulgarian feta is a rich, creamy, salty sheep's milk cheese. When Communism tumbled, the controls on Bulgarian feta were relaxed, and the cheese became a sad reminder of its former glory. Happily, there's now a great new Bulgarian feta called Tangra. This artisanal feta comes from mountain-pastured sheep, whose milk produces a very white cheese with great flavor, tang, and crumble. (For retail sources for Tangra, call the importer at 800-249-0272.)

❧ This salad is so good that you should try it even if you can't find Tangra. Substitute Greek, Israeli, or French feta.

❧ Some people find that whole parsley leaves are too big, so you may want to chop them first.

❧ The small pickling cucumbers called kirbys are especially tasty. Two or three will do.

❧ Feta is quite salty, so taste carefully before you add the salt.

salads

SOURCE: *San Francisco Chronicle*
COOK: Tara Duggan

green bean salad with olives, goat cheese, and basil vinaigrette

GREEN BEAN SALADS ARE USEFUL RECIPES to have in your arsenal, because green beans are readily available and hold up well when dressed. Unfortunately, many versions are humdrum, but here's one that is lively and up-to-date. Although we're not one hundred percent sure what boiling the beans in super-salty water does, they end up full of flavor and perfectly crisp-tender. Be sure to refresh them in ice water as soon as they're boiled, so that they retain maximum color. For a colorful presentation, use half green beans and half yellow wax beans.

serves 4

VINAIGRETTE

- 2 tablespoons Champagne vinegar (see note)
- 4 teaspoons finely chopped fresh basil
- Salt and freshly ground black pepper
- $1/4$ cup extra-virgin olive oil

SALAD

- $1/4$ cup kosher salt, plus more to taste
- 1 pound green beans, or $1/2$ pound green beans and $1/2$ pound yellow wax beans
- $1/2$ cup cherry tomatoes, halved if large
- $1/2$ cup pitted kalamata or other briny black olives, halved lengthwise
- 4 ounces aged goat cheese, rind trimmed, cubed (see note)
- Freshly ground black pepper, to taste

TO MAKE THE VINAIGRETTE

Combine the vinegar, basil, and salt and pepper to taste in a small bowl. Let the basil steep in the vinegar for a few minutes, then whisk in the oil in a steady stream until emulsified. Set aside.

TO MAKE THE SALAD

Have ready a large bowl of ice water. Bring 6 quarts of water to a boil in a large pot, then add the ¼ cup kosher salt. Return to a rolling boil and add the green beans (do this in two batches if using two types of beans). Return to a boil and blanch, uncovered, until crisp-tender, 2 to 5 minutes. Immediately drain the beans and plunge them into the ice water. As soon as the beans are completely cool, drain again and pat dry.

TO ASSEMBLE

Toss the beans with the tomatoes, olives, goat cheese, and vinaigrette. Season with salt and pepper and serve.

cook's notes

- While Champagne vinegar is preferable for its clean, sharp taste, you can substitute any good-quality white wine vinegar. Whatever you do, avoid the harsh distilled white vinegar sold for pickling.
- In place of an aged cheese, you can also use fresh goat cheese, spooned or rolled into bite-size balls.
- The individual elements of this salad may be prepared a few hours in advance and assembled just before serving.

tip

Goat cheese balls rolled in chopped pistachios are a delicious addition to salads, especially a roasted beet salad. Mix together 2 ounces softened goat cheese, 1 teaspoon heavy cream, 1 teaspoon sherry vinegar, 1 tablespoon finely chopped shallot, 1 tablespoon finely chopped fresh chives, the leaves from 2 sprigs of thyme, and salt and freshly ground black pepper in a small bowl. Chill for 15 minutes. Form the cheese mixture into 4 balls. Roll each ball in chopped unsalted pistachios. The cheese balls may be made ahead and refrigerated until needed. (From Roasted Beef and Endive Salad with Chèvre and Pistachio Vinaigrette, in *Chef Daniel Boulud: Cooking in New York City* by Daniel Boulud and Peter Kaminsky.)

SOURCE: *Gourmet*
COOK: Gina Marie Miraglia

zucchini, corn, and tomato salad

IF YOU HAVEN'T HAD THE PLEASURE of raw zucchini, you're in for a treat. In this salad, it's cut like skinny pasta, then salted to get rid of its excess water and paired with tomatoes, fresh corn, and basil. Halving the little tomatoes means you get lots of delectable juice, so be sure there's bread available to make the most of it.

It's hard to imagine a better summer salad. It goes with everything, from barbecue to picnic fare to fish.

serves 4

1 1/2 pounds medium zucchini
1 1/4 teaspoons salt
1 cup fresh corn kernels (cut from 2 ears)
2 tablespoons fresh lemon juice
1/2 teaspoon sugar

1/4 teaspoon freshly ground black pepper
1/4 cup extra-virgin olive oil
8 ounces grape or cherry tomatoes, halved lengthwise (2 cups)
1/4 cup thinly sliced fresh basil leaves

Cut the zucchini into thin strips, turning the vegetable as you go, using a mandoline with a julienne blade or a julienne peeler (see note). Discard the seedy cores.

Toss the zucchini strips with 1 teaspoon of the salt in a colander set over a bowl and let drain, covered and refrigerated, for 1 hour.

Gently squeeze handfuls of the zucchini to remove excess water and pat dry with paper towels. Set aside.

Cook the corn in a small saucepan of boiling water until tender, about 3 minutes. Drain, then rinse under cold water and pat dry with paper towels.

Whisk together the lemon juice, sugar, pepper, and the remaining 1/4 teaspoon salt in a large bowl, then add oil in a slow stream, whisking. Add the zucchini, corn, tomatoes, and basil, toss well, and serve.

cook's notes

- Although we usually think small zucchini are the tastiest, they'll be harder to work with than medium ones in this recipe, because there's a lot less zucchini flesh on each one.

- The julienne peeler is a new gizmo (from Kuhn Rikon and Oxo) that looks like a tiny rake and turns vegetables like carrots and daikon into elegant little strands. You can also prepare the zucchini by using a potato peeler to cut wide strips off the zucchini, then stacking them on a cutting board and cutting them into skinny strips.

- You can put the salad together up to 4 hours ahead, minus the dressing and the basil. Keep the salad at room temperature, covered, and just mix everything together before serving.

SOURCE: Elisa Bosley in *Delicious Living*
COOK: John Ash

zucchini salad with lemon and mint

CALIFORNIA CHEF-AUTHOR JOHN ASH transforms zucchini from a rather weary summer vegetable into a lively salad with a steam-and-smash technique and some lemon zest, fresh herbs, and a splash of top-quality olive oil. The salad is perfect for a picnic — just be sure to let it come to room temperature before serving.

serves 4

1¹/₂ pounds zucchini, cut crosswise into 2-inch lengths (see note)

4 tablespoons extra-virgin olive oil

1 medium white onion (about 8 ounces), sliced

2 tablespoons slivered fresh garlic

1 tablespoon finely grated lemon zest (from 1 large lemon)

1 tablespoon chopped fresh mint

1 tablespoon chopped fresh parsley

Sea salt and freshly ground black pepper

Lemon wedges, for garnish

Plain whole-milk yogurt, for garnish

Steam the zucchini until just softened but still bright green, 8 to 10 minutes. With a fork, mash the zucchini in a colander to press out as much water as possible. The zucchini will look very roughly chopped. Set aside.

Heat 3 tablespoons of the oil in a large sauté pan over medium heat. Sauté the onion and garlic until crisp-tender and just beginning to color, about 5 minutes. Remove from the heat and let cool. Gently stir in the zucchini and lemon zest.

Transfer the mixture to a medium bowl and stir in the mint, parsley, and remaining 1 tablespoon oil. Season to taste with salt and lots of pepper. Serve at room temperature with lemon wedges for squeezing over the salad and a dollop of yogurt.

cook's notes

- Young, tender-skinned zucchini are best in this salad. If you can't find any, cut the zucchini in half lengthwise and then cut them into 2-inch lengths.
- White onion is specified here because it retains a firmer texture and has a cleaner flavor, but you can use a yellow or red onion instead.
- The salad can be prepared up to a day ahead and stored, covered, in the refrigerator. Let the salad come to room temperature before serving.

SOURCE: David Pasternack with Florence Fabricant
in the *New York Times*
COOK: David Pasternack

italian-style tuna salad with green beans, potatoes, and red onion

THE STAR OF THIS SALAD IS THE TUNA, but it doesn't come from a can. You start with primo fresh fish from the seafood counter, cook it slowly in olive oil with garlic cloves, and then leave it to cool in the oil. The tuna comes out thoroughly cooked, yet so rich, tender, and flavorful that you'll never want to eat this fish any other way. We're so devoted to it that we make extra just to have a jar in the refrigerator to toss onto pasta, stir into a bean salad, or simply eat on toast.

The cooking technique and the salad come from the talented David Pasternack, chef at Esca in Manhattan. While he dresses up his salad with all sorts of chef-like ingredients — romano beans, fingerling potatoes, and lovage — we've made it with ordinary supermarket green beans, red potatoes, and celery leaves with great success.

serves 4

TUNA

1^1/$_2$ pounds fresh tuna (see note)
   Sea salt and freshly ground black
      pepper
2 large garlic cloves
^{3}/$_4$–1 cup extra-virgin olive oil
3 fresh lemon thyme sprigs
   (or plain thyme plus 1 teaspoon
   lemon zest)
2 bay leaves

SALAD

4 large salt-packed anchovies
   or 8 oil-packed anchovies
^{1}/$_4$ cup extra-virgin olive oil, plus
   more if using salt-packed
   anchovies
^{3}/$_4$ pound small potatoes, preferably
   fingerlings
1 pound green beans, romano
   or regular, trimmed
1 small red onion, sliced paper thin
^{1}/$_2$ cup fresh flat-leaf parsley leaves
^{1}/$_4$ cup fresh lovage leaves or inner
   leaves from celery
^{1}/$_4$ cup red wine vinegar
   Salt and freshly ground black
   pepper

TO MAKE THE TUNA

Cut the tuna in 1¹/₂-inch chunks. Season well with salt and pepper. Place in a saucepan with the garlic and oil, so that the tuna is just covered. Bring to a gentle simmer, and cook over low heat for about 10 minutes, taking care that the oil does not boil. Remove from the heat, add the lemon thyme or thyme and lemon zest and bay leaves, and set aside to cool to room temperature. This will take at least 1 hour. The tuna may be used at this point, but is better if left to marinate overnight. Transfer the contents of the pan to a bowl, cover, and refrigerate overnight. Bring to room temperature at least 1 hour before serving.

TO MAKE THE SALAD

If using salt-packed anchovies, soak them in water for 2 hours, drain, remove the bones, cut into ¹/₂-inch pieces, and toss with a little olive oil. If using oil-packed anchovies, drain and cut into pieces.

Place the potatoes in a pot of salted water, bring to a boil, and cook until tender, about 20 minutes. Drain, peel when cool enough to handle, and halve lengthwise. Place in a large bowl.

Have ready a large bowl of ice water. Bring 6 quarts salted water to a boil in a large saucepan. Add the beans and cook until tender, 5 to 7 minutes. Drain, and chill immediately in the ice water. When cool, drain well, pat dry with paper towels, and add to the potatoes. Add the anchovies, onion, parsley, and lovage or celery leaves. Drain the tuna, reserving the oil. Break the tuna into pieces and add to the bowl.

In a small bowl, whisk the vinegar with the ¹/₄ cup olive oil and ¹/₄ cup of the oil from the tuna. Season with salt and pepper. Pour the dressing over the salad and fold together. Season again with salt and pepper and serve.

cook's notes

- Yellowfin or albacore tuna is best, preferably sushi or sashimi quality.
- The tuna tastes even better the day after you make it. It will keep for a few days covered in oil in the refrigerator. Let it come to room temperature before serving. You may also gently warm it for serving with pasta. Don't serve it too hot or too cold.
- The tuna is delicious in salade niçoise.

salads

SOURCE: *Let the Flames Begin*
by Chris Schlesinger and John Willoughby
COOKS: Elmer Sanchez and Amilcar Baraca

corn bread salad with grilled sausage and spicy chipotle dressing

WE FIND OURSELVES LOOKING FOR EXCUSES to make corn bread (and whisking it away from the table before someone innocently finishes it) just so we can have leftovers for this bold salad.

Pretty much any corn bread will do, as long as it's firm enough to cut up into big croutons and toast. The dressing has earned the title "smoky lava," and it's about the spiciest we've ever tasted. You could certainly tame its fire-power by using less chipotle, but where's the fun in that?

Serve this salad as a starter course for an entire meal from the grill.

serves 4

DRESSING

1/2 cup olive oil

1/4 cup fresh lime juice (about 2 limes)

1/4 cup chipotle chiles in adobo sauce, pureed

1 tablespoon ground cumin
    Kosher salt and freshly ground black pepper

SALAD

2 ripe tomatoes about the size of baseballs, cored and cut into large dice

1 ripe Hass avocado, cut into medium dice

1/2 red onion, cut into small dice

1/3 cup coarsely chopped fresh cilantro or flat-leaf parsley

1 pound fresh sausage links (see note)

2 cups 3/4-inch cubes corn bread, toasted until golden brown (see note)

Build a fire in your grill and let it die down to medium (you should be able to hold your hand about 5 inches above the grill grid for 4 or 5 seconds).

TO MAKE THE DRESSING

Meanwhile, in a large bowl whisk together the olive oil, lime juice, chiles, cumin, and salt and pepper.

Add the tomatoes, avocado, onion, and cilantro or parsley to the dressing and toss gently to combine. Set aside.

Put the sausage on the grill and cook well, 5 to 8 minutes per side. To check for doneness, cut into one and peek to be sure it's cooked through, with no trace of pink inside. When the sausages are done, slice them neatly on the bias so they keep their shape.

Add the toasted corn bread to the salad and toss gently. Divide the salad among 4 plates, fan the sausage slices over the top, and serve.

cook's notes

- Choose whatever sausage you favor for this recipe, even chicken sausage, if you like. Avoid any super-spicy sausage, since this dressing carries enough BTUs on its own.
- To toast the corn bread, spread out the cubes on a baking sheet and bake them at 325 to 350 degrees for about 10 minutes.
- If you can't get outdoors to fire up the charcoal grill, you can certainly broil or pan-fry the sausages.

tip

If you love the butteriness of avocados, you might want to try a trick we learned from the grill-meisters Schlesinger and Willoughby in *Let the Flames Begin*. Next time you set out to make guacamole, fire up the grill to medium. Cut the ripe avocados in half and remove the pits, but leave the skin on. Rub the cut sides with olive oil and season generously with salt and pepper. Grill the avocados, cut side down, until you can see grill marks and the flesh is nicely softened, 3 to 4 minutes. Remove them from the grill and as soon as they are cool enough to handle, scoop the avocado pulp into a bowl, mash it, and proceed with your favorite guacamole recipe. The guacamole will be even richer than usual, with a nice whiff of smokiness.

SOURCE: *Happy Days with the Naked Chef*
by Jamie Oliver
COOK: Jamie Oliver

the easiest, sexiest salad in the world

THIS SALAD FEATURES AN INSPIRED COMBINATION of flavors: salty ham, mild, milky cheese, sweet figs (the sexy part), and a punctuation mark of basil, all bathed in a honey-lemon dressing.

As with all great simple recipes, the quality of the ingredients is everything. In this case it's the figs and the mozzarella. Oliver likes his figs to come from Italy or Greece, but we don't always have that option; American figs can be fine. Good ones start arriving in June and usually stay around until late fall. If real buffalo mozzarella is nowhere to be found, you can make the salad with good, handmade mozzarella from a gourmet shop or an Italian market. This salad makes lots of delicious juices, so be sure there's plenty of bread on the table to sop them up.

serves 4

4 green or black figs, so ripe they're about to burst

4 slices prosciutto or Parma ham

2 slices fresh mozzarella, preferably buffalo mozzarella, quartered

Fresh green or purple basil

DRESSING

6 tablespoons extra-virgin olive oil

3 tablespoons fresh lemon juice

1 tablespoon good honey

Sea salt and freshly ground black pepper

Remove the fig stems and cut a cross into the figs, almost all the way to the bottom. Squeeze the base to open the figs and expose their interiors.

Arrange the figs on a platter. Weave the prosciutto or ham slices around the figs and add some mozzarella slices to the platter around them. Tear the basil into pieces and scatter it over the salad.

TO MAKE THE DRESSING

Combine the olive oil, lemon juice, and honey in a small bowl and season to taste with the salt and pepper.

TO ASSEMBLE

Drizzle everything with the dressing, making sure it gets right down into the center of the figs.

breakfast and brunch

SOURCE: *The Zuni Cafe Cookbook* by Judy Rodgers
COOK: Judy Rodgers

eggs with crunchy bread crumbs

JUST WHEN YOU THINK THERE'S NO NEW WAY in the world to cook something so simple as a fried egg, along comes this delightful recipe, in which the eggs are cooked right over crisp bread crumbs. The combination of the familiar floppy eggs, the rich yolks, the crunchy crumbs, and a final sizzle of vinegar is amazingly good. Judy Rodgers likes to have these eggs for dinner when she's eating alone, but the dish also appears on the lunch menu at her San Francisco restaurant, Zuni Cafe, accompanied by bacon or sausage and grilled vegetables or roasted mushrooms.

You'll need a very large pan or two pans to make this dish for four. This is a terrific breakfast for houseguests.

serves 1

3 tablespoons packed bread crumbs (see note)

Salt

About 2 tablespoons extra-virgin olive oil

A few fresh thyme or marjoram leaves (optional)

2 large eggs

About 1 teaspoon red wine vinegar, balsamic vinegar, or sherry vinegar

Sprinkle the bread crumbs with salt to taste in a small bowl and add enough olive oil to just oversaturate them.

Add the crumbs to a 6- or 8-inch French steel omelet pan or nonstick skillet over medium heat. (If you like your eggs over easy, reserve some of the oiled crumbs to sprinkle over the eggs just before you flip them.) Let the crumbs warm through, then swirl the pan as they begin drying out — they'll make a quiet, staticky sound. Stir once or twice.

The moment you see the crumbs begin to color, quickly add the remaining oil and the thyme or marjoram, if using, then crack the eggs directly onto the crumbs. Cook the eggs as you like them.

Slide the eggs onto a warm plate. Immediately add the vinegar to the pan, swirling it once. Pour the sizzling vinegar over the eggs and serve.

cook's notes

- By "bread crumbs," Rodgers doesn't mean the kind you buy in a container at the supermarket. She's talking about good chewy peasant bread, such as ciabatta, that's slightly stale. You can grate the crumbs by hand or in a food processor. If you're making the eggs for more than four people, it's easiest to prepare the crumbs ahead in the oven instead of the skillet. Toast them in a 425-degree oven until they are the color of weak tea, then scatter them in the skillet and proceed with the rest of the olive oil and the eggs.

- The herbs are a very nice touch, if you have them available. Rodgers also suggests rosemary, but we found it a little strong for this dish. You can also add a subtle garlic flavor by rubbing the bread with a cut clove of garlic before you grate the crumbs.

- Making this dish is a bit like making a stir-fry: have everything at hand, and you won't have any trouble. If you're searching for the vinegar or plucking the herbs at the last minute, things can get tricky.

SOURCE: *Gourmet*
COOK: Lori W. Powell

baked eggs and mushrooms in ham crisps

WE FIRST DISCOVERED THESE LITTLE BEAUTIES one weekend in the country when we wanted something special but didn't feel like a trip to the store. Made from ordinary ingredients, eggs and ham, with the added surprise of creamy sautéed mushrooms, this breakfast is elegant enough to serve to fancy company yet simple enough to make just for yourself. The recipe is easily scaled up or down accordingly, as long as you have the right number of muffin tins. Small ramekins work too. The mushrooms can be prepared the night before, so all you need do in the morning is crack the eggs.

serves 6

- 2 tablespoons unsalted butter
- 3/4 pound button mushrooms, finely sliced
- 1/4 cup finely chopped shallots
- 1/2 teaspoon salt
- 1/4 teaspoon freshly ground black pepper
- 2 tablespoons crème fraîche or sour cream

- 1 tablespoon finely chopped fresh tarragon, plus whole leaves for garnish (see note)
- 12 slices Black Forest or Virginia ham (preferably without holes or tears; about 10 ounces)
- 12 large eggs
  Buttered brioche, challah toast, or other toast, for serving

Preheat the oven to 400 degrees. Lightly oil twelve 1/2-cup muffin cups. Heat the butter in a large heavy skillet over medium heat. Add the mushrooms, shallots, salt, and pepper and cook, stirring, until the mushrooms are tender and the liquid they give off has evaporated, about 10 minutes. Remove from the heat and stir in the crème fraîche or sour cream and tarragon.

Fit a slice of ham into each of the 12 muffin cups (the ends will stick up and hang over the edges of the cups). Divide the mushrooms among the cups and crack 1 egg into each. Bake in the middle of the oven until the egg whites are cooked but yolks are still runny, about 15 minutes. Season the eggs with salt and pepper. Lift from the muffin cups carefully using 2 spoons or small spatulas. Serve immediately on the brioche or other toast, garnished with tarragon leaves.

cook's notes

- For a quicker version, try the recipe without the mushrooms — just a thin slice of ham cradling a single baked egg. Or play around with other fillings, such as a bit of leftover sautéed spinach or creamed chicken — but nothing too watery.

- If you make the mushrooms ahead, let them come to room temperature or add a few minutes to the baking time.

- If you don't have fresh tarragon on hand, use a scant teaspoon of dried and skip the garnish.

- If there are holes or tears in the ham slices, overlap or patch them as best you can.

- The eggs come out with runny yolks and just-set whites. If you like your eggs cooked more, just leave them in the oven for a few minutes longer.

tip

If you find that you're always fishing bits of shell out of the egg after you crack it, you might try this advice from Alton Brown in *I'm Just Here for the Food*. Instead of cracking an egg on the edge of a bowl, which drives the shell fragments into the egg, try cracking it with a flat blow on the counter. It may take a little practice to get the amount of force right, but you'll find that the shell breaks cleanly.

SOURCE: *Eula Mae's Cajun Kitchen*
by Eula Mae Doré and Marcelle R. Bienvenu
COOK: Eula Mae Doré

creamy scrambled eggs for a crowd

THIS METHOD CREATES SOME OF THE FLUFFIEST, softest scrambled eggs we've ever tasted.

We were skeptical about making them in the microwave, but faced with a gang of overnight guests, we decided to give it a try. The technique worked like a charm. While this recipe is not lightning fast (you do have to start and stop the microwave a few times), it takes only about 10 minutes and leaves the stove free for bacon, sausage, or whatever else you're cooking. And if you choose a decent-looking microwave-safe bowl, you can serve the eggs directly from it, meaning less to clean up.

Eula Mae is the chef of the McIlhenny empire on Avery Island, the spot where Tabasco sauce is made. Here's what she has to say about these eggs: "I can tell you that this dish will make your head and tummy feel a lot better after a long night of partying." Let the *bon temps rouler*!

serves about 12

16 jumbo eggs (or 20 large)
1 8-ounce package cream cheese, softened
1 teaspoon Tabasco sauce
1/2 teaspoon salt

1/4 teaspoon Accent seasoning (see note)
1/4 teaspoon freshly ground black pepper
2 cups milk

Whisk together all the ingredients in a large microwave-safe bowl. Microwave on high for 2 minutes.

Remove from the microwave and stir. Microwave for 1 to 2 minutes more, then stir. Repeat the process until the eggs are set but still moist, about 8 minutes total. The cooking time will vary according to the microwave. Serve hot.

cook's notes

🌿 Leave the wrapped cream cheese out overnight so it's softened in the morning when you're ready to make these eggs.

🌿 If you don't keep Accent seasoning in your spice drawer, just use a pinch more salt.

🌿 A heatproof rubber spatula works well for stirring the eggs as they cook.

🌿 This recipe is adaptable and can be made for fewer or more people by adjusting the amount of eggs, cream cheese, and milk.

🌿 Put the salt shaker and pepper grinder on the table, since you may find that some people like their eggs a bit more seasoned.

tip

According to R. W. Apple in the *New York Times*, the scrambled eggs at Bill's café in Sydney, Australia, have been described as the best scrambled eggs in the world. The secret to getting them soft, creamy, and amazingly light is in the technique. To serve 1 or 2 people, melt a sliver of butter in a nonstick skillet over high heat. Whisk together 2 eggs, ½ cup cream, and a pinch or two of salt. (It's best if the eggs and cream are at room temperature.) Add the egg mixture to the skillet and do nothing for 20 seconds, then very slowly fold and stir the eggs with a wooden spoon, and pause for 20 seconds more. Repeat the gentle stir-and-fold, then remove the skillet from the heat and let the residual heat finish the cooking. Give one last gentle stir and serve. Make the eggs in batches if you're feeding a crowd so you don't overfill the pan.

SOURCE: *A Return to Cooking*
by Eric Ripert and Michael Ruhlman
COOK: George Davis

george davis's pancakes

HOW MANY TIMES ARE WE LURED into making a certain dish by a gorgeous photograph only to find that the result looks nothing like the photo? Well, these pancakes are a happy exception to that rule. They come out beautifully browned, with lightly crispy edges and fluffy, soft insides — picture-perfect — and they taste as good as they look. The two tricks are vinegar and bacon fat. The bit of vinegar in the batter interacts with the baking soda and gives the cakes their light texture. And frying them in bacon fat gives the exterior a light crunch that you don't get with butter.

serves 6

2 cups all-purpose flour
2 teaspoons baking powder
1 teaspoon baking soda
1 teaspoon salt
2 cups milk

3 large eggs
1/4 cup canola oil
2 tablespoons white vinegar
3 tablespoons bacon fat
Maple syrup, for serving

Whisk together the dry ingredients in a large bowl.

Whisk together the milk, eggs, and oil in a medium bowl. Add the vinegar and whisk to combine. Add the liquid ingredients to the dry and whisk until the batter is just combined. The batter should still be lumpy.

Heat a large heavy skillet (cast iron works great) over medium heat. Add 2 teaspoons of the bacon fat. Using a 2-ounce ladle (or 1/4-cup measure) for each pancake, pour the batter into the skillet. When bubbles start to form on the tops of the pancakes and the edges look set, flip. Cook until golden brown on the second side. Transfer to a plate or plates, and continue with the remaining bacon fat and batter. Serve hot. Pass the maple syrup at the table.

❧ If you first cook up enough bacon for 6 people (12 slices), you should have just the right amount of bacon fat for frying the pancakes. Hold the bacon in a warm oven while you make the pancakes.

❧ Although the pancakes are at their best when served directly from the skillet, you can hold them briefly on a baking sheet in a warm oven.

❧ Be certain to use pure maple syrup here. These pancakes are too good to waste on the imitation stuff. Eric Ripert prefers syrup from Vermont, and we won't argue with that.

SOURCE: *Mollie Katzen's Sunlight Café*
by Mollie Katzen
Cook: Mollie Katzen

amazing overnight waffles

THERE'S NOTHING LIKE SOME WAFFLES to brighten a morning, especially if they're homemade. It's hard to say if these are superb because they're so easy or because they're so delicious. Now you have no more excuses not to make the real thing, since you mix the batter the night before and all you have to do in the morning is beat an egg, melt some butter, and stir. At the very most, there's 15 minutes of work here. Yeast gives the waffles a special subtle quality that sets them apart from the usual baking powder and baking soda kind.

They make a great birthday breakfast. Although you could certainly offer some fancy toppings, we're partial to the classic butter and maple syrup.

makes 6 to 8 waffles

2 cups all-purpose flour
1 tablespoon sugar
1 teaspoon active dry yeast (about $^1/_2$ packet)
$^1/_2$ teaspoon salt
2 cups milk

1 large egg, lightly beaten
6 tablespoons ($^3/_4$ stick) unsalted butter, melted, plus more for the waffle iron
Nonstick spray

Combine the flour, sugar, yeast, and salt in a large bowl. Whisk in the milk until blended. Cover the bowl tightly with plastic wrap and let stand overnight at room temperature. (If it's warmer than 70 degrees, refrigerate the batter.)

The next morning, heat the waffle iron. Beat the egg and the 6 tablespoons melted butter into the batter, which will be quite thin.

Spray the hot waffle iron with nonstick spray, and rub on a little butter with a paper towel or a piece of bread. Add just enough batter to cover the cooking surface, about $1^1/_3$ cups for a Belgian waffle, $^2/_3$ cup for a standard.

Cook the waffles until crisp and brown but not too dark, 2 to 3 minutes each. Serve hot.

℃ Use all the batter and freeze any leftover waffles individually. Reheat them in a toaster oven.

tip

Yeast comes in several different forms. One envelope contains 2¹/₄ teaspoons of active dry or instant yeast. Fresh compressed yeast, which is sold in the refrigerator section of the supermarket, comes in 1-ounce foil-wrapped squares. Although some sources say you should use 25 percent less instant yeast than other types, *The Baker's Catalogue* from King Arthur Flour says there's not enough difference to make measuring worthwhile.

SOURCE: *The Foster's Market Cookbook*
by Sara Foster with Sarah Belk King
COOK: Sara Foster

buttermilk scones

FOSTER'S MARKETS, IN DURHAM AND CHAPEL HILL, North Carolina, are just the kind of jazzy take-out markets we all wish we had right around the corner, with cases jammed with gorgeous prepared foods and counters loaded with tempting baked goodies. When we learned that this scone recipe is the most requested one at the market, we took note. Made with buttermilk and more butter than we've ever seen in a batch of scones, these magnificent pastries are light and flaky, with great flavor and just the right amount of crunch around the edges. While we were tempted by many of the variations — especially pecan-praline and lemon-almond — in the end the plain ones prevailed. Some things are just too good to mess with.

makes 12 scones

4^1/$_2$ cups all-purpose flour (see note)
^{1}/$_2$ cup sugar
2 teaspoons baking powder
^{1}/$_2$ teaspoon baking soda
^{1}/$_2$ teaspoon salt
24 tablespoons (3 sticks) cold unsalted butter, cut into ^{1}/$_4$-inch pieces

1^1/$_4$ cups buttermilk, plus more as needed
1 large egg beaten with 2 tablespoons milk, for the egg wash

Preheat the oven to 400 degrees. Lightly grease two baking sheets.

Combine the flour, sugar, baking powder, baking soda, and salt in a large bowl. Add the butter and cut it into the flour using a pastry blender or two knives until the mixture resembles cornmeal. (Or use a food processor fitted with the metal blade to cut the butter into the flour mixture by pulsing 10 to 12 times. Transfer the mixture to a large bowl to continue.) Do not overwork the dough.

Add the 1^1/$_4$ cups buttermilk and mix until just combined and the dough begins to stick together. Add additional buttermilk, 1 tablespoon at a time, if the dough seems too dry. It should just hang together but not be at all wet or sticky.

Turn the dough out onto a lightly floured surface and roll or pat it into two 6-inch rounds about 1¹/₂ inches thick. Cut each round in half, then cut each half into 3 triangles (pie-shaped wedges) and place them on the baking sheets. Brush the tops with the egg wash.

Bake until golden brown and firm to the touch, 30 to 35 minutes. Remove from the oven and serve immediately.

cook's notes

- For best results, measure the flour carefully using the spoon-and-sweep method: spoon the flour into a dry measuring cup until it's piled above the rim, then level the measure by sweeping the back side of a knife across the top. Never pack or tamp down the flour.
- If you want to add a little something to the basic recipe, toss 1¹/₄ cups toasted, chopped pecans into the dry ingredients before adding the buttermilk.
- We generally end up needing an additional 2 to 6 tablespoons buttermilk. Just go easy so you don't end up with a soggy dough.

tip

If you've already taken advantage of powdered buttermilk, you know that you sift it first, mix it into the dry ingredients, and then add plain water in place of buttermilk. A reader of *Fine Cooking* has a good tip: keep powdered buttermilk in the refrigerator to extend its shelf life.

SOURCE: *Everything Tastes Better with Bacon*
by Sara Perry
COOK: Sara Perry

never-a-leftover breakfast bread pudding

THIS SAVORY BREAD PUDDING IS FULL of exciting flavors: olives, smoked Gouda, roasted red peppers, and applewood-smoked bacon. Sara Perry is right on two counts: everything *does* taste better with bacon, and you probably won't have any leftovers.

Fortunately, this bread pudding has to be put together the night before, because it needs at least 6 hours for the bread to absorb the liquid and let the flavors develop. Then it's just a little over an hour — no actual morning work — before breakfast is ready.

serves 4 to 6

8 thick slices artisan-style applewood-smoked bacon (about 8 ounces), cut crosswise into 1-inch pieces (see note)

2 cups half-and-half

6 large eggs

1 tablespoon Dijon mustard

1/4 teaspoon kosher or coarse sea salt

1/2 teaspoon freshly ground black pepper

1 loaf (about 15 ounces) olive ciabatta, cut into 12–15 slices, slightly stale (see note)

1 1/4 cups grated smoked Gouda cheese (about 5 ounces)

1/2 cup julienned jarred roasted red bell peppers

Grease a 9-inch square baking pan.

In a medium heavy skillet, cook the bacon pieces over low to medium-low heat, turning as needed, until brown but not crisp. Using a slotted spoon, transfer to paper towels to drain.

Whisk together the half-and-half, eggs, mustard, salt, and pepper in a medium bowl until blended.

Arrange half the bread slices in the bottom of the prepared pan and top with half of the cheese, three fourths of the bacon, and three fourths of the roasted peppers. Arrange the remaining bread slices over the first layer. Top with the remaining cheese, bacon, and peppers.

Carefully pour the egg mixture over the bread. With the back of a spatula, lightly press the assembled pudding. Cover loosely with aluminum foil and refrigerate for at least 6 hours, preferably overnight.

Preheat the oven to 375 degrees. Bake the pudding, covered, for 35 minutes. Remove the foil, reduce the oven temperature to 275 degrees, and bake until golden brown, 15 to 20 minutes more. Let stand for 15 minutes before serving.

cook's notes

- The quality of the bacon is important. If you can't find Nueske's, the brand Sara Perry recommends, look for Niman Ranch bacon or a good local dry-cured bacon. Jones thick-sliced smoked bacon is available almost everywhere.
- We can't usually find olive ciabatta. If you can't either, just use regular ciabatta and toss a few pitted chopped olives over each bread layer. For stale bread slices, dry them in the oven at 200 degrees for 20 minutes or leave them on a wire rack at room temperature overnight.
- If you can't find or don't like smoked Gouda, use good Swiss cheese instead.

SOURCE: *A Real American Breakfast*
by Cheryl Alters Jamison and Bill Jamison
COOK: Ellen Stelling

sausage and cheese grits casserole

THERE'S NO REASON SOUTHERNERS should get to keep this splendid soufflé-like casserole to themselves. This version comes from South Carolina, and it's as great for supper as it is for breakfast. It's also surprisingly light.

If you're in a rush, you can use quick-cooking grits to eliminate about 20 minutes of prep time (see note). The casserole won't be quite as spiffy as the classic version, but it will be really good.

You can put the casserole together the night before and just bake it in the morning.

serves 6

- 3/4 teaspoon salt, or more to taste
- 1 cup stone-ground grits (see note)
- 1 pound breakfast sausage, crumbled and fried until well browned
- 1/4 pound mild or smoked cheddar cheese, grated (about 1 cup)
- 3 tablespoons unsalted butter
- 1/4 teaspoon Tabasco, Texas Pete, or other hot pepper sauce
- 3 large eggs, lightly beaten
- 1–2 scallions

Preheat the oven to 350 degrees. Butter a medium baking dish. Bring 4 cups water and 3/4 teaspoon salt to a boil in a large heavy saucepan over high heat. Whisk in the grits, a handful at a time. Reduce the heat to a bare simmer and cook the grits until thick and soft, 30 to 40 minutes. Stir the grits occasionally as they cook, more frequently as they thicken, scraping them off the bottom to prevent scorching. If the grits become too stiff to stir easily before they are cooked through, add a bit more hot water.

Remove the grits from the heat and stir in the sausage, cheese, butter, and hot sauce. Check the seasoning, adding more salt and hot pepper sauce if you wish. Mix in the eggs, stirring briskly. Spoon into the prepared baking dish. (The casserole can be made to this point, covered, and refrigerated overnight. In the morning let it sit at room temperature for 20 to 30 minutes before baking.)

Bake until puffed and lightly set, 35 to 40 minutes.

Meanwhile, slice the scallions, both white and green parts, into sections about 2 inches long. Cut each section into long, thin strips.

When the casserole is ready, spoon it onto plates immediately or let it cool for about 10 minutes and then cut it into soft-textured squares. Garnish each portion with a little shower of scallion strips, and serve.

cook's notes

- To use quick-cooking grits instead, reduce the amount of cooking water to the amount listed on the package. Be sure not to use instant grits.
- The casserole is only as good as the sausage you use. If you don't have a good local country sausage, look for nationally distributed brands like Jones or Jimmy Dean.

main dishes

main dishes

SOURCE: Alain Ducasse with Florence Fabricant
in the *New York Times*
COOK: Alain Ducasse

olive mill pasta

THIS SUPERB RECIPE REMINDS US that there's always something new to be discovered about cooking. The technique comes from the farm families who run olive mills in Liguria, on the Italian Riviera, and it was brought to our attention by the esteemed chef Alain Ducasse. When Monsieur Ducasse announced that since learning this technique he will not cook pasta any other way, we decided that was good enough for us.

The deal is this: rather than boil the pasta in a vat of salted water and then apply a sauce, you take advantage of the pasta's natural starch and cook it as you would Arborio rice for risotto. First sauté some of the flavoring ingredients — onions and potatoes in this instance — then add the pasta and stir it around. Add hot broth, little by little, and simmer until the pasta is cooked and the whole dish is creamy and richly concentrated. Finish it with a good measure of Parmigiano-Reggiano, a final drizzle of extra-virgin olive oil, and the bright taste of fresh basil. *Squisito!*

serves 4

$1/2$ cup extra-virgin olive oil

4 tablespoons ($1/2$ stick) butter

$1/4$ pound potatoes, preferably fingerlings, peeled and cut into $1/4$-inch-thick slices

2 medium-small onions, minced
About $5^1/2$ cups vegetable or light chicken stock

14 ounces artisanal short-cut dried pasta, such as strozzapreti (see note), penne, gemelli, or fusilli

Salt and freshly ground black pepper

2 medium-size ripe tomatoes, peeled, squeezed of seeds and juice, or $2/3$ cup diced dry-packed sun-dried tomatoes, covered with boiling water, then drained

8 fresh basil or arugula sprigs, leaves removed and slivered and stems lightly crushed

1 garlic clove, crushed

1 bunch scallions, trimmed, slant-cut into 1-inch lengths

3 ounces freshly grated Parmigiano-Reggiano cheese (about 1 cup)

Heat $1/4$ cup of the oil in a large sauté pan (preferably 12-inch) over medium heat. Add the butter. When it melts, add the potatoes and onions. Cook, stirring gently, until they begin to turn golden.

Bring stock to a slow simmer in a small saucepan.

Add the pasta to the sauté pan and stir gently. Lightly season with salt and pepper, and add the tomatoes, basil or arugula stems, and garlic. Add 1½ cups of the stock. Cook, stirring gently, until nearly all the stock has been absorbed or evaporated. Add the scallions and another cup of stock and cook, stirring, adding additional stock from time to time so there is always some liquid in the pan, until the pasta is al dente, about 18 minutes. Remove garlic and herb stems.

Fold in the cheese and 3 tablespoons of the remaining oil. Add the slivered basil or arugula. Season with additional salt and pepper as needed. Transfer to warm soup or pasta bowls, taking care that the ingredients are well distributed. Drizzle the remaining 1 tablespoon oil over each bowl and serve.

cook's notes

- The secret to this recipe is, not surprisingly, the pasta. You have to use a high-quality short-cut pasta. Lesser supermarket brands won't hold up, and long noodles just don't work. Look for brands made from 100 percent semolina and shaped with old-fashioned bronze dies, such as Latini. These pastas are usually labeled "artisanal" and have better flavor and a rougher texture that absorbs the sauce.

- The original recipe calls for strozzapreti, a short, thick, twisted pasta that translates literally as "priest stranglers."

- If you can't find fingerling potatoes, use any smallish potato. Baby Yukon Golds or small red creamer potatoes are good choices.

- You want a light stock or broth here so it doesn't overpower the dish. If you buy a 1-quart package of broth, add 1½ cups of water to thin it. This will give you the 5½ cups you'll need.

- Use the back of a chef's knife to bruise the basil or arugula stems. This releases their flavors more quickly.

- If you like to ad-lib, use this recipe as a blueprint and follow the technique with other ingredients. The potatoes contribute additional starch, which helps make things creamy, but cooked white beans, such as cannellini, would work too.

SOURCE: Sheryl Julian and Julie Riven in the
Boston Globe Magazine
COOK: Daniele Baliani, after his aunt Adriana

spaghettini with tuna sauce

WHEN A FIRST-CLASS CHEF LIKE DANIELE BALIANI, who has worked in the kitchens of Daniel Boulud and Fauchon, among other prestigious places, treasures a hand-me-down recipe from his family, you know it's going to be good. Although we saw several spaghettinis with tuna sauce this year, when we did a mini cook-off, this one was the clear winner. It's just a little spicy, with bursts of surprising flavor. In winter, you can use little cherry tomatoes (don't bother peeling them).

Except for some fresh tomatoes and parsley, everything here is more or less a staple, so you can make this dish on the spur of the moment. It's served at room temperature, and the balance of flavors is truly remarkable. No cheese, please.

serves 4 to 6

1 tablespoon salt
1/4 cup olive oil
2 tablespoons pine nuts
2 garlic cloves, finely chopped
3–4 anchovy fillets, preferably white (see note)
1 teaspoon capers, coarsely chopped
1 teaspoon crushed red pepper flakes

1 28-ounce can whole peeled tomatoes, crushed in a bowl, with their juices
4 vine-ripened tomatoes, cored, peeled, and finely chopped
1 6- to 8-ounce can Italian tuna in olive oil, partially drained
1/4 cup golden raisins
1 pound spaghettini
1/4 cup chopped fresh parsley
Freshly ground black pepper

Bring a large pot of water to a boil. Add the salt to the water.

Meanwhile, in a large flameproof casserole, heat the oil over medium heat. Cook the pine nuts, stirring frequently, for 2 minutes, or until lightly golden.

Add the garlic, anchovies, capers, and red pepper flakes. Cook, stirring often, for 2 minutes, breaking up the anchovies as you stir.

Add the canned and fresh tomatoes and bring the sauce to a boil, stirring occasionally. Reduce the heat to low and simmer, stirring occasionally, for 30 minutes, or until the sauce thickens.

Stir the tuna and the raisins into the sauce. Break up the tuna into small pieces as you stir. Return the sauce to a simmer, then remove from the heat and set aside.

Add the spaghettini to the boiling water and return to a full boil, stirring. Cook the spaghettini for 6 minutes, or until it is not quite cooked through.

Drain the pasta in a colander and immediately transfer the pasta to the sauce. Add the parsley and pepper to taste. Toss well to coat the spaghettini. Set it aside to cool and serve at room temperature.

cook's note

As always, first-rate ingredients count for a lot in this dish. You probably won't find white anchovies unless you're a chef yourself, but of course you can use ordinary anchovies — look for the ones packed in small jars, which are likely to be higher quality than the tinned ones. Good canned tomatoes, either from the San Marzano area of Italy or Muir Glen organic tomatoes, are crucial, as is a good artisanal pasta, such as Latini. Don't substitute water-packed tuna. Two good brands of Italian tuna to look for are Progresso and Genoa.

SOURCE: Cooking class handout from
Robert Sinskey Vineyards
COOK: Craig Stoll

spaghetti with plum tomato sauce

MADE FROM THE SIMPLEST INGREDIENTS POSSIBLE — tomatoes, garlic, olive oil, and basil — this spaghetti recipe is nothing less than brilliant. It's what we dream of when we think of spaghetti and red sauce. It recalls those silky bowls of pasta that we used to get as a side dish in real Italian restaurants but could never come close to recreating at home, the ones in which each bite of pasta is infused with the smooth, sweet taste of the tomato sauce.

The first step is a long, lazy simmer. The cue that the sauce is ready is that the olive oil will go from sitting on the surface to becoming absorbed into the sauce. The other secret to this dish is cooking the spaghetti only partway and finishing it in the sauce. The result is a classic bowl of spaghetti: juicy, shiny, and full of flavor, with no pool of sauce sitting in the bottom of the bowl.

serves 4 (with leftover sauce)

2 28-ounce cans peeled
  whole plum tomatoes
4 garlic cloves
  Kosher salt
1/2 cup extra-virgin olive oil, plus
  more for serving (optional)
3 cups water

Freshly ground black pepper
Crushed red pepper flakes
1/2 bunch fresh basil, leaves only
1 pound spaghetti
  Freshly grated Parmigiano-
  Reggiano cheese, for serving

Working over the top of the can, break open each tomato and pull out the seeds. Let the seeds and juice fall back into the can. Drop the tomatoes into a separate container as you work. When finished, squeeze the tomatoes with your hands to break them up slightly, then strain the juice from the can over them. Discard the seeds.

Smash the garlic with the side of a knife and smear it slightly with a sprinkling of salt. Combine the garlic and the 1/2 cup oil in a heavy stainless steel pot over medium-low heat. Cover and stew the garlic slowly until soft but not browned, about 10 minutes.

Add the tomatoes and their juice and the water. Season lightly with salt, pepper, and a touch of red pepper flakes. Increase the heat to medium-high, bring to a boil, and skim the foam that rises to the surface, being careful not to skim off the oil. Reduce the heat to a quick simmer and cook, uncovered, until the sauce is reduced by two thirds and the oil is emulsified into the sauce, $1^1/_2$ to 2 hours.

Remove the sauce from the heat and pass two thirds of it through a food mill fitted with the medium disk. Stir the puree back into the remaining sauce. Tear the basil leaves into pieces and add them to the sauce. Season to taste with salt, pepper, and red pepper flakes.

To serve, place $2^1/_4$ cups pasta sauce in a large sauté pan (see note). If the sauce is cold, bring it to a gentle simmer. If it's still hot, keep it over low heat to stay warm.

Meanwhile, cook the pasta in a large pot of lightly salted water for 6 minutes. It should be quite al dente. Drain the pasta, reserving $1^1/_2$ cups of the cooking water. Add the spaghetti to the sauce along with 1 cup of the cooking water. Increase the heat to medium-high and cook, stirring frequently, until the pasta is thoroughly cooked and has completely absorbed the sauce, about 5 minutes, adding more pasta cooking water if necessary. Adjust the seasoning with salt, pepper, and red pepper flakes. Serve immediately in warm pasta bowls. Drizzle with a thread of top-quality extra-virgin olive oil, if you like, and pass grated Parmigiano at the table.

cook's notes

- You'll need a really big sauté pan to accommodate all of the sauce and the full pound of cooked spaghetti. If you don't have one, simply use two smaller sauté pans on two burners, and divide everything in half.
- For making 4 servings or fewer, here are the proportions per serving: 1 generous cup sauce, 4 to 6 tablespoons cooking water, and $1/_4$ pound dried spaghetti.
- Since it's easiest to make this sauce in large quantities — enough to serve 8 — you'll have leftover sauce. Freeze it in small containers for a quick supper later on. The sauce can be refrigerated for several days or frozen for a couple of months.

main dishes

SOURCE: Sarah Lydon in *Saveur*
COOK: Giuliano Gargani

pasta with citrus zest and cream

BE FOREWARNED THAT THIS PASTA DISH is rich beyond belief, but it's also elegant and wildly delicious. It's the type of thing we might serve as a first course for a New Year's Eve feast or whip up on the spur of the moment on a weeknight. The tantalizing combination of orange, lemon, and mint is a pleasant change from ordinary creamy pasta dishes and serves to undercut some of the richness.

The recipe comes from a small, lively trattoria in Florence where, as the story goes, evening celebrations are apt to include the patrons and the staff and merrily stretch through till morning. Perhaps it's the pasta?

Fresh pasta is the best choice for this delicate sauce.

serve 4

1 large lemon
1 orange (see notes)
1 cup heavy cream
1 cup half-and-half
2 tablespoons cognac

Leaves from 4 fresh mint sprigs
Salt
10 ounces fresh pasta, preferably tagliarini or linguine
1 cup freshly grated Parmigiano-Reggiano cheese

Bring a large pot of water to boil over high heat.

Meanwhile, gently scrub the lemon and orange under warm running water to remove any waxy residue, then pat dry with paper towels. Finely grate the zest from the lemon and orange.

Combine the cream, half-and-half, and citrus zests in a large skillet over medium heat. Bring to a boil, stirring frequently with a wooden spoon, and cook until reduced by about one fourth, about 10 minutes. Add the cognac and mint and cook until some of the alcohol evaporates, about 2 minutes. Season to taste with salt.

When the pot of water boils, add 2 generous pinches of salt. Add the pasta and cook, stirring frequently, until just tender, $1^1/_2$ to 2 minutes. Using tongs, transfer the pasta to the skillet with the sauce. Add the cheese and cook over medium heat, stirring constantly, until the sauce thickens, about 1 minute more. Serve immediately.

cook's notes

- Choose a small orange if you can, or don't use all the zest. You want only a bit more orange zest than lemon. Otherwise, the orange will dominate.
- When grating the citrus zest, be sure to use only the outermost orange and yellow zest. Avoid getting down to the white pith, which is bitter.

tip

Pasta is always best served in warm pasta bowls, and here's a neat tip from Carla Cimarosti, a *Fine Cooking* reader. When you drain pasta, put the serving bowl (or bowls) in the sink under the colander and fill with hot water as you drain the pasta. The hot water warms the bowl(s) as you finish up the pasta. If you need to reserve some cooking water for the sauce, just measure it out before draining the pasta into the sink. There will be more than enough hot water for heating the bowls and finishing the sauce.

SOURCE: *Food & Wine*
COOK: Marcia Kiesel

three-cheese baked pasta

THIS SCRUMPTIOUS PASTA WILL REMIND YOU a lot of lasagna, but there's no layering. Instead, a single layer of sauced pasta is covered with a rich cheese topping — ricotta, mozzarella, and Parmesan. There's a surprise mixed into the sweet red peppers in the sauce: a smoky taste of chipotle powder (chipotles are smoked jalapeños) that gives it a little heat as well.

The pasta looks great, especially if you can find trenne (triangular tubes). Add a bottle of Chianti, a big green salad, and some garlic bread and you're set for company.

serves 6

1/4 cup extra-virgin olive oil

4 red bell peppers, thinly sliced

1 large onion, thinly sliced

6 garlic cloves: 4 halved, 2 minced
    Salt

1 teaspoon chipotle powder (see note)

1 28-ounce can plum tomatoes, drained, juices reserved

3 cups ricotta cheese

3/4 cup freshly grated Parmesan cheese

1/2 cup grated fresh mozzarella
    Freshly ground black pepper

1 pound trenne or rigatoni

1 tablespoon unsalted butter, melted

Heat the oil in a medium enameled cast-iron Dutch oven over medium heat. Add the bell peppers, the onion, the 4 halved garlic cloves, and a pinch of salt. Cover and cook, stirring occasionally, until the vegetables soften, about 15 minutes. Add the chipotle powder and cook uncovered, stirring, until the vegetables are lightly browned, about 5 minutes more. Add the tomatoes and their juices, cover, and simmer over low heat for 20 minutes. Scrape the sauce into a food processor and puree. Wipe out the Dutch oven. Strain the sauce into the Dutch oven and season with salt; keep warm.

Preheat the oven to 375 degrees. Butter a 10-x-14-inch glass baking dish. Combine the ricotta, 1/2 cup of the Parmesan, the mozzarella, and the minced garlic in a medium bowl. Season with salt and pepper.

Cook the pasta in a large pot of boiling salted water until almost al dente. Drain the pasta and return it to the pot, then toss with 2 cups of the sauce. Spread the pasta in the baking dish, then spread the ricotta mixture on top and drizzle with the melted butter. Sprinkle the remaining 1/4 cup Parmesan on top. Cover with aluminum foil and bake for 25 minutes, or until hot.

Preheat the broiler. Uncover the pasta and broil 4 inches from the heat for 2 minutes, or until the topping is evenly browned. Serve hot.

cook's notes

- Chipotle powder is available in gourmet specialty stores. To make your own, preheat the oven to 300 degrees. Pull the stems off the whole dried chipotles and slit them open, removing the seeds. Open them out flat on a baking sheet and toast for 3 to 5 minutes, or until they're completely stiff. Crumble them into a bowl and let cool. Grind in a spice grinder or coffee mill. The chile powder will keep, tightly sealed, for 3 months in the freezer.

- You can bake the pasta right up to the point of broiling, cool it, and freeze it. Bring the pasta to room temperature before heating it thoroughly and broiling.

SOURCE: *Seriously Simple*
by Diane Rossen Worthington
COOK: Diane Rossen Worthington

baked pasta
with sausage and tomato pesto

SERIOUSLY SIMPLE IS JUST WHAT WE'RE AFTER, and this great spicy party dish delivers the goods. It has all the crowd-pleasing appeal of lasagna, but it's much lighter, fresher, and more interesting. Mixing baby spinach right into the pasta gives it both a jolt of color and a new flavor. The smoked Gouda is an innovative touch that works brilliantly, subtly softening instead of melting.

The pasta is cook-friendly, too, since it relies on high-quality convenience products such as store-bought marinara and pesto sauces and spinach that's already cleaned and ready to use.

serves 6 to 8

SAUCE

- 1 pound hot Italian sausage, casings removed
- 1 onion, finely chopped
- 3 garlic cloves, minced
- 2 26-ounce boxes Pomi brand marinara sauce (see note)
- 6 tablespoons pesto sauce (store-bought is fine)
  Salt and freshly ground black pepper

PASTA

- 1 pound penne
- 8 ounces smoked Gouda or smoked mozzarella, finely diced
- 1 cup freshly grated Parmesan
- 1 6-ounce bag baby spinach leaves

TO MAKE THE SAUCE

Heat a large Dutch oven over medium-high heat and add the sausage and onion. Cook, breaking up the sausage with a spoon, for about 5 minutes, or until softened, stirring frequently to evenly cook the onion. Add the garlic and cook for 1 minute more. Add the marinara sauce and reduce the heat to medium. Simmer for 10 minutes, or until the sauce begins to thicken. Stir in the pesto and season with salt and pepper. Set aside.

TO MAKE THE PASTA

Cook the penne in a large pot of salted boiling water for about 10 minutes, or until al dente. Drain well.

TO ASSEMBLE

Preheat the oven to 375 degrees. Oil a 9-x-13-inch baking dish. Spread a thin layer of sauce over the bottom of the dish.

Combine the pasta with the remaining sauce, the Gouda or mozzarella, $1/3$ cup of the Parmesan, and the spinach in a large bowl, mixing well. Spoon the mixture into the prepared dish and sprinkle the remaining $2/3$ cup Parmesan over the top.

Bake for about 30 minutes, or until the casserole begins to bubble and the cheese is browned. Serve hot.

cook's notes

- If the Pomi brand isn't available at your market, use another high-quality prepared marinara sauce.
- Smoked gouda is available at all cheese shops and many supermarkets.
- Diane Worthington points out that the sauce can also be used to top cooked pasta or polenta.
- You can assemble the pasta in its dish up to 2 days ahead and keep it covered in the refrigerator. Remove from the refrigerator half an hour before baking.
- Make a double batch and freeze one for another day.

SOURCE: *The Whole Foods Market Cookbook*
by Steve Petusevsky
COOK: Unknown

southwest king ranch casserole

ACCORDING TO OUR SOURCES at Whole Foods Market, the origin of this recipe is a mystery. They tell us that it was created in one of their stores in the Southwest, but no one really knows where or by whom. They do know, however, that it's one of the most popular dishes at their take-out counters — a fact that didn't surprise us once we tried it.

The best way to describe this tasty, comforting casserole is as a cross between lasagna and enchiladas. Made with mostly prepared ingredients, this recipe delivers big flavor with a minimum amount of fuss. Simply load up the casserole dish with layers of tomatillo salsa (jarred is fine), corn tortillas, spicy shredded chicken (rotisserie is fine), sour cream, mild green chiles, and grated cheese. This is best made 1 to 3 days before serving so that the flavors meld, which makes it a great party dish. Just reheat it when it's time to serve. If you like, add a garnish of fresh cilantro.

serves 8

3 tablespoons canola oil
1¹/₂ cups diced yellow onions
2 garlic cloves, minced
   (about 1 teaspoon)
2 teaspoons paprika
1 teaspoon ground cumin
1 teaspoon salt
¹/₂ teaspoon coarsely ground
   black pepper
3 cups shredded cooked boneless
   chicken (see note)

¹/₂ cup chopped fresh cilantro
2 cups grated Monterey Jack cheese
1 cup grated cheddar cheese
2 cups prepared tomatillo sauce
   (see note)
8 corn tortillas
1¹/₂ cups sour cream
¹/₂ cup canned chopped green chiles,
   drained (see note)

Preheat the oven to 350 degrees. Heat the oil in a large sauté pan over medium-high heat. Add the onions and cook until translucent, 2 to 3 minutes. Stir in the garlic, paprika, cumin, salt, and black pepper. Add the chicken and heat through. Remove from the heat and stir in the cilantro.

Combine the cheeses in a small bowl.

Spread 1 cup of the tomatillo sauce on the bottom of an 8-inch square baking pan. Arrange 4 of the tortillas on top of the sauce, overlapping as necessary. Spread ³/₄ cup of the sour cream evenly over the tortillas. Add ¹/₂ cup of the remaining tomatillo sauce, 1¹/₂ cups of the chicken mixture, 1 cup of the cheeses, and ¹/₄ cup of the green chiles.

Top with the remaining 4 tortillas and the remaining ³/₄ cup sour cream, ¹/₂ cup tomatillo sauce, and chicken mixture. Follow with 1 cup of the cheese and the remaining ¹/₄ cup green chiles. End with the remaining 1 cup cheese sprinkled on top. Bake until hot and bubbly, for about 25 minutes. Serve.

cook's notes

- We particularly like the darker, more flavorful thigh meat in this recipe, but any combination works. You can also use an already-cooked rotisserie chicken from the market. One small one should yield just enough for this casserole.
- Look for jarred tomatillo sauce in the Mexican section of your grocery store. A mild green salsa may be substituted.
- A 4-ounce can of chopped green chiles equals the ¹/₂ cup needed here.
- To make ahead, bake the casserole, cool, cover, and refrigerate until needed. Reheat at 350 degrees for about 30 minutes, or until heated through.

SOURCE: *Chile Pepper*
COOK: Claudia M. Caruana

spicy baked rice

THIS DELICIOUS CASSEROLE with a soft, almost creamy center and a crusty top is a sure hit. It's even good served cold or at room temperature. The technique of baking uncooked rice with mixture of sauce, ground meat, raw eggs, and cheese comes from Malta and was unfamiliar to us but works beautifully.

For color and taste, stir a handful of fresh or frozen peas into the rice when it first comes out of the oven.

serves 4 to 6

5 tablespoons olive or vegetable oil

1 large onion, chopped

1 large frying pepper or bell pepper, seeded and chopped

1 jalapeño pepper, minced (optional)

1–5 garlic cloves, minced

1 pound lean ground beef or pork, or a combination

4 cups cold water, plus more if needed

4 cups plain tomato sauce (see note)

1–3 fresh basil leaves, shredded

1–2 fresh flat-leaf parsley sprigs, chopped

Salt and freshly ground black pepper

2 large eggs

2 large egg whites

1/4 cup freshly grated Parmesan cheese

1 1/2 cups uncooked white rice, soaked in warm water for 30 minutes and drained

Preheat the oven to 400 degrees. Spray a 2 1/2- to 3-quart baking dish with non-stick spray (see note).

Heat the oil in a large skillet over medium heat. Sauté the onion, frying pepper or bell pepper, jalapeño (if using), and garlic until the onion becomes translucent, 5 to 10 minutes. Add the ground meat and cook, stirring, until the meat is no longer pink. Drain off and discard the fat. Add the water, tomato sauce, basil, parsley, and salt and pepper to taste. Simmer, stirring occasionally, for 25 minutes, to break up any clumps of meat. Set aside to cool.

Mix together the eggs, egg whites, and Parmesan in a medium bowl. Stir into the cooled meat mixture.

Place the uncooked rice in the prepared baking dish. Carefully ladle the ground meat mixture onto the rice. Bake for 30 minutes. Remove the baking dish from the oven and stir the rice mixture thoroughly. Bake until the top is browned, about 1 hour more. If the rice appears to be drying out too soon, add more water and stir again. The top should be crunchy and blackened slightly in spots. Serve hot or cold.

cook's notes

- You can use jarred tomato sauce — just buy one that has no corn syrup in the ingredients.
- Feel free to increase the amount of parsley and basil in the sauce for more freshness and flavor.
- Control the spiciness by adding more or less garlic and including the jalapeño or not.

SOURCE: *Nancy Silverton's Sandwich Book*
by Nancy Silverton with Teri Gelber
COOK: Nancy Silverton

scrambled eggs, long-cooked broccoli, and feta cheese sandwich

SANDWICH RECIPES SEEMED TO BE EVERYWHERE this year, and we were having trouble choosing even before we opened *Nancy Silverton's Sandwich Book,* an impressively diverse collection. This open-faced sandwich got our vote because its components are fabulous on their own and even better when stacked together. Stewing the broccoli in olive oil transforms it into something altogether irresistible. Parboiling it first in the salty water helps it keeps its texture. Silverton's eggs come out creamy, with large, billowy curds, and the salty, slightly sharp feta adds just the right balance.

serves 4

LONG-COOKED BROCCOLI

1–2 heads broccoli (about 1³/4 pounds)

1/4 cup plus 2 teaspoons kosher salt, plus more to taste

1 small onion, thinly sliced

4 garlic cloves, thinly sliced

1 whole dried red chile pepper

1/2 cup plus 2 tablespoons extra-virgin olive oil

BREAD

4 slices white or whole wheat sourdough bread

1 garlic clove

SCRAMBLED EGGS

8 extra-large eggs

1/2 teaspoon kosher salt

2 tablespoons unsalted butter

TOPPING

1–2 teaspoons fresh lemon juice, or to taste

Salt and freshly ground black pepper

4–6 ounces feta cheese, preferably French Valbreso or Bulgarian

1/4 cup finely chopped fresh chives

TO MAKE THE BROCCOLI

Trim off and discard 1 inch from the bottoms of the broccoli stalks. Cut the heads off the stalks, leaving about 1 inch of the stalk still attached to the florets. Set aside. Slice the outer layer of fibrous peel off the main stalks, and cut them vertically into long, flat slices, about 1/4 inch thick and 1 inch wide. (If the broccoli seems extra tough and fibrous, slice the stalk on the extreme diagonal into 1/4-inch-thick pieces.) Slice all the way through the broccoli top, cutting it vertically into 1-inch-thick pieces, cutting each into florets when necessary. You should have several long pieces of broccoli.

Bring 8 cups water and $^1/_4$ cup of the salt to a boil in a large pot. Have a large bowl of ice water handy. Cook the broccoli in the boiling water until it turns bright green, about 2 minutes. Drain and place the broccoli in the ice water to chill. Drain well, then pat dry with paper towels.

Combine the broccoli, onion, garlic, chile, the remaining 2 teaspoons salt, and the oil in a large heavy skillet over very low heat. Cook, stirring occasionally, for about 1$^1/_2$ hours, or until the broccoli is very soft and tender. Season with salt.

TO PREPARE THE BREAD

Grill or toast the bread. Rub one side of the bread with the garlic clove. Place the slices on serving plates, garlic side up. Set aside.

TO MAKE THE SCRAMBLED EGGS

Whisk 4 of the eggs and $^1/_4$ teaspoon of the salt in a medium bowl. Melt 1 tablespoon of the butter in a large nonstick skillet over medium heat. When the butter starts to bubble, pour the eggs into the skillet. Using a heatproof rubber spatula, scrape down the sides and bottom of the skillet, letting the uncooked egg run underneath around the edges, folding the egg over itself, keeping it moving continuously. Cook for 2 to 3 minutes, or until very softly scrambled with large curds. Repeat with remaining eggs, salt, and butter.

TO ASSEMBLE THE SANDWICHES

Arrange the broccoli over the bread and squeeze a few drops of lemon juice over it. Pile the scrambled eggs on top, leaving a border of broccoli around the edge. Sprinkle with salt and pepper to taste. Crumble about 2 tablespoons feta on top of each, sprinkle with chives, and serve.

cook's notes

- Make extra broccoli to have on hand as a snack or for pasta, omelets, and pizza.
- The broccoli can be stewed one or two days ahead, covered, and refrigerated.
- Look for a feta cheese that is creamy, rather than chalky or crumbly.

SOURCE: *The Convent Cook* by Maria Tisdall
COOK: Maria Tisdall

convent chicken

THIS SUBTLY FLAVORED, unsweetened barbecued chicken, which can be grilled outdoors or baked in the oven, is a bit unusual — it has both garlic powder and fresh tarragon, ingredients you almost never see together, and it also has a huge amount of fresh lemon juice. As Maria Tisdall, who really does cook for a convent, notes, people always eat more of it than you expect they will. If by chance there are any leftovers, it's also excellent cold.

Tisdall writes that people always seem to like the thighs best, and they're our favorite too. Count on about 18 of them if you decide to use all thighs.

serves 6 to 8

4 chicken breast halves, skin on
6 chicken legs, skin on
6 chicken thighs, skin on
1 cup low-sodium soy sauce
1/2 cup fresh lemon juice

2 tablespoons chopped fresh tarragon or 2 teaspoons dried
2 teaspoons garlic powder
1 teaspoon paprika
1/2 teaspoon freshly ground black pepper

Rinse the chicken pieces under cold running water and pat dry with paper towels. Combine the soy sauce, lemon juice, tarragon, garlic powder, paprika, and pepper in a bowl. Divide the chicken evenly between two large zip-top plastic bags. Divide the marinade evenly between the bags. Roll the tops of the bags down to expel as much air as possible before sealing. Massage the marinade into the chicken to coat evenly. Place in the refrigerator and marinate for at least 3 hours, or preferably overnight. Turn the bags several times to redistribute the marinade.

Prepare a hot fire in a charcoal grill or preheat a gas grill until very hot. Place the chicken, skin side down, on the grill rack. Discard the bags and marinade. If using a charcoal grill, move the chicken away from the hottest area. If using a gas grill, reduce the flame to medium-low. Cover the grill. (This will allow the chicken to cook thoroughly without drying out.) Turn the chicken frequently so it cooks evenly and thoroughly. It should be ready in about 35 minutes, or when the internal temperature reaches 165 degrees. (When it's done, the chicken will be golden brown.)

To serve, place the chicken on a large serving platter and let your family and friends go to town.

cook's note

If you want to cook the chicken in the oven, it will take about 45 minutes at 375 degrees. Use a baster to drain off any excess liquid, or let the chicken drain in a colander for half an hour before you cook it.

SOURCE: *New York Times*
COOK: Amanda Hesser

braised chicken with prunes

THE COMBINATION OF CHICKEN, PRUNES, AND WHITE WINE is a culinary epiphany. The dark meat of the chicken becomes juicy and succulent after simmering in the wine and fruit. The prunes' richness amplifies the fruitiness of the wine, while the wine's acidity (along with a bit of vinegar) cuts the overall richness. The result is a quick weeknight meal — it takes less than 45 minutes start to finish — that's tasty enough to serve to company.

Serve a side of mashed potatoes or buttered egg noodles to soak up the juices. Pour a rather forceful red wine to accompany the meal. This is one chicken dish that can stand up to it.

serves 4

- 4 chicken thighs, skin on
- 4 chicken drumsticks, skin on
- Kosher salt and freshly ground black pepper
- 1/2 cup all-purpose flour

- 3 tablespoons olive oil
- 1 cup dry white wine
- 1/4 cup white wine vinegar
- 12 large, plump dried prunes (see note)

Generously season the chicken pieces with salt and pepper. Spread the flour in a wide shallow bowl and dredge the chicken pieces until well coated. Shake off any excess flour.

Heat a deep sauté pan (just large enough to hold the chicken pieces in a single layer) over medium-high heat for a minute or two. Add the oil and heat until it shimmers. Arrange the chicken pieces in the pan, skin side down, and don't move them until the undersides are browned, about 3 minutes. Turn the chicken, and let sit again until browned on the other side, 3 to 4 minutes.

Add the wine, vinegar, and prunes. Cover, reduce the heat to low, and simmer, basting occasionally, until the chicken is tender and almost falling off the bone, about 30 minutes.

Using a slotted spoon, transfer the chicken to a platter and keep warm. Increase the heat to high and reduce the pan juices for 1 to 2 minutes. Pour the juices over the chicken and serve.

cook's notes

- Some cooks like to remove the chicken skin before braising, but we're glad to see that it's left on here. It adds flavor and richness.
- Be sure to follow the instruction that tells you not to move the chicken while browning it. Moving it around will slow the browning and change the timing of the recipe.

SOURCE: **Bret Begun** in *Newsweek*
COOK: **Bobby Flay**

roasted turkey with herbs

YOU WANT TO ROAST A TRULY GREAT, interesting bird, but you also want to avoid spending hours in the kitchen fussing with it. Bobby Flay's got the solution, and we loved it. All you need besides a big bird is fresh sage leaves, butter, salt, and pepper. If you want to make Flay's pomegranate sauce, which is sweetly good, it will take a little longer, but not much.

The turkey tastes really buttery, and the sage perfumes the whole kitchen with Thanksgiving fragrance. This bird also has eye appeal, because the sage leaves are visible through the crisp skin.

serves 12

1 16-pound fresh turkey, at room temperature (see note)

20 fresh sage leaves

16 tablespoons (2 sticks) unsalted butter, melted

Salt and freshly ground black pepper

Pomegranate Sauce (recipe follows)

Preheat the oven to 450 degrees. Discard the neck and gizzard (or save them for stock). Rinse the turkey with cold water and pat dry with paper towels. Loosen the skin of the breasts and drumsticks and slip the sage leaves underneath the skin. Rub the turkey with ¼ cup of the melted butter. Sprinkle the skin and cavity with salt and pepper. Truss the turkey and place it on a rack in a large roasting pan.

Roast the turkey for 45 minutes, basting with butter every 10 minutes. Reduce the oven temperature to 350 degrees and roast for about 1¼ hours more, or until an instant-read thermometer inserted in the inner thigh reads 180 degrees. If the legs or breasts brown too quickly, cover them with aluminum foil. Let the bird rest for 20 to 30 minutes on a cutting board before carving. Serve with Pomegranate Sauce, if desired.

cook's notes

✥ Should you buy an organic, free-range, or kosher turkey? We tried all three this year, and while they were all good, the kosher turkey was the juiciest and tastiest, because the salt develops flavor and helps to retain the juices. Kosher turkeys aren't available everywhere, but keep an eye out for them. (They also have a few quills left in; you need to go after these with tweezers before you do anything else to the turkey.) This year's darling is the heirloom turkey, big proud ones that look like the birds in our storybooks about the Pilgrims and with suitable names like Narragansett. These turkeys are meaty and delicious — if you can find one, grab it.

🍂 It will take a 16-pound turkey about 4 hours to come to room temperature, so plan accordingly.

tips

🍂 Peck's Market, a full-service supermarket in New York's Hudson Valley, offered a similar turkey breast recipe in their annual calendar. They used fresh thyme and rosemary as well as sage and laid out the leaves under the skin in a beautiful pattern.

🍂 Just after Thanksgiving, we caught Linda Wertheimer on NPR interviewing Judy Rodgers of Zuni Cafe in San Francisco on the subject of what to do with turkey leftovers. Judy likes to make turkey salad. She warms bits of turkey in leftover drippings and adds strips of red bell pepper, toasted pine nuts, currants, croutons, ribbons of fennel, and a handful of bitter greens. Whisk together a red wine vinaigrette, and you've got lunch.

pomegranate sauce

3 tablespoons unsalted butter
1 medium Spanish onion, finely diced
1 tablespoon minced garlic
1 tablespoon whole black peppercorns
1 cup port
6 cups homemade chicken stock

2 cups pomegranate juice (see note) or cranberry juice
2 tablespoons pomegranate molasses (see note)
2 tablespoons light brown sugar
Salt and freshly ground black pepper
1/2 cup pomegranate seeds
3 tablespoons finely chopped fresh chives

Melt the butter in a large saucepan over medium heat. Add the onion and garlic and sweat until the onion is tender, about 3 minutes. Add the peppercorns and cook for 3 minutes. Add the port and stir until most of it evaporates. Add the stock, pomegranate or cranberry juice, pomegranate molasses, and brown sugar. Increase the heat to medium-high and reduce slowly until you have a sauce consistency. Season to taste with salt and pepper. Remove from the heat and garnish with the pomegranate seeds and chives.

❧ Pomegranate juice can be found in some Middle Eastern markets, health food stores, and California farmers' markets and supermarkets. We generally make our own from fresh pomegranates. Each large pomegranate yields $^3/_4$ to 1 cup seeds or $^1/_2$ cup of juice, so figure on 4 to 6 pomegranates for this recipe. To make the pomegranate juice, whir the seeds in batches ($1^1/_2$ to 2 cups at a time) in a food processor or blender. Strain through a cheesecloth-lined sieve. If you want to skip the food processor, just put the seeds in a clean dish towel or double layer of cheesecloth and twist and squeeze to extract the juice. The juice will keep for 5 days in the refrigerator. It also freezes well.

❧ A good pomegranate should feel heavy, indicating that it is full of juice, and the skin should be thin, tough, and unbroken.

❧ Pomegranate molasses, a sweet-and-sour syrup made from pomegranate juice, is available from Dean & DeLuca (800-999-0306).

tip

Here's a no-mess way to seed a pomegranate,
from the California Pomegranate Web site (www.pomegranates.org):

1. Cut off the crown end with a sharp knife.

2. Lightly score the rind into quarters.

3. Immerse the fruit in a bowl of cold water for 5 minutes.

4. Holding the fruit under the water, break the sections apart. Separate the seeds from the membrane and let them sink to the bottom of the bowl.

5. Skim off and discard the membrane and rind.

6. Pour the seeds into a colander to drain. Pat dry.

SOURCE: *Legends of Texas Barbecue Cookbook*
by Robb Walsh
COOK: Lady Bird Johnson

lady bird johnson's barbecue sauce

PRESIDENT LYNDON BAINES JOHNSON loved his barbecue, so we weren't at all surprised that this quick barbecue sauce devised by his wife is first-rate. In fact, if you wrote Lady Bird at the White House asking for a recipe, this is the one you'd get. We're betting the garlic in the recipe was made optional for genteel White House correspondents, not for Texans.

Butter is a traditional ingredient in old Southern-style barbecue sauces, and it's responsible for a lot of flavor here. This is a thin, tasty sauce that both goes over the meat while it's being grilled and gets passed at the table, warm.

makes about 1 cup

4 tablespoons (1/2 stick) butter
1/4 cup vinegar (see note)
1/4 cup ketchup
1/4 cup fresh lemon juice
1/4 cup Worcestershire sauce

Tabasco sauce, to taste
1 tablespoon minced garlic (optional)
Salt and freshly ground black pepper, to taste

Melt the butter in a small saucepan, stir in the remaining ingredients, and bring to a boil. Serve warm.

cook's note

℮ No particular kind of vinegar is specified here, but we'd vote for apple cider vinegar, preferably an organic one.

SOURCE: *CookSmart* by Pam Anderson
COOK: Pam Anderson

oven-roasted ribs

REAL PIT-BARBECUED RIBS ARE BEST LEFT TO THE PROS, but you can still make some mighty tasty ribs at your house, with or without a grill. We're drawn to the latter option, used in this recipe, especially when the weather's bad or when we're too lazy to fire up the grill. If you miss that smoky flavor, you can add a little liquid smoke to the glaze.

This sweet, slightly spicy, garlicky rub is just right, and the mustard smeared over the ribs before cooking makes a big difference to the final flavor. The technique of baking the ribs directly on the oven rack is key, along with the very low heat. This works best with baby back ribs, which aren't quite as juicy as the big guys but will be tenderer when roasted this way. If you decide to use regular spareribs, the cooking time may be much longer if they're especially meaty.

serves 6 to 8

6 tablespoons light or dark brown sugar

6 tablespoons paprika

3 tablespoons garlic powder

3 tablespoons freshly ground black pepper

1 1/2 teaspoons salt, plus more for the ribs

2 teaspoons liquid smoke (optional)

1/2 cup plus 1 tablespoon Dijon or yellow mustard

4 slabs baby back ribs or 3 slabs pork spareribs

Barbecue sauce or one of the glazes that follow (optional)

Adjust one oven rack to the low position and remove the other rack. Preheat the oven to 250 degrees. Mix a dry rub of brown sugar, paprika, garlic powder, pepper, and 1 1/2 teaspoons salt in a small bowl. If you're using liquid smoke, mix it with the mustard in another small bowl.

Lay the ribs directly on the removed oven rack and lightly sprinkle them with salt. Brush both sides of each slab with mustard, then sprinkle them with the dry rub (see note).

Line a jelly roll pan with a large sheet of heavy-duty aluminum foil, extending the foil so it will cover the oven rack when you place the pan in the oven.

Slide the rack with the ribs into the upper-middle position and place the foil-lined pan on the lower oven rack, making sure that the foil covers the rack. Roast the ribs until fork-tender, $1^{1}/_{2}$ to 2 hours for baby back ribs and 2 to 3 hours or longer for spareribs.

If coating the ribs with barbecue sauce or one of the glazes, remove the pan from the oven and pour off the excess fat. Transfer the ribs to the foil-lined pan, meat side down. Turn on the broiler.

Brush the ribs with half the sauce or glaze, and broil until the glaze bubbles vigorously. Turn the ribs over, brush with the remaining glaze, and broil again. Let stand for 5 to 10 minutes, then cut the slabs into individual ribs and serve.

glazes for ribs

SWEET-AND-SOUR ORANGE GLAZE

1 cup orange marmalade
$1/_{4}$ cup rice vinegar
1 teaspoon dried thyme

APRICOT-SHERRY GLAZE

1 cup apricot jam
$2^{1}/_{2}$ tablespoons sherry vinegar
2 teaspoons ground cumin

To make the glazes, mix all the ingredients in a small bowl and brush onto the ribs as directed above.

cook's notes

- A lot of supermarkets don't sell full-size spareribs by the slab, but rather by the package. A slab of spareribs will weigh close to 3 pounds; baby back slabs weigh more like $1^{1}/_{2}$ pounds.
- When you're seasoning the ribs, you can save yourself a big mess by putting a layer of newspaper under the rack they're sitting on. That way, any falling spices can be rolled up and dumped along with the newspaper.
- Don't worry that the oven rack will be hard to clean. Because the heat stays low in the oven, nothing gets baked on tenaciously; the rack just needs a warm, soapy soak to loosen any clinging bits.

SOURCE: *The Babbo Cookbook* by Mario Batali
COOK: Mario Batali

pork chops milanese with arugula and cherry tomatoes

WHAT A GOOD IDEA THIS RECIPE IS! TV's ebullient chef Mario Batali devised this smart way to dress up the otherwise rather pedestrian center-cut pork chops available in every supermarket. He pounds them thin, breads them, and pan-fries them in olive oil and butter, following the Milanese technique. The meat stays tender and moist, a great contrast to the lovely golden crunchy bread coating.

The spicy arugula and cherry tomato salad that accompanies the pork makes this a year-round one-dish meal. If you can find yellow teardrop tomatoes, they look best. Don't forget to serve with lemon wedges — a good squeeze of fresh lemon at the table adds just the right edge.

serves 4

PORK

4 1-inch-thick, center-cut pork chops, preferably boneless
  Kosher salt and freshly ground black pepper
2 extra-large eggs, lightly beaten
1 cup fresh bread crumbs, lightly toasted (see note)
1/4 cup extra-virgin olive oil, plus more if needed
1 tablespoon unsalted butter

SALAD

1 bunch arugula, stems removed
1/2 pound cherry tomatoes, preferably teardrop, halved lengthwise
3 tablespoons extra-virgin olive oil
1 tablespoon fresh lemon juice
  Kosher salt and freshly ground black pepper
1 lemon, cut into 4 wedges, seeds removed

TO MAKE THE PORK

Remove the bones from the chops if they are not boneless. Using a meat mallet, carefully pound the pork chops on a chopping block until they are uniformly 1/4 inch thick. Season with salt and pepper. Dip each chop into the beaten egg, letting the excess drip off. Dredge each chop in the bread crumbs and set on a plate.

In a 14- to 16-inch sauté pan, heat the ¼ cup oil over medium heat until just smoking. Add the butter and let it foam for 10 to 15 seconds. Add the chops and cook until light golden brown on one side, about 5 minutes. Using tongs, carefully turn the chops and cook on the other side until light golden brown, about 5 minutes more. Add more oil if necessary, ½ tablespoon at a time, to avoid scorching the breading. Watch the heat level so that the pan doesn't get too hot.

TO MAKE THE SALAD

Combine the arugula and tomatoes in a large bowl. Add the oil, lemon juice, and salt and pepper and toss to coat the greens.

TO ASSEMBLE

Place a pork chop on each of four warmed dinner plates. Divide the arugula salad evenly among the plates, place a lemon wedge on each plate, and serve immediately.

cook's notes

- Don't be shy about pounding the pork. Pork chops are quite a bit sturdier than other meats, so you may have to put some muscle into it to pound them down to ¼ inch.
- Fresh bread crumbs are the only choice. Use a mix of fine and medium crumbs for the best texture. The fine crumbs adhere and coat, while the larger crumbs add crunch. To toast them, place them on a baking sheet and bake at 350 degrees until lightly toasted.
- If you don't have a 14- to 16-inch sauté pan, just use two sauté pans side by side. The idea is not to crowd the pan: the chops should not overlap at all, but there shouldn't be large spaces between them either.
- Monitor the heat closely; if the breading starts to get too dark, reduce the heat a bit. It should take the full 10 minutes to cook the chops.

SOURCE: *The Pleasures of Slow Food*
by Corby Kummer
COOKS: Ben and Karen Barker

roasted fresh ham with salsa verde

THE BARKERS COOK AT THE HIGHLY ESTEEMED Magnolia Grill in Durham, North Carolina, and they have a fearless motto: "Not afraid of flavor." Certainly not in this recipe, which is designed to feed a happy party of porcophiles. The seasoning paste is eyebrow-raising: three heads' worth of roasted garlic, a cup of cilantro leaves, and four jalapeños, together with olive oil and salt. Don't be scared of the garlic or the jalapeños — they all mellow out.

After an overnight snooze in this heady emollient, the pork goes into the oven for a long, slow roast. A recipe for a salsa verde with fresh herbal flavors and punchy anchovies follows, but the roast is also great all by itself.

You must start the pork the day before to allow it time to marinate.

serves 8

1 cup packed fresh cilantro leaves
1/2 cup roasted garlic puree
    (about 3 heads garlic; see note)
4 jalapeño peppers, seeded
    and minced

2 1/2 tablespoons kosher salt
1/2 cup olive oil
1 8-pound bone-in fresh ham
    or pork shoulder (see note)
Salsa Verde (recipe follows)

Combine the cilantro, garlic, jalapeños, salt, and oil in a small bowl. Rub all over the pork. Cover and refrigerate overnight.

Remove the pork from the refrigerator about 1 1/2 hours before roasting and place on a rack set in a roasting pan.

Preheat the oven to 400 degrees. Roast the pork for 45 minutes. Reduce the oven temperature to 300 degrees and roast for 2 to 3 hours more, or until an instant-read thermometer inserted in the center of the meat reads 155 degrees. Remove from the oven, cover loosely with aluminum foil, and let rest for 25 to 30 minutes.

Cut the ham or pork across the grain into 1/3-inch-thick slices. Pass the Salsa Verde, if using, at the table.

♌ Don't confuse the whole fresh ham called for here with smoked ham. Fresh ham is a pork leg, and you'll probably have to special-order it at your market. It may weigh more than 8 pounds — and will likely take more than 4 hours to cook. A whole leg can also take up to 5 hours to come to room temperature, and that too can affect the cooking time. Boston butt is a good alternative. Cook it to a slightly higher temperature — 160 degrees on an instant-read thermometer — because it has more fat and more gristle. Even a much smaller Boston butt needs a longer cooking time: our 5¹/₂-pounder took about 4 hours.

♌ Chopping the cilantro leaves makes it easier to get them to stick on the roast.

♌ To roast the garlic: put 3 heads of garlic, pointy ends up, in a baking dish and drizzle with olive oil. Roast at 375 degrees for about 35 minutes, or until the cloves are completely soft but not mushy. Cut off the tops and squeeze the garlic out from the root end. Any extra keeps well, tightly covered in the refrigerator, for at least 1 week.

salsa verde

¹/₄ cup packed fresh lemon verbena leaves or ¹/₄ cup packed fresh parsley leaves plus the grated zest of 1 lemon

¹/₄ cup packed fresh cilantro leaves

1 jalapeño pepper, seeded and coarsely chopped

4 garlic cloves

1 salt-packed anchovy, filleted and rinsed

1 tablespoon capers, rinsed

¹/₂ cup olive oil

Salt

In a mortar or food processor, pound or puree everything together but the oil and salt. Transfer to a small bowl, stir in the oil, and season with salt. Set aside for up to 1 hour before serving.

cook's note

♌ If you can't get salt-packed anchovies, or don't want to fuss with them, just use about 6 oil-packed anchovy fillets, rinsed.

SOURCE: *Fast Entrées*
by Hugh Carpenter and Teri Sandison
COOKS: Hugh Carpenter and Teri Sandison

best-ever grilled asian beef

WE TEND TO STEER CLEAR OF "BEST-EVER" RECIPES because we're so often disappointed. But when we looked at the list of ingredients for these Asian grilled steaks, we knew they just had to be good. The marinade, which doubles as a basting sauce, takes no time at all to assemble and delivers an uncanny depth of flavor. We especially love the way the sauce caramelizes on the surface of the beef as it grills.

serves 4

2 pounds beef tenderloin steaks, 1 inch thick (see note)

3/4 cup hoisin sauce

1/2 cup plum sauce

1/4 cup oyster sauce

1/4 cup dry sherry

2 tablespoons dark sesame oil

1 tablespoon Asian chili sauce

2 tablespoons finely minced fresh ginger

4 garlic cloves, finely minced

1/2 teaspoon five-spice powder

Place the steaks in a shallow baking dish. Combine the remaining ingredients in a medium bowl. Reserve 1/2 cup of the sauce for basting. Pour the remaining sauce over the steaks and turn to coat evenly. Cover and refrigerate for at least 10 minutes and up to 8 hours, turning occasionally.

Prepare a medium-hot fire in a charcoal grill or preheat a gas grill to medium. Brush the grill rack with oil and place the meat on the rack, discarding the marinade. Grill, turning once and basting with the reserved sauce, for about 4 minutes on each side, or until the meat is done to your liking. (To be sure, use an instant-read thermometer and take the meat off the grill at 120 degrees for rare or 130 degrees for medium-rare.) Transfer to warm dinner plates and serve at once.

cook's notes

❦ If you don't want to spring for tenderloin, shop for other types of tender steaks, such as flank, New York strip, or rib-eye. Just be sure they are 1 inch thick. If not, adjust the cooking time accordingly.

❦ Lamb chops are another excellent choice for this recipe. Look for 1-inch-thick center-cut loin chops or boneless lamb leg steaks. Use the same doneness test for lamb as for beef.

❦ If you don't have Asian chili sauce, you can substitute your favorite hot sauce.

❦ This sauce is such a hit that you might consider whipping up a big batch during grilling season and keeping it in the refrigerator for last-minute dinner inspiration. It keeps indefinitely. Try it on chicken or seafood.

SOURCE: *Welcome to My Kitchen*
by Tom Valenti and Andrew Friedman
COOK: Tom Valenti

porcini-crusted filet mignon with wilted arugula

WHEN YOU'RE IN THE MOOD for a luxurious taste, try this terrific quick pan sauté. Porcini powder creates a little crust on the steak and gives it a richer beef flavor. This is one great steak.

The arugula salad has just the right bite for the filet, and the scrap of garlic brings it into focus. Best of all, this recipe is quick to put together and the ultimate low-carb meal when it's time for a celebration.

serves 4

WILTED ARUGULA

2 tablespoons olive oil
1 garlic clove, minced
1 pound arugula, washed and left a little wet

FILET MIGNON

4 7- to 8-ounce filets mignons
   Coarse salt and freshly ground black pepper
   Porcini powder (see note)
4 tablespoons (^{1}/$_2$ stick) unsalted butter
2 tablespoons olive oil

TO MAKE THE ARUGULA

Heat the oil and garlic in a large sauté pan over medium heat. When the garlic begins to sizzle, add the arugula and cook until wilted but still vibrant, about 1 minute.

Turn the arugula out onto a baking sheet to cool. Set aside.

TO MAKE THE STEAK

Preheat the oven to 450 degrees. Season the filets on all sides with salt and pepper, then dredge in the porcini powder, shaking off the excess.

Heat 2 tablespoons of the butter and the oil in a large ovenproof sauté pan over medium-high heat. Add the filets and sear on all sides, about 1 minute per side. Drain the grease from the pan, temporarily removing the filets if necessary.

Add the remaining 2 tablespoons butter, return the filets to the pan, if necessary, and transfer the pan to the preheated oven. Cook for 3 to 4 minutes for rare or 5 to 6 minutes for medium rare, basting every minute or so with the pan juices.

TO ASSEMBLE

Mound some wilted arugula in the center of each of four plates, place a filet alongside, and serve.

cook's note

You can buy porcini powder from Zingerman's (www.zingermans.com), or you can make your own. All you need is a 1½-ounce package of dried porcini mushrooms. Preheat the oven to 275 degrees and arrange the porcini in a single layer on a baking sheet. Let the porcini dry thoroughly in the oven, 10 to 12 minutes, then grind to a powder in a spice mill, coffee grinder, or food processor. Porcini powder will keep, tightly sealed, for several months in a cool, dry place.

tip

Heard on *Dish*, Ed Levine's New York food radio show: Michael White, chef at Manhattan's Fiamma Osteria, says South African porcini taste just like Italian ones but are bug-free because they're grown wild on rocks. They're also much cheaper.

SOURCE: Matt Lee and Ted Lee, in
Martha Stewart Living
COOK: Martha Stewart Omnimedia, Inc.

chili for a crowd

THIS CHILI ISN'T EXCESSIVELY SPICY but uses real chiles as well as the Mexican touch of chocolate, which mellows the flavor.

And we love the special garnish that goes on top of it: lumpy guacamole. You can also serve bowls of sour cream, a mix of shredded Monterey Jack and cheddar cheeses, and some extra roasted hot green chiles or minced jalapeños.

This chili makes a wonderful all-day buffet dish; it would be great for New Year's Day, for instance. To accompany it, consider what the Lee brothers serve: a green salad with avocado, toasted sesame seeds, and an orange vinaigrette. And don't forget the tortilla chips.

serves 12

1 pound dried pinto beans, soaked overnight

7 tablespoons corn oil

3 1/2 pounds fresh plum tomatoes (about 18)

2 1/2 pounds medium yellow onions (about 7), stem ends trimmed, quartered lengthwise with the skins left on

10 garlic cloves, unpeeled

4 mulato chiles (see note)

3 ancho chiles (see note)

1 14 1/2-ounce can low-sodium beef broth

1 cup water

5 pounds ground round or ground beef chuck

1 tablespoon coarse salt

2 ounces Mexican chocolate or semisweet chocolate, chopped (see note)

1/2 teaspoon freshly ground black pepper

Lumpy Guacamole (recipe follows)

Drain and rinse the soaked beans. Place them in a large saucepan with water to cover by 2 inches. Bring to a boil, reduce the heat to low, cover, and simmer gently until the beans are tender, about 1 1/2 hours. (The beans can be prepared up to 2 days ahead; let cool, cover, and refrigerate in their liquid.)

Heat 2 tablespoons of the oil in a 12-inch cast-iron skillet over medium heat. Add the tomatoes and cook, turning occasionally, until the skins begin to char, about 5 minutes. Cover the skillet, reduce the heat to medium-low, and continue to cook, turning, until the tomatoes have softened, 7 to 8 minutes more. Transfer to a large bowl. When cool enough to handle, peel and core the tomatoes. Set aside in a bowl.

Place two thirds of the onion quarters in the same skillet with 2 tablespoons of the oil. Cover and cook over medium heat, turning occasionally, until nicely charred and softened, 12 to 15 minutes. Transfer to a bowl to cool. Repeat with the garlic cloves, the remaining onion quarters, and another 1 tablespoon of oil. When cool enough to handle, peel the garlic and onion, cutting off and discarding the roots and peels and adding the flesh to the tomato bowl. Transfer the tomato-onion mixture and any juices to a blender in batches, filling it no more than halfway. Puree until nearly smooth and set aside in a large bowl.

Tear the chiles in half and discard the stems and seeds. Toast the chiles in the remaining 2 tablespoons oil in the same skillet over medium heat, turning with tongs, until smoky, about 3 minutes. Transfer to the blender.

Bring the broth and water to a boil in a small saucepan, pour over the chiles, and let stand until the chiles are pliable, about 5 minutes. Puree the chiles and broth, then stir into the tomato mixture.

Cook one third of the beef in a 7-quart Dutch oven over medium heat, breaking it up with a spoon and stirring occasionally, until nicely browned, about 8 minutes. Meanwhile, brown another one third of the beef in the skillet over medium heat. Add that batch to the first in the Dutch oven. Brown the remaining beef in the skillet; add to the Dutch oven. Drain the cooked beans and add them to the pot with the salt.

Bring the chili to a boil, reduce the heat to low, cover, and simmer gently, stirring occasionally, until the beef is tender and the sauce is thick, about $1\frac{1}{2}$ hours. Stir in the chocolate and pepper, heat for a few minutes, and serve with the guacamole and other toppings (see headnote).

If you can't find the Mexican chiles, you can substitute a good brand of chili powder, such as Gebhardt's, and add cumin, cayenne, and other spices for more complexity. It won't taste the same, but it will be very good. Taste as you go, and remember that a chili's heat develops slowly — what may taste very mild early in the day can be a lot spicier at dinnertime (and even better the next day).

It's easy to burn the chiles — if you're not an old hand, just heat them for a little less than half a minute on each side.

You can use unsweetened cocoa powder instead of chocolate.

tip

Our favorite leftover tip of the year comes from Texas, courtesy of Gordon Fowler, husband of legendary blues artist Marcia Ball. For Frito pie, slit open a bag of Fritos, dump hot leftover chili into the bag, and squish it around a bit. Top with chopped onions and shredded cheese, and dig in. (From *Saveur*.)

lumpy guacamole

6 ripe Hass avocados

4 plum tomatoes, finely diced

1 jalapeño pepper, minced (for
more heat, don't remove seeds)

3 garlic cloves, minced

$^1/_4$ cup fresh lime juice

$^1/_4$ cup fresh lemon juice

$1^1/_2$ teaspoons coarse salt

$^1/_2$ teaspoon freshly black ground
pepper, or to taste

Halve the avocados and remove the pits. Score the flesh into cubes with a small sharp knife and scrape it into a bowl. Stir in the tomatoes, jalapeño, garlic, and lime and lemon juice. Season with the salt and pepper to taste, and serve.

cook's notes

- We're incapable of serving guacamole — or chili, for that matter — without cilantro, so we'd suggest adding a side bowl of chopped fresh cilantro.

- You can make the guacamole a day ahead if you press plastic wrap directly on the surface and refrigerate it. Bring to room temperature before serving.

SOURCE: Niman Ranch e-mail newsletter
COOK: Jayne Cohen

pomegranate-braised brisket with onion confit

BRAISING IS EVERYWHERE THIS YEAR — a development that we're more than a little pleased about. This old-fashioned cooking method creates supreme comfort food: a hunk of tough meat is transformed into sumptuousness through long, slow cooking in a covered pot with a little bit of liquid. While this is a good technique for pot roast, shoulder cuts, and shanks, the daddy of all braising cuts is brisket, the breast portion of beef.

Pomegranate juice brightens the flavors of this dish, and the deep red juice makes an appealing amethyst-colored gravy. The crowning touch is a jammy onion confit that cooks on the stovetop while the brisket simmers in the oven.

As with most braised dishes, this tastes better the next day or even the day after.

serves 8

3 tablespoons olive or vegetable oil

1 brisket (about 6 pounds), trimmed of excess fat, wiped with a damp paper towel, and patted dry

2 medium onions, coarsely chopped (about 2 cups)

2 leeks, white and pale green parts, washed well and coarsely chopped

6 garlic cloves, crushed

2 large carrots, coarsely chopped

1 celery stalk with leaves, coarsely chopped

2 cups pomegranate juice (see note, page 114)

2 cups chicken stock

3 fresh thyme sprigs or 2 teaspoons dried

2 fresh rosemary sprigs

2 bay leaves

Salt and freshly ground black pepper

Onion Confit (recipe follows)

Heat the oil in a large heavy roasting pan over medium-high heat, using two burners if necessary, in a wide 6-quart Dutch oven or flameproof casserole. Add the brisket and brown well on both sides, about 10 minutes. Transfer the brisket to a platter and set aside.

Preheat the oven to 325 degrees. Pour off all but 1 tablespoon of the fat in the pan and add the onions, leeks, garlic, carrots, and celery. Cook, over medium-high heat, stirring occasionally, until the vegetables are softened, 5 to 7 minutes.

Add 1 cup of the pomegranate juice and bring to a boil, scraping up the browned bits from the bottom of the pan with a spoon, until the liquid is reduced by about half. Add the remaining 1 cup pomegranate juice, the stock, thyme, rosemary, and bay leaves and bring to a simmer. Season to taste with salt and pepper.

Lightly salt and pepper the brisket on both sides. Add it to the pan, fat side up, spooning the vegetable mixture over the meat. Cover the pan tightly and braise the brisket, basting every half hour, until very tender, 2½ to 3½ hours. (If the liquid in the pot begins to bubble rapidly, reduce the oven temperature to 300 degrees — it should be a slow simmer.)

Meanwhile, make the onion confit.

Transfer the brisket to a cutting board and cover loosely with aluminum foil. For the gravy, strain the braising liquid, discarding the thyme, rosemary sprigs, and bay leaves and reserving the vegetables. Skim and discard as much fat as possible from the surface of the liquid. Puree the vegetables and 1 cup of the degreased braising liquid in a food processor or blender. Transfer the pureed mixture and the remaining braising liquid to a skillet over high heat and reduce the gravy to the desired consistency. Taste for seasoning.

Cut the brisket into thin slices across the grain at a slight diagonal. Spread the onion confit on a serving platter and arrange the sliced brisket on top. Ladle over the hot gravy and serve.

cook's note

❦ Unless you own an enormous Dutch oven, chances are you'll need to use a roasting pan to accommodate the full brisket. Just be sure to cover it tightly with aluminum foil before sliding it into the oven.

onion confit

3 tablespoons olive oil

4 large onions (about 2$\frac{1}{2}$ pounds), very thinly sliced

Salt and freshly ground black pepper

$\frac{1}{2}$ cup dry red wine

$\frac{1}{4}$ cup chicken stock

$\frac{1}{2}$ cup pomegranate seeds (see tip, page 114)

Heat the oil in a 10- to 12-inch skillet over low heat. Add the onions, season lightly with salt and pepper, and toss to coat with the oil. Cook, tightly covered, over the lowest heat, stirring occasionally, until the onions are very soft and brown in color, about 1 hour. Add additional salt and pepper to taste, the wine, and the stock. Increase the heat and boil, uncovered, stirring constantly, until all the liquid has evaporated and the onions are deeply colored. Taste again for seasoning — the confit tends to take a bit of salt. Remove from the heat, cover, and keep warm. Stir in the pomegranate seeds just before serving.

SOURCE: *Real Stew* by Clifford A. Wright
COOK: Clifford A. Wright

apulian lamb and fennel stew

THIS TREASURE OF A RECIPE was adapted from a traditional southern Italian recipe by the scholarly cookbook author Cliff Wright. While the authentic version — made with wild fennel and sheep's milk and simmered in a clay *caldariello* — is undoubtedly wonderful, we've made this over and over again with supermarket ingredients in a regular stew pot. There's none of the dredging in flour and browning of the meat that most stews require. Instead, everything is pretty much tossed into the pot and simmered. Serve with pieces of toasted or grilled country bread — you won't want to leave a drop of sauce behind.

serves 4

1 small fennel bulb, thinly sliced, leaves and stalk chopped (see note)

1 medium onion, sliced

Leaves from 1 small bunch fresh flat-leaf parsley, finely chopped

2 large garlic cloves, finely chopped

1 teaspoon freshly ground fennel seeds

$1/2$ cup extra-virgin olive oil

$1^1/2$ cups whole milk

1 cup heavy cream

$1^3/4$ pounds boneless leg of lamb, trimmed of any large pieces of fat and cubed

Salt and freshly ground black pepper

Combine the fennel, onion, parsley, garlic, fennel seeds, oil, milk, and cream in an earthenware stew pot set on a heat diffuser over high heat. Reduce the heat to low before it comes to a boil. (If you are not cooking with earthenware and a diffuser, begin on medium heat.)

Once the liquid is just quivering on the surface, add the lamb and season with salt and pepper. Simmer over low heat, using the heat diffuser if necessary, stirring occasionally, until the lamb is fork-tender, about $2^1/2$ hours. It is important the liquid never come to a boil. If it does, it won't affect the taste, but the cream may curdle. Serve hot.

cook's note

If you can get wild fennel, use two small handfuls of it in place of the fennel and fennel seed.

main dishes

SOURCE: *Sara Moulton Cooks at Home*
by Sara Moulton
COOK: Sara Moulton, after Kemp Minifie

rosemary-scallion–crusted rack of lamb

WE CAN'T THINK OF A CUT OF MEAT AS ELEGANT as rack of lamb, with its delicate baby chops all strung together — and few are as expensive. It always says Special Occasion, or at least Dinner Party or Big Treat.

In this recipe, a mustardy mayonnaise coating keeps the lamb's juices in as well as providing a base for its crunchy scallion-rosemary bread-crumb crust. It's not a new idea — *Gourmet* senior food editor Kemp Minifie created it in the mid-Eighties — but Moulton has never found another lamb dish she likes as well. So well, in fact, that she suggests you count on a whole rack for just two people.

serves 4

3 tablespoons olive oil
1/2 teaspoon crushed red pepper flakes
2 garlic cloves, minced
1 small bunch (6 or 7) scallions, white and 1 inch of the green parts, thinly sliced
2 teaspoons dried rosemary
1 cup fresh bread crumbs

Kosher salt and freshly ground black pepper
2 1 1/4-pound trimmed and frenched racks of lamb (7 or 8 ribs each)
1/4 cup mayonnaise
2 teaspoons Dijon mustard
Fresh watercress sprigs, for garnish

Heat the oil in a large heavy ovenproof skillet over medium-high heat. Add the red pepper flakes and cook for 10 seconds. Add the garlic and cook until softened but not browned, about 30 seconds. Stir in the scallions and rosemary and cook until the scallions are slightly softened, about 10 seconds. Stir in the bread crumbs and remove from the heat. Season with salt and pepper. Transfer to a small bowl and set aside. Wipe out the skillet.

Preheat the oven to 400 degrees. Heat the same skillet over medium-high heat until almost smoking. Season the lamb with salt and pepper and place in the skillet, meat side down. Cook, turning often, until well browned on the sides and ends, about 5 minutes. Pour off all the fat from the skillet.

Mix the mayonnaise and mustard in a small bowl and spread over the meat side of the rack. Pat the crumb mixture evenly on top. Transfer to the oven and roast until an instant-read thermometer reads 130 degrees for medium-rare, 25 to 30 minutes. Let rest on a cutting board, uncovered, for 10 minutes. Cut down between the ribs or between every two ribs and arrange attractively on a warmed platter. (If the crumb mixture falls off, gently pack it around the round part of the meat before serving.) Garnish with the watercress and serve.

cook's notes

- To *french* means to scrape clean the long elegant bones of the rack. Have your butcher remove the chine bone and trim all the fat from the top of the meat. The mustard-mayonnaise crust will protect the meat from the heat.

- The crumb crust and mustard-mayonnaise can be made a day ahead. The meat can be seared, covered with the crust, and left to sit until you're ready to roast it, about 40 minutes before you plan to serve it.

- Don't skip the resting period; it's crucial to the ultimate flavor of the lamb.

SOURCE: *Bon Appétit*
COOK: Zarela Martínez

sautéed shrimp with chipotle chiles

FROM THE SIZZLING PORT CITY OF VERACRUZ comes this classic Mexican dish full of zingy flavor and some surprising ingredients, like soy sauce and Worcestershire.

The marinade needs to sit for an hour before you use it, but then the shrimp need only a quick 15-minute dip. Once that's done, it's just a few minutes until dinner. Serve with a bowl of rice and some plain tortillas.

serves 4

1 pound uncooked medium to large shrimp, peeled and deveined
1/2 recipe Seafood Marinade (recipe follows)
4 tablespoons extra-virgin olive oil
2 garlic cloves, minced

1 tablespoon minced canned chipotle chiles in adobo sauce
1/2 teaspoon dried oregano
Salt and freshly ground black pepper

Place the shrimp in a large bowl. Add the marinade and toss to coat. Cover and refrigerate for 15 minutes. Drain the shrimp and discard the marinade. Return the shrimp to the bowl.

Puree 2 tablespoons of the oil, 1 of the garlic cloves, the chipotles, and the oregano in a food processor until smooth. Add to the shrimp and toss to coat.

Heat the remaining 2 tablespoons oil in a large heavy skillet over medium-high heat. Add the remaining garlic clove and sauté for 1 minute. Add the shrimp and sauté until cooked through, about 5 minutes. Season to taste with salt and pepper.

seafood marinade

1   12-ounce bottle light-colored
    lager-style beer
3/4 cup fresh lime juice
1   teaspoon Worcestershire sauce
1   teaspoon soy sauce
1   teaspoon hot pepper sauce

6   garlic cloves, minced
1   teaspoon powdered chicken
    bouillon base (such as Knorr)
1   teaspoon freshly ground black
    pepper

Whisk together all the ingredients in a medium bowl. Let the marinade stand for 1 hour before using.

cook's notes

- The marinade can be prepared 1 week ahead and refrigerated; whisk before using. It makes twice as much as you'll need for the shrimp, but it's great on any fish. If you don't think you'll use all that marinade, just prepare half a recipe — and drink the rest of the beer while you cook.

- Marinate fish from 15 minutes to 1 hour before grilling or sautéing.

SOURCE: *Real Simple*
COOK: Kay Chun

chili shrimp and coconut rice

HERE'S A PRETTY SUPPER THAT'S SPECIAL enough for company yet simple enough to toss together for a weeknight meal. The recipe calls for leftover rice, but we've been known to cook up a fresh pot just for this recipe.

Don't worry that a quarter pound of shrimp per person won't be enough; the coconut milk adds a lot of richness.

serves 4

- 2 tablespoons olive oil
- 1 pound large shrimp, peeled and deveined
- 2 garlic cloves, minced
- 1 teaspoon kosher salt
- 1 14-ounce can coconut milk
- 2 tablespoons Asian chili paste (see note)

- 4 cups cooked rice, preferably a long-grain variety such as jasmine (see note)
- 1 cup bean sprouts
- 1 scallion, thinly sliced
- 1 tablespoon fresh lime juice
- Fresh basil leaves, for garnish

Heat the oil in a large sauté pan over medium heat. Add the shrimp, garlic, and salt and cook until the shrimp are pink and just cooked through, about 5 minutes. Remove the shrimp and set aside.

Add the coconut milk and chili paste to the pan and bring to a boil. Reduce the heat to low and simmer, stirring occasionally, until the sauce is thickened and reduced by half, about 5 minutes. Add the shrimp, rice, bean sprouts, scallion, and lime juice and cook until heated through. Serve immediately, garnished with basil leaves.

cook's notes

❧ Look for chili paste in the Asian section of your supermarket. There are several varieties. If you find one seasoned with garlic, omit or cut back on the fresh garlic in the recipe. The jar will last for months in your refrigerator.

❧ You'll need to cook 1⅓ cups raw rice for the 4 cups called for. Leftover Chinese take-out rice works too.

❧ If you're like us, you'll want to serve this with lime wedges.

SOURCE: *Asian Grilling by Su-Mei Yu*
COOK: Su-Mei Yu

grilled garlic-and-pepper shrimp with kumquats

SALT, GARLIC, AND WHITE PEPPERCORNS are a classic Thai flavor triumvirate, especially for grilled seafood. This marinade combines them with minced cilantro stems (more flavorful than the leaves), some sugar, and a shot of Thai fish sauce.

The grilled kumquats are so good that we like to make up a few extra skewers of them. If kumquats are not available — their season is limited to the winter holidays and just after — substitute thick lemon or lime slices.

Serve these shrimp as a starter (one skewer per person) or over aromatic long-grain rice for a main course (two skewers per person) and let guests remove the shells at the table.

serves 8 as an appetizer, 4 as a main course

24 large shrimp in the shell
1 tablespoon plus $1/4$ teaspoon sea salt
1 tablespoon whole white peppercorns
1 head garlic, separated into cloves, peeled, and coarsely chopped (about $1/2$ cup)

1 tablespoon minced fresh cilantro stems (without leaves)
1 teaspoon sugar
1 tablespoon Thai fish sauce (nam pla)
8 kumquats, halved crosswise and seeded
3 tablespoons vegetable oil
2–3 serrano peppers, slivered

Soak 8 bamboo skewers in water for 30 minutes, then drain and dry with paper towels. Set aside.

With scissors, snip the fins from the shrimp (these are the little "legs" on the inside of each shrimp), leaving the tails intact. Snip open the backs of the shells to expose the dark vein. Remove the veins, then rinse the shrimp under cold water. Put the shrimp in a colander, sprinkle 1 tablespoon of the salt over them, and massage it in lightly. Let sit for 5 to 10 minutes. Rinse the shrimp again with cold water and pat dry with paper towels. Set aside.

Dry-roast the peppercorns in a small skillet over medium-high heat, shaking the skillet to prevent burning, until the peppercorns emit a pleasant aroma, about 1 minute. Transfer to a small bowl and let cool. Grind in a spice grinder.

Combine the ground peppercorns, garlic, cilantro, sugar, the remaining ¹/₄ teaspoon salt, and the fish sauce in a large bowl. Add the shrimp and toss to coat. Cover and refrigerate for 30 minutes.

Build a fire in the grill with all the coals mounded on one side, leaving the other side empty.

Meanwhile, remove the shrimp from the marinade, shaking off the excess. Reserve the marinade. Thread the shrimp lengthwise onto the skewers, from the head through the tail, alternating with the kumquat halves so that each skewer has 3 shrimp and 2 kumquat halves tucked close together.

When the grill is medium-low, generously spray the shrimp with nonstick spray and lay the skewers on the grill. Arrange the skewers so the shrimp are over the coals and the exposed ends of the skewers are not, to prevent the skewer ends from burning. Grill the shrimp, turning frequently, until the shells are slightly charred and crispy and the shrimp are cooked through, 5 to 6 minutes. Transfer to a platter and tent with aluminum foil to keep warm.

Heat the vegetable oil in a skillet over high heat for 1 to 2 minutes. Add the reserved marinade and the serranos and cook, stirring constantly, until the garlic turns golden, about 3 minutes. Remove from the heat.

Remove the shrimp and kumquats from the skewers and place on the platter. Pour the sauce over them and serve.

cook's notes

- We had best success with 16- to 20-count shrimp.
- Dry-roasting the white peppercorns before grinding them brings out their floral, spicy character.
- If you don't have a charcoal grill, you can make these over a gas grill or even indoors under the broiler.

SOURCE: www.oregonlive.com
COOK: Maurizio Paparo

grilled shrimp
with prosciutto, rosemary, and garlic

THIS IS ONE OF THOSE PRICELESS RECIPES that you can manage with a quick trip through the supermarket express lane on the way home from work. You'll need to splurge on jumbo shrimp — otherwise the prosciutto would overpower the delicate taste.

A brief marinade of rosemary, garlic, and lemon adds just the right punch to the sweet flavor of the shrimp. The prosciutto protects them from the heat of the grill, so that they stay moist. Good choices for accompaniment are rice, risotto, and polenta. (The photograph is on the cover.)

serves 6

6 tablespoons extra-virgin olive oil
1/4 cup chopped fresh rosemary
2 tablespoons sliced garlic
2 teaspoons freshly grated lemon zest
1/2 teaspoon crushed red pepper flakes
Salt and freshly ground black pepper

24 jumbo shrimp (8–10 per pound), peeled and deveined, tails left intact (see note)
12 paper-thin slices prosciutto (about 4 ounces), preferably imported, cut in half crosswise
Lemon wedges, for serving

In a large bowl, combine the oil, rosemary, garlic, lemon zest, red pepper flakes, and salt and pepper to taste. Add the shrimp and toss to coat. Marinate for 1 hour, no longer.

Prepare the grill for direct grilling on medium-high heat.

Remove the shrimp from the marinade and snugly wrap each with a slice of prosciutto. (Because the prosciutto is so thin, it stays wrapped.)

Place the shrimp on the hot grill and cook, turning once, until firm and opaque, 2 to 3 minutes per side. Serve on a hot platter with lemon wedges.

- You can thread the shrimp on skewers if you like before grilling.
- You can either scrape the slices of garlic off the shrimp before wrapping them in prosciutto or leave them on. It depends on how much of a garlic lover you are, or what your plans are for later in the evening.
- To prevent the wrapped shrimp from sticking to the grill, rub the outside of the prosciutto with a bit of oil.
- Spring-loaded tongs are the best tools for flipping the shrimp.

tip

For the most part, shrimp are frozen at harvest, shipped, thawed, and then sold. A tip from Maurizio Paparo for reinvigorating previously frozen shrimp is to soak them for 20 minutes in salted water in the refrigerator (2 tablespoons salt to 1 quart cold water). Then drain, rinse, and pat dry with paper towels before proceeding with your recipe.

SOURCE: *Bon Appétit*
COOK: Bruce Aidells

smoky shrimp and halibut stew

IT RARELY OCCURS TO US to make fish stews, but this recipe called to us. This gratifying dish is also relatively light. There's no fuss here; bottled clam juice, canned chicken broth, and canned diced tomatoes speed things along. You can also make the stew ahead up to the point where you add the fish, which is just 3 minutes before serving, so it's a great last-minute supper. All you need is some coleslaw and warm biscuits.

serves 4

8 ounces smoked bacon slices, coarsely chopped

$2/3$ cup chopped onion

1 medium fennel bulb, coarsely chopped, with 2 tablespoons of the fronds, chopped

1 6-ounce red-skinned potato, unpeeled, cut into $1/2$-inch pieces

$1^1/4$ cups dry white wine

1 cup canned low-sodium chicken broth

1 8-ounce bottle clam juice

1 $14^1/2$-ounce can diced tomatoes, undrained

1 teaspoon chopped fresh thyme

$1^1/2$ pounds halibut fillets, cut into $2^1/2$-inch pieces

1 pound uncooked large shrimp, peeled

Salt and freshly ground black pepper

$1/4$ cup chopped fresh flat-leaf parsley

Sauté the bacon in a large pot over medium-high heat until crisp, about 10 minutes. Transfer one third of the bacon to a bowl and set aside.

Add the onion to the remaining bacon and drippings in the pot and sauté for 5 minutes. Add the fennel bulb and potato and sauté for 5 minutes more. Add the wine and bring to a boil. Add the broth, clam juice, tomatoes with their juices, fennel fronds, and thyme and return to a boil. Reduce the heat and simmer until the potato is tender, about 5 minutes.

Add the halibut and shrimp to the pot. Cover and cook until opaque in the center, about 3 minutes. Season with salt and pepper. Stir in the parsley and reserved bacon and serve.

cook's notes

- We found thinner potato slices, cut $1/8$ inch thick, cooked through more reliably.
- Our favorite canned tomatoes are Muir Glen organic.
- Halibut isn't always available and is sometimes expensive. You can substitute scrod or use a mix of halibut, scrod, and shrimp.

SOURCE: *New York Times Magazine*
COOK: Jason Epstein

scrambled eggs with scallops and bacon

WE'VE LONG BEEN IN FAVOR OF EGGS FOR SUPPER. They are about the easiest thing in the world to cook, and besides, there's something intimate and maybe even a bit reckless about a dinner for two that suggests breakfast. So when we spotted this recipe a few days before Valentine's Day under the heading "Sexy Feast," we were indeed seduced.

Scrambling the eggs in a double boiler assures that they'll stay creamy and soft. They're a perfect foil for the crisp bacon and tender scallops. Serve something chilled and sparkling, like Prosecco or Champagne, as an accompaniment. This makes a fine breakfast as well.

Bay scallops are what you want here. If you can find only sea scallops, buy the smallest ones available and slice them horizontally in half.

serves 2

4 slices lean bacon
6 large eggs
4 tablespoons butter
  Salt and freshly ground black
    pepper
2 tablespoons heavy cream,
    half-and-half, or milk, according
    to your conscience

1 large egg yolk (optional)
  Chopped fresh flat-leaf parsley,
    tarragon, or chives to taste
8 ounces very fresh bay scallops
4 slices brioche, lightly toasted,
    for serving

Broil or fry the bacon in a medium skillet over medium heat so that when the slices are done they lie flat. Drain on paper towels and set aside in a warm oven.

Set a colander over a cold double boiler or heatproof bowl and break the eggs into it. Using a whisk or wooden spoon, push the eggs through. Add 1 tablespoon of butter and salt and pepper to taste.

Cook the eggs in the top of a double boiler or in the bowl placed over a pan of simmering water over medium heat, whisking constantly, taking care to scrape the sides where the eggs first cook. When the eggs begin to thicken, add the cream, half-and-half, or milk. Some people add a raw egg yolk at this time to keep the eggs extra tender.

Remove the eggs from the heat when they have formed small, bright yellow curds, about 10 minutes. Add the chopped herbs, if using.

Meanwhile, pat the scallops dry with paper towels and melt the remaining 3 tablespoons butter in a 10-inch nonstick skillet over medium-high heat. When the butter bubbles but before it darkens and begins to smoke, add the scallops in a single layer. Cook until they turn brown, about 3 minutes. Turn and cook until browned on all sides, about 2 minutes more. Remove the scallops with a slotted spoon and drain on paper towels.

To serve, pile the eggs at one end of a warm platter and the scallops at the other. Arrange the bacon strips between the two. Serve with the toasted brioche.

cook's notes

- Cooking the bacon over medium rather than high heat helps to keep the slices from ruffling up. This not only keeps the entire strip crisper, but it's a handsomer presentation.
- Pushing the eggs through a colander may seem a bit odd, but it means that you don't have to whisk as hard to break them up. If you skip this step, just be sure to thoroughly beat the eggs without introducing too much air.
- Dry the scallops thoroughly before sautéing. Otherwise, they will hiss and steam and not brown up properly.

SOURCE: *Food & Wine*
COOK: Michael Romano

mussels
with smoky bacon, lime, and cilantro

OUR TESTING NOTES FOR THIS RECIPE start with one word — *Killer!*
Perhaps it's the combination of smoky bacon and jalapeño, maybe it's the little bit of ketchup, or the butter, lime juice, and cilantro swirled into the sauce
at the end. Whatever it is, we can't stop making this dish.

If your only experience with steamed mussels has been the standard version steamed in white wine with shallots, you owe it to yourself to try this bold
version from Michael Romano, chef at Union Square Cafe in New York City. It
will be a revelation. And don't forgo the crusty bread, because you really will
want to sop up every bit of juice.

serves 4

¹/₄ pound thick-sliced lean smoked
   bacon, cut into ¹/₂-inch pieces
   (see note)
 2 large shallots, thinly sliced
 1 large jalapeño pepper, thinly
   sliced into rings, seeds removed
   Salt and freshly ground black
   pepper
¹/₂ pound plum tomatoes, coarsely
   chopped (see note)

¹/₂ cup dry white wine
 2 tablespoons ketchup
3¹/₂ pounds medium mussels,
   scrubbed and debearded
 2 tablespoons fresh lime juice
¹/₄ cup chopped fresh cilantro
 2 tablespoons unsalted butter
   Crusty bread, for serving

Cook the bacon in a large enameled cast-iron Dutch oven over medium heat until crisp, about 8 minutes. Pour off all but 2 tablespoons of the fat. Add the shallots and jalapeño, season with salt and pepper, and cook, stirring occasionally,
until softened but not browned, about 4 minutes. Add the tomatoes and cook
for 3 minutes. Add the wine and ketchup and simmer until reduced by half,
about 4 minutes.

Increase the heat to high and add the mussels. Cover and cook, shaking the pan a few times, until the mussels open, about 5 minutes.

With a slotted spoon, transfer the mussels to four large shallow serving bowls. Remove the Dutch oven from the heat and stir in the lime juice, cilantro, and butter. Ladle the sauce over the mussels and serve at once with the bread.

cook's notes

- Look for a thick-cut, smoked bacon with a good bit of lean. It will make a difference. This recipe was developed using smoked bacon from Niman Ranch, a top-quality producer of natural, hormone-free pork products. You can find it at www.nimanranch.com.

- If fresh tomatoes are out of season, substitute one 14-ounce can whole peeled tomatoes, drained.

- For the freshest mussels, don't debeard until immediately before you plan to cook them. To do so, grab the thin wiry threads (or beards) that extend from the shell and yank or cut them off with a small knife. Some farm-raised mussels will have only the thinnest beards, which take no force at all to remove.

- If you don't have a large enameled cast-iron Dutch oven, use a stainless steel or other nonreactive pot with a tight cover.

SOURCE: *American Classics*
by the editors of *Cook's Illustrated*
COOKS: *Cook's Illustrated* staff

pan-fried fresh salmon cakes

SALMON CAKES HAVE A LOT OF THE CHARM of crab cakes without the extreme richness, so they're a treat you can make for a weeknight supper. What's so good about these is their crunchy coating, especially if you use the Japanese bread crumbs called panko, which are starting to turn up in a lot of supermarkets. The panko goes over a flour-and-egg breading to assure a super crunch.

These little cakes have a bright, delicate flavor. You may feel that they would benefit from a little sauce — the Creamy Lemon Herb Sauce is just a flavored mayonnaise, made in moments. It's very good, but we like them best with just a squeeze of fresh lemon juice.

serves 4

1¼ pounds salmon fillets, skinned, any bones removed

1 slice high-quality white sandwich bread, such as Pepperidge Farm, crusts removed and white part very finely chopped (about 5 tablespoons)

¼ cup finely grated onion

2 tablespoons chopped fresh flat-leaf parsley leaves

2 tablespoons mayonnaise

¾ teaspoon salt

1½ tablespoons fresh lemon juice

½ cup all-purpose flour

2 large eggs

1½ teaspoons plus ½ cup vegetable oil

1½ teaspoons water

¾ cup plain dry bread crumbs, preferably panko (see above)

Lemon wedges or Creamy Lemon Herb Sauce (recipe follows), for serving

Chop the salmon into ¼-inch pieces and mix with the chopped bread, onion, parsley, mayonnaise, salt, and lemon juice in a medium bowl. Scoop a generous ¼-cup portion and use your hands to form it into a patty measuring roughly 2½ inches in diameter and ¾ inch thick. Place on a parchment-lined baking sheet and repeat with the remaining salmon mixture to make 8 patties. Freeze the patties until the surface moisture has evaporated, about 15 minutes.

Meanwhile, spread the flour in a shallow dish. Beat the eggs with 1½ teaspoons of the oil and the water in a second shallow dish. Spread the bread crumbs in a third. Dip the chilled salmon patties in the flour to cover and shake off the excess. Transfer to the beaten egg and, with a slotted spatula, turn to coat; let the excess drip off. Transfer to the bread crumbs, shaking the dish to coat the patties completely. Return the breaded patties to the baking sheet.

Heat the remaining $1/2$ cup oil in a large heavy skillet over medium-high heat until shimmering but not smoking, about 3 minutes. Add the salmon patties and cook until medium golden brown on the bottoms, about 2 minutes. Flip the cakes over and cook until medium golden brown on the other side, about 2 minutes more.

To remove any excess oil, transfer the cakes to a plate lined with paper towels and let them drain about 30 seconds. Serve immediately with lemon wedges or the sauce.

---

creamy lemon herb sauce

makes about $1/2$ cup

$1/2$ cup mayonnaise
$2^1/2$ tablespoons fresh lemon juice
1 tablespoon minced fresh
    flat-leaf parsley leaves
1 tablespoon minced fresh
    thyme leaves

1 large scallion, white and green
    parts, minced
$1/2$ teaspoon salt
Freshly ground black pepper

Mix all ingredients except the pepper in a small bowl. Season to taste with the pepper. Cover and refrigerate until the flavors blend, about 30 minutes, before serving. The sauce can be refrigerated for several days.

SOURCE: *Fine Cooking*
COOK: Kim Landi

caramel-braised cod

DESPITE ITS EXOTIC-SOUNDING TITLE, this dish is quick to make and something that even the least adventuresome eaters will enjoy. The method of simmering fish (or meat or poultry) in a mahogany-colored, spicy-savory caramel sauce is widely used in Vietnamese cooking. If you've never tasted this sauce, here's a great place to start. After a brief simmer, the cod fillets take on a delectable flavor that combines a little heat from the chile flakes, depth from the fish sauce, and a hint of sweetness from the caramelized sugar. This recipe uses only one pan, requires almost no slicing or dicing, and is ready in less time than it takes to cook the accompanying rice.

serves 4

1 teaspoon crushed red pepper flakes, or more to taste

1 teaspoon plus $1/4$ cup sugar

$1/4$ teaspoon salt

$1^1/2$ pounds cod fillets, 1 inch thick

$3/4$ cup water

3 tablespoons fish sauce (see note)

2 tablespoons olive oil

Cooked jasmine rice or other long-grain rice, for serving

1 scallion, white and light green parts, thinly sliced

Combine the red pepper flakes, 1 teaspoon of the sugar, and the salt in a small bowl. Rub the cod with half of the mixture and set aside. Combine the other half of the mixture with $1/4$ cup of the water, fish sauce, and oil. Set aside.

Put the remaining $1/4$ cup sugar in a large heavy sauté pan with straight sides. Cook over high heat, without stirring, until the sugar starts to melt at the edges and turns golden brown, about 2 minutes. Reduce the heat to medium and stir energetically with a wooden spoon. When the caramel is a reddish mahogany brown, 1 to 2 minutes more, remove from the heat. Stirring gently, slowly add the remaining $1/2$ cup water to the pan. Be careful: the caramel may steam or spatter. If the caramel doesn't dissolve completely, return the pan to medium heat and stir until dissolved. Stir in the fish sauce mixture.

Put the fish in a single layer in the sauté pan. Bring to a gentle simmer over medium-low heat and braise the fish, uncovered, using a soupspoon to baste the fish with the sauce occasionally. After 7 minutes, gently flip the fish and continue to braise and baste until the fish is opaque throughout, 5 to 7 minutes more. Serve with the sauce over the rice, sprinkled with the scallion slices.

cook's notes

- Fish sauce is available in many supermarkets and most Asian markets. Vietnamese fish sauce is called nuoc mam. Thai fish sauce is nam pla. If your brand of fish sauce contains sugar, omit the sugar in the seasoning mixture.

- You may want to turn on your kitchen exhaust fan when cooking the sugar, since it can produce a fair amount of smoke.

side dishes

Green Beans with Lemon and Mint 156

Zucchini with Cilantro and Cream 158

Chard with Ginger 159

Greens with Garlicky Toasted Bread Crumbs (Pancotto) 160

Fennel-Roasted Vegetables 162

Brussels Sprouts Puree 165

Spiced Braised Red Cabbage 166

Turnip Flapjacks 168

Garlicky Smashed Potatoes and Greens 170

Greek-Style Potatoes with Olives and Feta 172

Sweet Potatoes with Ginger and Apple Cider 174

Roasted Portobello and Potato Gratin 176

Corn Pudding with Basil and Cheddar 178

Quick, Soft, Sexy Grits 180

Orange-Raisin Couscous with Almonds and Parsley 181

Texas Rice 182

Minted Fried Rice 183

Apricot and Pistachio Baked Rice 184

Cumin-Scented Barley 186

Instant Black Beans 187

New Orleans Red Beans 188

Giant Popover with Wild Mushrooms 190

Bread Stuffing with Fennel and Swiss Chard 192

Kumquat and Cranberry Compote 194

SOURCE: *Lemon Zest* by Lori Longbotham
COOK: Lori Longbotham

green beans with lemon and mint

SINCE VIRTUALLY EVERY ONE of Lori Longbotham's recipes is a keeper, we agonized over which to choose. These beans don't seem particularly unusual at first glance, but they have a wonderfully refreshing quality that we just can't seem to get enough of, summer or winter. Longbotham saves this dish for warm weather, but we found it just as useful at a groaning-board Thanksgiving; the diners at our table loved its fresh, cleansing quality.

There are three kinds of lemon flavor here — lemon juice, lemon zest, and lemon oil (olive oil infused with lemon) — and two fresh herbs, mint and parsley. They do wonders for the humble green bean. If you're serving this in summer, use half yellow wax beans for an especially pretty dish.

serves 6

1 pound green and/or yellow wax beans

1/4 cup packed fresh flat-leaf parsley leaves

1/4 cup packed fresh mint leaves

1 teaspoon finely grated lemon zest

2 tablespoons fresh lemon juice

2 tablespoons lemon-infused olive oil or extra-virgin olive oil

1 teaspoon salt

1/4 teaspoon freshly ground black pepper

Cook the beans in a large pot of boiling salted water until crisp-tender, about 5 minutes. Drain, refresh under cold running water, and drain again. Pat dry with paper towels.

Meanwhile, chop together the parsley, mint, and lemon zest. Transfer to a serving bowl and stir in the lemon juice, lemon oil or olive oil, salt, and pepper.

Add the beans to the bowl and toss with the parsley mixture. Serve at room temperature.

If the finished dish sits for a long time, the beans will turn an unappealing khaki color. If you need to make it ahead, toss the beans with the dressing just before serving.

tip

Like all good-quality cold-pressed oils, lemon-infused olive oil is perishable and should be used up quickly. It's available from Zingerman's (www.zingermans.com), and the folks there suggest drizzling it on slices of fresh fennel, adding a few slivers of Parmigiano-Reggiano, and some toasted walnuts or pine nuts for a lively winter salad. They also recommend brushing it on top of broiled fish, drizzling it on warm pasta tossed with fresh cheese and toasted pine nuts, or sprinkling it over cinnamon-raisin toast for a dessert "bruschetta."

SOURCE: *Bon Appétit*
COOK: Helene Wagner-Popoff

zucchini with cilantro and cream

THIS QUICK RECIPE IS INSPIRED by the subtle flavors of Corsican cooking as well as the products of the author's bountiful backyard garden on the island.

It's hard to put your finger on why these tastes are so sensational together. If this were a Mexican dish, it would have chiles in it, and that's not at all a bad idea, but unsubtle by comparison.

Serve it as a side dish or use it as a sauce, spooned over roasted fish.

serves 4

2 tablespoons butter
2 large garlic cloves, minced
1³/4 pounds zucchini, trimmed and cut into ¹/3-inch-thick rounds

4 tablespoons chopped fresh cilantro
¹/3 cup whipping cream
Salt and freshly ground black pepper

Melt the butter in a large heavy skillet over medium heat. Add the garlic and sauté for 10 seconds. Add the zucchini and 2 tablespoons of the cilantro and sauté until the zucchini is crisp-tender, about 5 minutes. Add the cream and simmer until the juices just slightly thicken, about 1 minute. Season with salt and pepper, sprinkle with the remaining 2 tablespoons cilantro, and serve.

SOURCE: Cooking class handout,
Cooking at The Gardener, Healdsburg, California
COOK: Niloufer Ichaporia King

chard with ginger

THIS VERY WELL TRAVELED DISH was taught to Niloufer King, a San Francisco cook born in Bombay, by a chef from the Seychelles. The recipe works for virtually all greens, though some tougher ones, like kale, need a quick parboil first.

The simple seasonings here are key: fresh ginger, chiles, and garlic, with a bit of salt and oil to pull it together. The leaves and stems of the greens are shredded and cooked in just the moisture clinging to them after being washed. The ginger adds a wonderful zingy touch, but you can take the greens in another direction by using just the garlic and a bit of chile. Adding the salt to the oil, says Niloufer, is an old Chinese trick that brings everything into focus.

One of the best things about this uncomplicated preparation is that it can be served at room temperature.

serves 4

About 15 leaves of Swiss chard or other greens
2 tablespoons olive or peanut oil
Salt to taste

1–2 inches fresh ginger, peeled, sliced, and shredded (optional)
1–2 red chiles, fresh or dry
2 garlic cloves, chopped

Wash and shred the greens. Heat the oil in a wok or deep skillet over medium-high heat. Add the salt, ginger, chiles, and garlic. When the ginger is sizzling, add the greens and stir them around. The greens will quickly cook down; if they seem resistant, cover them briefly. They're done when they are tender and wilted. Serve at room temperature.

cook's notes

- If you have fresh chiles (and of course green ones are good too), slit them lengthwise up to the stem; leave the dried ones whole, to be eaten by the intrepid.
- For a very mild garlic flavor, use the garlic whole or cut it in half lengthwise; remove it from the pan just as it begins to color.
- For a crowd, cook the greens in batches.

SOURCE: www.faithwillinger.com
COOK: Faith Heller Willinger
after Bernardino Lombardo

greens with garlicky toasted bread crumbs (pancotto)

PANCOTTO (LITERALLY "COOKED BREAD") is a southern Italian specialty, one of those loaves-and-fishes creations made out of the simplest of leftovers: in this case, cooked greens and stale bread. The bread absorbs the olive oil, garlic, and the juices from the greens while bringing body and crispness to the dish. Serve this as a side dish or even for lunch along with a platter of salami, cheese, and tomatoes.

Bernardino Lombardo, chef-owner of La Caveja, a hilltown inn near Naples, learned to make this dish from his grandmother. As Willinger points out, you can use virtually any vegetable, from leeks to red radicchio — even beans. We love it best with broccoli rabe.

serves 4

1 pound turnip greens, broccoli rabe, or wild field greens (such as dandelion)
1/4 cup coarse sea salt (see note)
1/2 cup best-quality extra-virgin olive oil, plus more if needed

2 garlic cloves
1 dried chile, halved
2–4 cups 1/2-inch cubes stale rustic bread
Fine sea salt

Bring a large pot with at least 4 quarts of water to a rolling boil. Meanwhile, clean the greens, discarding any tough stems. Add the coarse sea salt to the boiling water, add the greens, and cook for 5 minutes or until they are tender — a central leaf rib should be soft when pinched. Drain the greens in a colander, reserving 2 cups of the cooking water. Cool the greens under cold running water, squeeze out the excess water, and coarsely chop them.

Heat 1/4 cup of the oil in a large skillet over medium heat. Add the garlic and chile and sauté until the garlic begins to brown. Discard the garlic and chile pepper, add the chopped greens, and sauté until they absorb the oil. Add the bread cubes and 1/2 cup of the reserved cooking water. Sauté over high heat until the bread absorbs the juices from the greens and the seasoned oil.

Taste and add fine sea salt if necessary. Add more reserved cooking water, $^1/_2$ cup at a time, if necessary. *Pancotto* should be moist but not soupy.

Remove from the heat, add $^1/_4$ cup or more oil, stir, and serve.

cook's notes

- We thought the greens were delicious cooked in this amount of salt — they didn't taste salty at all — but of course you can use less if you like.
- The right bread is one with no added fat, such as ciabatta.
- If you'd like the bread cubes to be crisp and browned a bit, add them to the seasoned oil in the pan a couple of minutes before you add the greens. Don't add the cooking liquid right away; save it until you're just about ready to serve. It helps to brown the bread if you push the cubes down to the bottom of the pan while the greens are cooking.
- This is a delicately flavored dish. If you'd like more garlic flavor, smack the garlic cloves to break them open before they go in the pan and use more garlic, up to 6 cloves.
- If you have no whole dried chiles, you can use $^1/_4$ teaspoon crushed red pepper flakes and add them along with the greens.
- Even if you don't use the bread, this is a great way to cook broccoli rabe.

SOURCE: *Michael Chiarello's Casual Cooking*
by Michael Chiarello with Janet Fletcher
COOK: Michael Chiarello

fennel-roasted vegetables

CARAMELIZED, FRAGRANT, AND TENDER — these roasted vegetables are sensational alongside meat, poultry, or fish or with a big pot of rice for a vegetarian main course. Once you master the technique of parboiling any slow-cooking vegetables first and adding the tenderer varieties later on, you can use this recipe as a template, adding and subtracting other vegetables as you like. The Fennel Spice Mix is optional (ground fennel seeds work very nicely in its stead), but if you have the inclination to make the spice mix, we guarantee you'll find all sorts of good uses for it — roasts, chops, steaks, fish, soups, stews, and so on.

serves 8

$3/4$ pound Yukon Gold potatoes, unpeeled, cut into 1-inch cubes

2 large carrots, peeled and cut on the diagonal into $1/2$-inch-thick slices

5 tablespoons extra-virgin olive oil

$1/2$ pound red onions, each halved and cut into 6–8 wedges through the root end

1 fennel bulb, halved lengthwise and cut into $1/2$-inch-wide wedges through the core

$3/4$ pound asparagus, tough ends trimmed, cut on the diagonal into $1^1/2$-inch lengths

2 zucchini, ends trimmed, halved lengthwise, and cut on the diagonal into $1^1/2$-inch-thick slices

$1^1/2$ teaspoons Fennel Spice Mix (recipe follows), or 1 tablespoon fennel seeds, crushed in a mortar or spice grinder

Sea salt

Preheat the oven to 425 degrees. Put the potatoes in a large pot of cold, well-salted water. Bring to a boil, adjust the heat to maintain a gentle simmer, and cook until almost tender, about 7 minutes. Add the carrots and simmer for about 1 minute more. Drain.

Heat a very large ovenproof skillet over high heat. Add 4 tablespoons of the olive oil. When the oil is hot, add the potatoes and carrots. Cook for about 1 minute, then add the onions and cook, turning occasionally with tongs, until the vegetables are nicely browned, about 10 minutes. Reduce the heat if needed to keep them from burning.

Add the fennel bulb, asparagus, zucchini, Fennel Spice Mix or crushed fennel seeds, and salt to taste. Toss well to distribute the seasonings. Drizzle with the remaining 1 tablespoon oil and toss again. Transfer the skillet to the oven (see note) and roast until the vegetables are deeply caramelized, 20 to 25 minutes, stirring occasionally so they cook evenly. Serve immediately.

cook's notes

- When oven-roasting vegetables, be sure not to overcrowd the pan. So unless you have a truly large, restaurant-scale skillet, you're better off using a roasting pan or baking sheet for the final roasting. Brown the onions and carrots in the skillet, as directed, then transfer them to a roasting pan or baking sheet. Add the remaining vegetables and seasonings then proceed with the recipe.
- If you're using crushed fennel seeds in place of the spice mix, add a few cranks from the pepper grinder along with the salt.

fennel spice mix

makes about 1¹/₄ cups

1 cup fennel seeds
3 tablespoons coriander seeds

2 tablespoons whole white
  peppercorns
3 tablespoons kosher salt

Toast the fennel seeds, coriander seeds, and peppercorns in a small heavy skillet over medium heat. Watch carefully, tossing the seeds frequently so they toast evenly. When they are fragrant and beginning to brown, pour them onto a plate to cool. (They must be cool before grinding, or they will gum up the blender blade.)

Pour the cooled seeds into a blender and add the salt. Blend to a powder, removing the blender jar from the base and shaking occasionally to redistribute the seeds. Store in an airtight container in a cool, dark place for up to 4 months, or freeze for up to 1 year.

cook's note

⚘ If you have a spice grinder, you can easily cut this recipe in
  half. With a blender, you'll need the full amount, because
  anything less won't grind properly.

SOURCE: *New York Times Magazine*
COOK: Julia Reed

brussels sprouts puree

FOR MANY PEOPLE, BRUSSELS SPROUTS embody the worst character-istics of cabbage. But that's only because they don't know how to cook them.

As this recipe proves, brussels sprouts can be stunningly good. Chopped up into slawlike threads, they have a nutty sweetness that goes very well with cold-weather roasts. This happens to be the easiest, fastest, tastiest brussels sprouts dish we've ever seen.

serves 4 to 6

1 pound brussels sprouts
1 cup heavy cream
3 tablespoons butter
$1/2$ teaspoon salt, plus more to taste

$1/4$ teaspoon freshly ground white pepper, plus more to taste
Pinch of freshly grated nutmeg

Steam the brussels sprouts until tender but not soft, about 6 minutes. When the sprouts are just cool enough to handle, slice them in half and pulse in a food processor until finely chopped.

Heat the cream in a small saucepan until almost boiling and add to the sprouts along with the butter. Process until smooth. Add the salt, white pepper, and nut-meg, process well, and adjust the seasonings to taste. Serve warm.

cook's note

The white pepper adds a delicate note, something quite different from black pepper's exclamation point. If you don't have any, it's worth getting some to make this dish.

SOURCE: Aquavit newsletter
COOK: Marcus Samuelsson

spiced braised red cabbage

MARCUS SAMUELSSON, THE WILDLY TALENTED New York City chef, is known for putting contemporary and global twists on traditional Swedish dishes. Here he adds garam masala and maple syrup to the usual sweet-and-sour red cabbage, then gives it a long, slow simmer to ensure that no one flavor dominates.

In the Swedish Christmas tradition, this cabbage would accompany the turkey; it's also good year-round with almost any roast meat. And for game or meatballs, there is simply no better side dish.

serves 6 to 8

About $^1/_2$ cup chopped pork fat scraps or $^1/_2$ cup chopped bacon

2 large red onions, finely chopped

1 3-inch piece fresh ginger

1 2-inch cinnamon stick

2 heads red cabbage (about 2 pounds each), trimmed, quartered, and cored

2 fresh marjoram sprigs

1 teaspoon garam masala (see note)

1 cup red wine vinegar

1 cup ruby port

$^1/_2$ cup pure maple syrup

Cook the pork scraps or bacon in a large skillet over low heat, stirring occasionally, until the fat has rendered, about 20 minutes.

Add the onions, ginger, and cinnamon stick. Increase the heat to medium and cook, stirring occasionally, until the onions have softened, about 5 minutes.

Add the cabbage, marjoram, garam masala, vinegar, and port. Stir well, reduce the heat to medium-low, and cover. Simmer for 1 hour, removing the cover from time to time and stirring to make sure that the cabbage is not sticking to the bottom of the skillet.

Remove the cover and cook, stirring frequently, for 15 minutes. Stir in the maple syrup, and cook for 15 minutes more, or until most of the liquid has cooked away. Discard the cinnamon stick, ginger, and marjoram sprigs. Transfer to a serving bowl and serve.

cook's note

🍃 Garam masala is a currylike spice mix from India that's been used in Swedish cooking since the eighteenth century. It's available in gourmet markets and many supermarkets.

SOURCE: *Savoring America*
COOK: Kerry Conan

turnip flapjacks

TO APPRECIATE THE GOODNESS OF TURNIPS, you have to cook them right, and here's a great place to start. These flapjacks make the most of the vegetable's lightly spicy, faintly mustardy, and just barely sweet character. Since turnips have very little natural sugar, the griddle cakes brown slowly, which gives them time to develop a creamy, soft interior while the edges get good and crispy. Serve these savory cakes as a side to meaty roasts or rich stews. They also make a nice addition to a big bacon-and-egg breakfast.

serves 4

6 tablespoons (^{3}/4 stick) unsalted butter

2 large or 3–4 medium turnips (about 1 pound)

1 cup half-and-half

1 large egg

^{1}/2 teaspoon kosher salt

1 cup all-purpose flour

Milk, for thinning the batter, if needed

^{1}/2 cup sour cream (optional)

^{1}/4 cup minced fresh chervil (optional)

Melt 2 tablespoons of the butter and set aside. Peel the turnips. Using the large holes on a box grater, shred the turnips into ribbons as long as possible. You should have 2 cups packed. Toss with the melted butter in a medium bowl.

Beat together the half-and-half, egg, and salt in a large bowl. Stir in the flour and mix to just combine. Fold in the shredded turnips until evenly coated. Thin with a little milk if the turnip mixture seems too dry. It should just coat the turnips.

Heat a large heavy skillet over medium heat. Sprinkle with a few drops of water. If they dance around for a moment and then evaporate, the temperature is correct. If they vaporize immediately, the surface is too hot. Coat with just enough of the remaining 4 tablespoons butter to prevent sticking.

For each flapjack, spread a heaping forkful of turnip batter in the skillet to form thin, wispy 3-inch cakes. Fry, turning once, until both sides are deeply browned, about 5 minutes per side. Transfer to a platter and keep warm in a low oven. Butter the pan as needed to prevent sticking between batches. Serve immediately, either plain or garnished with sour cream and chervil, if desired.

cook's notes

- When shopping for turnips, look for ones that feel heavy in your hand. Light turnips are apt to be spongy, dried out, and bitter.

- To get these flapjacks right, it's important that the skillet be neither too hot nor too cool. Use the readiness test described in the recipe, and make sure that the cakes cook for the full 5 minutes per side. If they cook too fast, the insides will be gummy.

tip

Another excellent way to prepare turnips is to make them into fries. Preheat the oven to 450 degrees. Cut 4 medium peeled and trimmed turnips into 1/2-inch-thick sticks and toss in a bowl with 1/4 cup olive oil, 1/4 cup grated Parmigiano-Reggiano, 2 pinches grated nutmeg, and salt and freshly ground black pepper. Spread the turnips out on an oiled baking sheet. Bake until golden, 18 to 20 minutes. Serves 4. (From *Saveur*, adapted from a recipe by vegetarian cooking authority Deborah Madison for rutabaga fries, which are made the same way and are also really great.)

SOURCE: *Make It Italian* by Nancy Verde Barr
COOK: Nancy Verde Barr

garlicky smashed potatoes and greens

THE GREAT THING ABOUT SMASHED POTATOES is how quick and satisfying they are. You boil the spuds in their jackets and then thrash them with a handheld masher until you've got a lovely soft mass. And even better than plain smashed potatoes are these, embellished with garlic cloves, some leafy greens, and a few glugs of good olive oil. These are best served warm soon after smashing. If they have to wait, drizzle the top with a bit more olive oil and keep them covered and warm.

serves 4 to 6

2 pounds small boiling potatoes, preferably Yukon Golds, scrubbed

3–4 large garlic cloves

1¹/2 teaspoons salt per quart of water, plus more for seasoning

1 pound chard, beet greens, or escarole, washed, trimmed, and torn into palm-size pieces

3 tablespoons extra-virgin olive oil, or as needed

Freshly ground black pepper

Put the potatoes and garlic in a large saucepan — the potatoes should not be too crowded — and cover with cold water by 1 inch. Add enough salt so the water tastes lightly salty. Bring to a boil, and cook for 8 minutes after the water comes to a boil. Add the greens to the pan and return to a boil. Cook until the potatoes are tender in the center when pierced with a cake tester, 7 to 14 minutes more.

Drain the potatoes and greens, reserving 1 cup of the cooking water. Using a potato masher, smash the potatoes and greens with the olive oil. If the potatoes are too stiff, mash in some of the reserved cooking water. Season with salt and pepper and serve immediately.

❧ Use potatoes that are 1¹/₂ to 2 inches in diameter for this recipe. If you can't find small enough Yukon Golds, look for any other waxy variety, such as Red Bliss or yellow finns.

❧ Tenderer greens, such as spinach and arugula, may be substituted. Just add them a little later in the cooking, since they don't take as long to cook as the heartier varieties listed in the recipe.

tip

Garlic skins slip right off if you zap them for a few seconds in the microwave. The Oven Sensations Web site (www.ovensensations.com) suggests 12 seconds, but 5 or 6 seconds works for us. The timing varies from microwave to microwave. Just be sure not to leave the garlic in so long that it begins to cook.

SOURCE: *Cook's Illustrated*
COOK: Adam Reid and Meg Suzuki

greek-style potatoes with olives and feta

WHAT'S GREEK ABOUT THESE STOVETOP POTATOES is their substantial flavor of garlic and lemon — both zest and juice. You can leave out the olives and feta, but they're very tasty. The herb used is fresh oregano, but if you have access to some good dried Greek oregano or even Mexican oregano, it will be excellent.

The technique is unusual: the potatoes are cooked in a skillet until they're crusty brown, then covered to cook through, and only then are the seasonings added. Because you're using Yukon Golds, they cook relatively quickly, in a little over 20 minutes, so you can have this dish on the table in well under half an hour.

serves 4 to 6

1 tablespoon vegetable oil (see note)

1 tablespoon unsalted butter

4 medium Yukon Gold potatoes (about 2 pounds), peeled and cut lengthwise into 8 wedges

4 medium garlic cloves, minced or pressed

2 tablespoons minced fresh oregano leaves or 2 teaspoons dried

1 teaspoon lemon zest

2 tablespoons fresh lemon juice

1 tablespoon extra-virgin olive oil

1 teaspoon salt

1/2 teaspoon ground black pepper

2 tablespoons minced fresh flat-leaf parsley leaves

1/3 cup crumbled feta cheese (optional)

8 kalamata olives, pitted and sliced (optional)

Heat the vegetable oil and butter in a heavy 12-inch nonstick skillet over medium-high heat until the butter melts and the foaming subsides, swirling the skillet occasionally. Add the potatoes in a single layer and cook until golden brown (the pan should sizzle but not smoke), about 6 minutes. Using tongs, turn the potatoes so the second cut sides are down. Cook until deep golden brown on the second side, about 5 minutes more. Reduce the heat to medium-low, cover tightly, and cook until the potatoes are tender when pierced with the tip of a paring knife, about 5 minutes.

Meanwhile, combine the garlic, oregano, lemon zest, lemon juice, and olive oil in a small bowl. When the potatoes are tender, add the garlic-lemon mixture and salt and pepper and stir carefully to distribute.

Cook, uncovered, until the seasoning mixture is heated through and fragrant, 1 to 2 minutes. Sprinkle the potatoes with the parsley and the feta and olives, if using, and stir gently to distribute. Serve immediately.

cook's notes

- We beg you to use olive oil instead of vegetable oil with the butter in this recipe.
- If you want to make the potatoes for a crowd, you can brown them, uncovered, in a large pan in the oven in a single layer at 400 degrees, cover with foil, and cook until tender.

SOURCE: *Bon Appétit*
COOK: Rozanne Gold

sweet potatoes with ginger and apple cider

WITH HER USUAL MINIMALIST APPROACH to cooking, cookbook author Rozanne Gold adds only two ingredients to pureed sweet potatoes (three, if you count the butter) and thus transforms a bland side dish into something altogether wonderful. An entire quart of apple cider (get the fresh, unfiltered stuff) is reduced to a deeply concentrated apple syrup spiked with fresh ginger. Indeed, after tasting these sweet-and-spicy potatoes at Thanksgiving last year, one guest called over a week later to say that she couldn't stop thinking about them.

serves 6

$2^1/_2$ pounds sweet potatoes
(about 3 medium)
4 cups apple cider

$^1/_4$ cup minced peeled fresh ginger
2 tablespoons butter

Place the potatoes in a large pot and add enough water to cover by 2 inches. Bring to a boil over high heat. Reduce the heat to medium-low and simmer until very tender, about 40 minutes. Drain and let cool. Peel the potatoes and cut them into large chunks. Transfer to a food processor.

Bring the cider to a boil in a medium, heavy saucepan over high heat. Reduce the heat to medium-low and simmer until the cider is reduced to 1 cup, about 30 minutes. Transfer the cider, ginger, and butter to the food processor with the potatoes and process until very smooth. Season with salt and pepper. Serve hot.

cook's notes

- Instead of boiling the sweet potatoes, you can roast them at 400 degrees until quite tender, about 1 hour. They will have a slightly richer, more concentrated flavor.
- Avoid filtered clear apple juice. You want cloudy, unfiltered fresh cider if you can find it. In the fall, most health food stores will carry it.

tip

When boiling cider (or any other liquid) to reduce it dramatically in volume, we found the following advice from Ken Haedrich, author of *Apple Pie Perfect,* helpful. Start with a large saucepan, but not one that's too heavy, because at the end you'll be pouring the cider back and forth into a measuring cup to check the volume and if the pan is too heavy, this is too much work. Then when you think you're getting close, check by pouring the cider into a heatproof measuring cup. If the liquid is not quite reduced enough, pour it back into the pan and continue boiling, checking again in a few minutes.

SOURCE: Florence Fabricant in the *New York Times*
COOK: Eric Ripert

roasted portobello and potato gratin

LIKE SO MANY ELITE FRENCH CHEFS, Eric Ripert, executive chef and co-owner of Manhattan's celebrated fish restaurant Le Bernardin, is a sucker for homey dishes. He especially loves gratins, those crunchy-topped cold-weather side dishes that are served at the table. After a little experimenting, he came up with this one, which is a bit lighter and less overwhelming than traditional versions — though it doesn't stint on the cream.

The surprise ingredient is portobello mushrooms. This is an excellent holiday dish, good with roast beef, ham, or even turkey.

serves 6 to 8

4 large portobello mushrooms, stems discarded, caps peeled

4 large garlic cloves

4 fresh thyme sprigs

1/4 cup extra-virgin olive oil

Sea salt and freshly ground white pepper

2 tablespoons unsalted butter

1 large onion, chopped

1 1/2 cups heavy cream

1/2 cup whole milk

4 Idaho (russet) potatoes (about 2 pounds)

1/4 teaspoon freshly grated nutmeg

1/4 cup dry bread crumbs

Preheat the oven to 400 degrees. Line a rimmed baking sheet with a sheet of parchment. Place the mushrooms gill side up on the parchment. Thinly slice 3 of the garlic cloves and scatter over the mushrooms. Place a thyme sprig on each mushroom, drizzle the caps with the olive oil, and sprinkle with salt and white pepper. Roast until soft and releasing liquid, 10 to 15 minutes. Remove from the oven and let cool. Leave the oven on.

Melt 1 tablespoon of the butter in a skillet over medium-low heat. Add the onion and sauté until soft and beginning to color. Add the cream and milk, bring almost to a boil, then remove from the heat. Use the remaining 1 tablespoon butter to grease a 9-inch gratin dish. Rub the dish with the remaining garlic clove.

Remove and reserve the garlic from the mushrooms. Discard the thyme. Slice the mushrooms 1/2 inch thick.

Peel and thinly slice the potatoes. Place one third of the potatoes in the gratin dish, season with salt, white pepper, and nutmeg, and scatter with half the reserved garlic. Arrange half the mushroom slices on top. Repeat the layers. Layer the last third of the potatoes on top. Season with salt and white pepper. Pour the onion mixture over the potatoes. Strew the bread crumbs on top.

Place the gratin dish on a baking sheet and bake for 1 hour, or until potatoes are tender and the liquid has thickened. If the top browns too fast, cover with aluminum foil. Let stand for 10 minutes, then serve.

cook's notes

- The portobellos are peeled because their skins can be tough. This is a good basic preparation for these mushrooms that can be applied to many other portobello recipes.
- To peel the caps, start at the edge of the mushroom cap with a paring knife and your thumb and peel back the outermost layer.

tip

If your portobellos taste bitter, says Ripert, it means they're too old.

SOURCE: *Barefoot Contessa Family Style*
by Ina Garten
COOK: Ina Garten

corn pudding with basil and cheddar

WE'RE ALWAYS GAME for new and improved versions of old favorites, and this lovely corn pudding is exactly that. It's as sweet and custardy and chock-full of corn kernels as any good corn pudding should be, but the flavor's been amped up with fresh basil and plenty of extra-sharp cheddar cheese. As much as we love to make this in August, it's also great for Christmas dinner. Thankfully, this is just as good with frozen shoepeg corn.

serves 8

- 8 tablespoons (1 stick) unsalted butter
- 5 cups corn kernels (6–8 ears)
- 1 cup chopped yellow onion (1 onion)
- 4 extra-large eggs (see note)
- 1 cup milk
- 1 cup half-and-half
- 1/2 cup yellow cornmeal
- 1 cup ricotta cheese

- 3 tablespoons chopped fresh basil leaves
- 1 tablespoon sugar
- 1 tablespoon kosher salt
- 3/4 teaspoon freshly ground black pepper
- 3/4 cup grated extra-sharp cheddar cheese (about 6 ounces), plus more to sprinkle on top

Preheat the oven to 375 degrees. Grease an 8- to 10-cup baking dish. Melt the butter in a very large sauté pan over medium-high heat. Add the corn and onion and sauté for 4 minutes. Cool slightly.

Whisk together the eggs, milk, and half-and-half in a large bowl. Slowly whisk in the cornmeal and then the ricotta. Add the basil, sugar, salt, and pepper. Add the corn mixture and cheddar. Pour into the prepared baking dish. Sprinkle the top with more cheddar.

Place the dish in a larger pan and fill the pan halfway up the sides of the baking dish with hot tap water. Bake the pudding for 40 to 45 minutes, or until the top begins to brown and a knife inserted in the center comes out clean. Serve warm.

cook's notes

- You can substitute large eggs for the extra-large with no worries.

- A large gratin dish works well for baking this pudding. It's pretty enough to carry to the table as well.

- A large roasting pan makes a good water bath for baking the pudding.

SOURCE: *Food & Wine*
COOK: Jan Birnbaum

quick, soft, sexy grits

WE'VE BEEN BRAINWASHED FOR SO MANY YEARS by traditionalist Southerners that we automatically turn up our noses at quick-cooking grits. But the fact is, they're very good. Jan Birnbaum has all the right credentials for good grits; he's a big-guy Louisiana-born chef in the grand tradition. This recipe produces a dish exactly like its name in just over 10 minutes. This is soul food for all of us.

serves 6

6 cups chicken stock
  or canned low-sodium broth

2 cups heavy cream

4 tablespoons (¹/₂ stick)
  unsalted butter

2 large garlic cloves, minced

2 teaspoons kosher salt, plus more
  to taste

Freshly ground black pepper

2 cups quick grits

Tabasco sauce

In a large saucepan, combine the stock, cream, butter, and garlic. Add the 2 teaspoons salt and ¹/₄ teaspoon pepper and bring to a boil. Slowly whisk in the grits and cook over low heat, whisking often, until thick and completely smooth, about 10 minutes. Season with salt, pepper, and Tabasco and serve.

SOURCE: *Let the Flames Begin*
by Chris Schlesinger and John Willoughby
COOKS: Chris Schlesinger and John Willoughby

orange-raisin couscous
with almonds and parsley

WE'VE LONG BEEN IMPRESSED by the way the "grill guys" — Chris Schlesinger and John Willoughby — pair flavors to create new and exciting dishes, and this couscous dish is no exception. The primary flavorings here are orange juice and a good dose of crushed coriander seeds, and when you taste these two together, you may experience one of those "Eureka! Why didn't I think of that?" moments. We certainly did.

Using instant couscous makes this a recipe a cinch, and because it's good either warm or at room temperature, it's ideal for a buffet.

serves 4

- 1 cup orange juice (fresh-squeezed is best)
- 1/2 cup olive oil
- 1 cup uncooked instant couscous
- 1/3 cup raisins
- 1/3 cup toasted chopped almonds
- 1/2 cup coarsely chopped fresh flat-leaf parsley
- 3 tablespoons crushed coriander seeds
- Kosher salt and freshly cracked black pepper

Bring the orange juice to a simmer in a small saucepan over medium heat. Remove from the heat and stir in the oil. Place the couscous in a medium bowl and pour the hot orange juice mixture over it. Cover and let stand for 5 minutes.

Uncover the bowl and fluff the couscous with a fork. Stir in the raisins, almonds, parsley, and coriander seeds. Season to taste with salt and pepper. Serve the couscous warm or at room temperature.

cook's notes

- Fresh orange juice really makes a difference. Count on 2 juicy oranges for 1 cup, 3 if the oranges are small.
- Toast almonds in a small dry skillet on medium-high heat, stirring for about 2 minutes, or until they smell toasty and are lightly browned.
- Whole coriander seeds are a must here — ground won't do. Crush the seeds with a mortar and pestle or put them on a cutting board and chop them coarsely with a chef's knife. Sprinkling the seeds with a few drops of water before chopping will prevent them from shooting out from under the knife.

side dishes

SOURCE: *Los Angeles Times*
COOK: Abby Mandel

texas rice

OH, TO BE IN TEXAS, eating some great barbecue and Texas rice! Now you can make this very light dish to serve alongside your own barbecued ribs, or with ham or fried chicken or almost any other down-home dish.

serves 4

1 tablespoon vegetable oil

1 cup uncooked rice

1 cup minced white onion

$^1/_3$ cup diced green bell pepper

1 jalapeño pepper, seeded, if desired, and minced

1 tablespoon minced garlic

$^1/_2$ teaspoon ground cumin

$^1/_2$ teaspoon coarse salt

$1^1/_2$–$1^3/_4$ cups low-sodium canned chicken broth

$^1/_2$ cup canned diced tomatoes in sauce

$^1/_4$ cup fresh cilantro leaves

Heat the oil in a medium saucepan over medium-high heat. Add the rice and cook, stirring frequently, until lightly browned, about 5 minutes. Add the onion, bell pepper, jalapeño, garlic, cumin, and salt. Cook, stirring frequently, until the onion softens, 4 to 5 minutes.

Stir in $1^1/_2$ cups of the broth and the tomatoes. Bring to a boil, then reduce the heat and simmer, covered, until the liquid is absorbed and the rice is tender, about 15 minutes. Let stand, covered, for 10 minutes. The rice can be served immediately, after stirring in the cilantro, or it can be made a day ahead and refrigerated (see note).

cook's note

You can make the rice a day ahead and reheat it before serving. If made ahead, reheat, covered, in a 350-degree oven for about 45 minutes. Add more hot broth if the rice is too dry. Stir in the cilantro and serve hot.

SOURCE: *Martin Yan's Chinatown Cooking*
COOK: Martin Yan, after Christina Yau

minted fried rice

WHAT AN EASY AND APPETIZING WAY to use up leftover plain rice — especially the kind that comes in the take-out Chinese containers and never seems to get eaten. A bit of ginger and jalapeño add just enough heat and spice, but it's the fresh mint that really does the trick. Serve it with seafood, chicken, pork, or as part of a multicourse Chinese feast.

serves 4

3 tablespoons vegetable oil
1/2 red or green jalapeño pepper, cut into thin rings
1 teaspoon minced fresh ginger
1 large egg, lightly beaten
3 cups cold cooked long-grain rice, grains separated

2 teaspoons oyster sauce
1/4 cup finely chopped fresh mint
1/2 teaspoon salt
1/4 teaspoon freshly ground white pepper

Heat a wok over high heat until hot. Add the oil and swirl to coat the sides. Add the jalapeño and ginger and cook, stirring, until fragrant, about 30 seconds. Add the egg and cook until lightly scrambled. Scatter the rice into the wok and stir until heated through.

Stirring constantly, add the oyster sauce, mint, salt, and pepper. Mix well and cook until heated through, 1 to 2 minutes. Scoop the rice onto a warmed platter and serve hot.

cook's notes

❧ You'll need about 1¼ cups raw rice to make 3 cups cooked.
❧ Break up the cold rice with a fork or your fingers before adding it to the wok, so that there are no clumps.
❧ A good way to cut fresh mint is to stack the leaves and cut them into thin strips.

side dishes

SOURCE: *Gourmet*
COOK: Katy Massam

apricot and pistachio baked rice

IF YOU'RE SEARCHING FOR A TASTY AND IMPRESSIVE rice dish to serve when company's coming to dinner, you've found it. Rinsing the rice (six times!) and then parboiling it takes the guesswork out of cooking perfect rice. All the rinsing guarantees ideally separate grains. It bakes in the oven for about 20 minutes — leaving you free to finish the rest of the meal — then comes out tender, aromatic, and not the slightest bit wet or sticky. The apricots, pistachios, and dried cherries (or dried cranberries) complement the exotic fragrance of long-grain basmati, giving the whole dish a marvelous Middle Eastern flair. If fresh apricots are available, by all means use them, but dried work just fine as long as your reconstitute them (see note). This is especially good with lamb and pork.

serves 8

1½ cups uncooked basmati rice

6 cups water

2 tablespoons kosher salt

2 tablespoons vegetable oil

¾ pound firm-ripe apricots (4 large), cut into ½-inch pieces (see above)

½ cup dried cherries or dried cranberries

⅓ cup shelled pistachios (not dyed red)

3 tablespoons dried currants

Wash the rice in six changes of cold water in a large bowl until the water is almost clear. Drain into a large sieve.

Bring the 6 cups water and the salt to a boil in a 4-quart heavy ovenproof pot with a tight-fitting lid. Stir in the rice and cook, uncovered, for 6 minutes (the rice will still be firm). Drain in the sieve. Dry the pot and return it to the stove.

Heat the oil in the dried pot over medium heat until hot but not smoking. Add the rice, stirring until well coated, then remove from the heat. Stir in the remaining ingredients.

Bake, tightly covered, in the center of the oven until the rice is tender, about 18 minutes. Fluff with a fork and serve immediately.

cook's note

❦ Dried apricots make a fine substitute for fresh. Soak a handful of dried apricots (about 6) in warm water for 8 hours or overnight. Drain, and cut them into pieces.

SOURCE: Jonathan Reynolds in the
New York Times Magazine
COOK: Karen MacNeil

cumin-scented barley

WINE WRITER KAREN MACNEIL, author of *The Wine Bible,* devised this fragrant dish to go with lamb shanks. MacNeil feels barley is the most under-rated grain, and if you make this lightly crunchy dish with its complex mix of flavors, you'll agree that it's like no barley you've ever tasted. Cooked this way, al dente, freshened with scallions and parsley, it achieves a new status at the table.

serves 4 to 6

2 tablespoons olive oil
2 cups chopped onions
1 1/4 cups uncooked pearl barley
4 tablespoons (1/2 stick) butter
2 tablespoons ground cumin
1/2 teaspoon freshly ground black pepper
5 cups chicken stock

1/4 cup sweet or dry Madeira (see note)
3/4 cup finely chopped scallions
3/4 cup chopped fresh flat-leaf parsley
1/3 cup toasted walnuts, chopped
3 tablespoons dark or golden raisins
Salt

Preheat the oven to 325 degrees. Heat the oil in an enamel or stainless-steel Dutch oven. Add the onions and sauté until softened, about 10 minutes. Add the barley and 1 tablespoon of butter, stirring until the barley is coated. Add the cumin and pepper and sauté until the barley starts to crackle, about 5 minutes. Add the stock and Madeira, bring to a boil, then cover. Cook in the oven until the barley is al dente and most of the liquid has been absorbed, about 45 minutes.

Remove from the oven and stir in the remaining 3 tablespoons butter, the scallions, parsley, walnuts, raisins, and salt to taste. Cover and let stand for 15 minutes before serving.

cook's notes

- No Madeira? Just use sherry, but not a very sweet one.
- To toast walnuts, place in a small dry skillet and toast over medium-high heat for about 3 minutes, or until fragrant.

SOURCE: Elaine Louie in the *New York Times*
COOK: Angela Pontual

instant black beans

MOST BRAZILIANS LIVING ABROAD don't go to Brazilian restaurants because they insist on good home-cooked food. That can be a problem, since the beloved traditional dishes are often cooked for an entire day. Angela Pontual, a writer and editor of Brazilian news for television in New York, became a speed cook out of necessity. Her streamlined version of black beans will be our gold standard from now on.

We've listed this recipe as a side dish, but it's hearty and would make a good weeknight dinner served over rice.

serves 4

2 strips bacon, chopped
6 ounces garlicky sausage, such as chorizo, linguiça, or kielbasa, diced
2 garlic cloves, finely chopped

2 $15^1/_2$-ounce cans Goya black bean soup
1 cup hot water
$^1/_2$ bay leaf, finely chopped

Fry the bacon until crisp in a large saucepan over medium heat. Add the sausage and sauté until browned, about 3 minutes. Add the garlic and sauté for 1 to 2 minutes more. Add the soup, water, and bay leaf and bring to a boil. Reduce the heat to medium-low and simmer uncovered until the mixture has thickened, 15 to 20 minutes. Serve hot.

cook's note

❦ If you're using chorizo, it can sometimes be unpleasantly hard. In that case you might want to grind the diced sausage in the food processor before adding it to the pan.

new orleans red beans

NEW ORLEANS RED BEANS ARE LEGENDARY, but up until recently we'd been mostly disappointed by the recipes we'd tried at home. Thanks to Frank Brigtsen, the chef and co-owner of Brigtsen's in New Orleans, we now have a version that excites us. Spicy and saucy, this dish is what red beans should taste like. The ingredient list may look long, but don't be daunted — aside from andouille sausage, it's all standard fare. Serve these beans as either a side dish or a great little supper.

serves 8

1 tablespoon plus 1 teaspoon minced garlic

Kosher salt

1 teaspoon dried oregano, crumbled

1/2 teaspoon dried thyme

1/4 teaspoon ground cumin

1/4 teaspoon freshly ground black pepper, plus more to taste

1/8 teaspoon freshly ground white pepper

1/8 teaspoon cayenne pepper

1 tablespoon olive oil

10 ounces smoked ham, cut into 1/2-inch dice (about 2 cups)

10 ounces andouille sausages (see note), halved lengthwise and sliced crosswise 1/4 inch thick (about 2 cups)

1 large Spanish onion, finely chopped

5 large celery ribs, finely chopped

1 large green bell pepper, cored, seeded, and finely chopped

2 bay leaves

4 cups chicken stock or canned low-sodium broth

4 cups water

1 pound dried red kidney beans, picked over and rinsed

4 tablespoons finely chopped fresh flat-leaf parsley

Steamed white rice or garlic bread, for serving

Combine the garlic, 4 teaspoons kosher salt, the oregano, thyme, cumin, black pepper, white pepper, and cayenne in a small bowl.

Heat the oil until shimmering but not smoking in a large heavy Dutch oven (preferably enameled cast iron) over medium heat. Add the ham and cook, stirring occasionally, until lightly browned, about 4 minutes. Add the andouille and cook, stirring occasionally, until lightly browned, 5 to 6 minutes. Add the onion, celery, bell pepper, and bay leaves and cook, stirring occasionally, until the vegetables soften, about 10 minutes. Add the spice mixture and cook, stirring, until fragrant.

Add the stock, the water, and the beans and bring to a boil. Cover and cook the beans over low heat for 1 hour. Stir in 2 tablespoons of the parsley and cook, uncovered, over medium-low low heat until the beans are tender and the liquid is thick, about 1 hour more. Stir in the remaining 2 tablespoons parsley and season with salt and black pepper. Ladle the beans into bowls and serve with white rice or garlic bread.

cook's notes

- Andouille sausage is widely available in well-stocked supermarkets and gourmet shops.

- When shopping for dried beans, look for ones with smooth, unwrinkled skins, and without dust or debris in the bottom of the bag. These will be fresher and have a better texture when cooked. A good place to buy dried beans is the bulk bin at a busy health food store.

- Like most slow-cooked dishes, this one tastes even better a day or two after it's made. If the beans thicken too much after sitting, just add a bit of water.

SOURCE: *Local Flavors* by Deborah Madison
COOK: Deborah Madison

giant popover with wild mushrooms

IF YOU LOVE POPOVERS, Yorkshire pudding, or Dutch babies (the sweet version of this puffy classic), you'll adore this sophisticated interpretation, which features cheese and wild mushrooms cooked with a little cream. The whole thing is baked in a skillet in the oven and brought hot to the table. For the fragrance alone the dish is worth it.

Although it's best made with chanterelles, oyster mushrooms, or other very woodsy wild mushrooms, you can also use regular button mushrooms.

The popover makes a great brunch dish. For breakfast, consider the delectable sweet version (see tip). Usually you have to serve popovers the minute they're cooked through, but this dish will survive 5 or 10 minutes out of the oven without losing its big puff. Still, it's best hot from the oven.

serves 4

1 pound chanterelles or other wild or cultivated mushrooms

4 tablespoons (¹/₂ stick) unsalted butter

4 large eggs

1 cup milk

Sea salt

³/₄ cup all-purpose flour

2–3 tablespoons freshly grated Parmesan or dry Monterey Jack cheese

2 tablespoons cream (optional)

Freshly ground black pepper

1 tablespoon minced fresh flat-leaf parsley leaves

1 scant teaspoon minced fresh thyme leaves

Clean the mushrooms: pick out any pine needles and brush off any forest dirt. If you're using morels, cut them in half lengthwise so you can brush out the centers. Don't dunk the mushrooms in water unless they're really dirty; instead wipe them with a damp cloth. Slice into attractive pieces that reveal the shapes of the mushrooms.

Preheat the oven to 400 degrees. Put a 10-inch cast-iron skillet in the oven with 2 tablespoons of the butter while you whisk together the eggs, milk, and ¹/₂ teaspoon salt in a medium bowl. Add the flour and whisk until smooth. When the butter has melted, brush it around the rim of the skillet, then stir it into the batter. Add the cheese, then pour the batter back into the hot skillet. Set in the center of the oven to bake. In 20 minutes it will have risen dramatically around the edges and be puffed in the center as if it were trying to lift itself out of the skillet.

Meanwhile, melt the remaining 2 tablespoons of butter in a large sauté pan over high heat. Add the mushrooms, salt them lightly, and sauté until they begin to give up their juices. Reduce the heat to medium and cook the mushrooms until tender, about 5 minutes, possibly longer for wild mushrooms. If there's a huge amount of juice, increase the heat to reduce it, but don't let it cook away completely. Stir the cream, if using, into the juices and allow them to mingle and thicken slightly. Season with pepper, then toss with the parsley and thyme.

Remove the popover from the oven and spoon the mushrooms into the center, or slice the popover into wedges and spoon the mushrooms over each serving. Serve immediately.

cook's notes

- A few shiitake caps are good to mix into the other mushrooms, as are some peeled portobello caps (see note, page 177).
- It can be hard to get the popover out of the pan with the mushrooms on it; transfer the whole popover to a platter and slice it, then spoon the mushrooms on top.
- You can serve the dramatic popover all by itself.

tip

Sweet version: For breakfast or even dessert, try this popover with pears. Peel and core two buttery ripe pears and cut them into $1/2$-inch-thick slices. Toss them with $1/2$ teaspoon ground cardamom, the juice of half a lemon, and 2 tablespoons sugar. Make the popover batter, omitting the cheese, adding to the milk $1/2$ teaspoon pure vanilla extract and $1/8$ teaspoon almond extract. Melt the butter in the pan and add the pears, cooking them over medium-high heat until they're tender, about 3 minutes. Pour the popover batter over the pears and bake as directed. (From *Local Flavors*, by Deborah Madison.)

SOURCE: S. Irene Virbilia in the *Los Angeles Times*
COOK: Suzanne Goin

bread stuffing with fennel and swiss chard

WE ALL KNOW SOMEONE WHO WOULD RATHER EAT the stuffing than the turkey, and if this were the stuffing in question, we would too. The recipe comes from the fabulously talented Suzanne Goin, the chef at Lucques in West Hollywood, and we don't think you need to roast a turkey (or even a chicken) to have an excuse to make it. The combination of sautéed fennel and currants adds a delightful sweet note, the chard keeps it earthy, and the chiles provide a hint of heat. If you're not a fan of chicken livers, leave them out — although they add good flavor. While we prefer to cook the stuffing in a baking dish so the top gets browned and crisp, you can, of course, use it to stuff a large roasting chicken or even the Thanksgiving turkey (see note). Besides being a fine accompaniment for roast poultry, it's good alongside roast beef, lamb, or pork.

serves 8

- $^3/_4$ pound good-quality rustic white bread
- $^3/_4$ cup extra-virgin olive oil
- 1 fresh rosemary sprig
- 2 dried red chiles
- 3 small or 2 medium onions, diced (about 2 cups)
- 1 fennel bulb, diced (about 1$^3/_4$ cups)
- 2 garlic cloves, minced
- 1 tablespoon ground fennel seeds

- 1 tablespoon minced fresh thyme
- $^1/_2$ teaspoon grated lemon zest
  Salt
- $^1/_3$ cup dried currants
- 4 fresh sage leaves, thinly sliced
- 1 bunch Swiss chard, roughly chopped
- 1 tablespoon butter
- $^1/_2$ pound chicken livers
  Freshly ground black pepper
- 2 tablespoons balsamic vinegar

Preheat the oven to 350 degrees. Butter a 9-x-13-inch baking dish.

Cut the crusts off the bread and discard. Tear the bread into 1-inch pieces; it's okay if they're slightly uneven in size. In a large bowl, toss the bread with $^1/_4$ cup of the oil. Place the bread on a baking sheet and bake until crispy on the outside but still tender on the inside, about 15 minutes. Let the croutons cool, then place them in a large bowl. Reduce the oven temperature to 325 degrees.

Meanwhile, heat $1/4$ cup of the remaining oil in a 12-inch skillet over medium-high heat. Add the rosemary and chiles and let them sizzle in the oil to release their flavors, about 30 seconds. Add the onions, fennel, garlic, fennel seeds, thyme, lemon zest, and $1/2$ teaspoon salt. Cook until browned, scraping the bottom of the pan with a wooden spoon frequently, about 15 minutes. Remove from the heat, fish out the rosemary sprig, and stir in the currants and sage. Add to the bowl with the croutons and toss well.

Return the skillet to medium-high heat. Add 2 tablespoons of the remaining oil and cook the chard until wilted, 6 to 7 minutes. Add to the bowl with the croutons.

Melt the butter in a small skillet over medium-high heat. Season the chicken livers with salt and pepper and cook, turning, until medium-rare, 4 to 5 minutes. They should be a little browned on the outside and a little pink inside. Chop and add to the bowl with the croutons. Toss well. Season the stuffing with the remaining 2 tablespoons oil and the balsamic vinegar. Mix with your hands, gently mashing the ingredients together so they are well blended.

Place the stuffing in the prepared baking dish, cover with aluminum foil, and bake for 20 minutes. Uncover and bake until the top is golden and crisp, 20 minutes more. Serve hot.

cook's notes

- Look for a plain but good-quality crusty country bread. Avoid any overly sour sourdough for this stuffing, because it will overpower the other ingredients.
- The recipe makes enough stuffing for two large roasting chickens (6 to 8 pounds each) or one 16- to 18-pound turkey. When cooking stuffed poultry, roast until the stuffing reaches 160 degrees. Bake any extra stuffing in a buttered baking dish as directed in the recipe.
- Red or rainbow-colored chard makes this dish even prettier.
- If you omit the chicken livers, you won't need the tablespoon of butter for frying them either.

SOURCE: *Gourmet*
COOK: Lori W. Powell

kumquat and cranberry compote

WE'VE NEVER MET A CRANBERRY COMPOTE we didn't like, but this not-too-sweet one takes the concept into the stratosphere. There's a subtle Asian flavoring: kumquats, fresh ginger, and a haunting, can't-quite-put-your-finger-on-it hint of star anise. The compote is great with the Thanksgiving turkey or with duck, ham, lamb, or any other rich cranberry-friendly meat. It's also delicious stirred into yogurt.

Gourmet notes that the compote tastes good without the kumquats, but we wouldn't dream of it.

serves 8 to 10

2 12-ounce bags fresh cranberries

9 ounces kumquats, trimmed and quartered lengthwise (about 1 1/2 cups)

1 1/4 cups sugar

2 tablespoons finely chopped fresh ginger

2 whole star anise pods

1/4 teaspoon salt

1 cup water

Combine all the ingredients in a heavy 4-quart saucepan. Simmer, uncovered, until the berries have burst, 10 to 12 minutes. Remove the star anise and cool completely before storing, covered, in the refrigerator.

cook's note

℞ If the kumquats have large seeds, you may want to seed them before you add them to the pot. You can also use them whole, which is prettier; they'll soften in the cooking. You can also eat kumquats raw.

breads

SOURCE: *Everything Tastes Better with Bacon* by Sara Perry
COOK: Debbie Putnam

buttermilk and cream biscuits

WE WERE TEMPTED TO RENAME THESE "dream biscuits," since the recipe works like a dream and the biscuits themselves are so tender and heavenly. The combination of buttermilk and cream translates into a rich dough with a good tangy edge. But what makes this recipe really stand out is the technique. There's none of the kneading or patting out of most biscuit recipes. Instead, the sticky, wet dough is scooped or spooned out, dropped into flour, and quickly shaped into individual biscuits. Once they are baked, you can brush the crusty biscuits with melted butter if you like. We do.

makes about 10 biscuits

2 cups self-rising flour
$1/8$ teaspoon baking soda
$3/4$ teaspoon salt
2 tablespoons sugar
4 tablespoons ($1/2$ stick) cold unsalted butter, cut into small pieces

$3/4$ cup buttermilk
$1/2$ cup heavy cream
1 cup all-purpose flour
2 tablespoons unsalted butter, melted (optional)

Preheat the oven to 500 degrees. Spray an 8-inch round cake pan with nonstick spray. Whisk together the self-rising flour, baking soda, salt, and sugar in a medium bowl. Add the cold butter. Using a pastry blender, two knives, or your fingertips, work the mixture together until the butter is the size of peas. Stir in the buttermilk and cream and let the dough stand for 2 minutes. It will be sticky and wet.

Place the all-purpose flour in a separate bowl. Flour your hands well. Scoop or spoon a lemon-size lump of wet dough into the flour. Coat it with flour, pick it up, and gently shape it into a soft round. Shake off the excess flour and place it in the prepared pan. Repeat with the remaining dough, placing the biscuits against each other, 8 around the edges and 2 in the center.

Bake the biscuits for 5 minutes. Reduce the oven temperature to 475 degrees and bake until the biscuits are very brown, about 17 minutes more. Remove from the oven and brush with the melted butter, if desired. Cool for 5 minutes before inverting the pan and removing the biscuits. Gently pull the biscuits apart and serve.

cook's note

The biscuits will keep for a day or two, but are best served warm. To rewarm, wrap the biscuits in aluminum foil and place in a 350-degree oven for a few minutes.

SOURCE: *Los Angeles Times*
COOK: Regina Schrambling

slow-rising pumpkin-thyme dinner rolls

NO MATTER HOW MUCH WE'VE ALL COME TO LOVE big, chewy loaves of crusty bread, there's no denying the pleasure of a well-made dinner roll: pull-apart tender, buttery and a wee bit sweet, and so soft that you just have to drag a piece across your plate to sop up the last bits of gravy. These rolls turn a lovely pale orange color from the pumpkin puree and have a nice whiff of thyme to balance the sweetness.

You can start them the night before and let them rise overnight in the refrigerator, which is ideal for big holiday feast days like Thanksgiving. The next day, shape the rolls, leave them to rise at room temperature, and then bake them while the turkey rests. As with most soft rolls, these are best eaten the day they are baked, although a leftover roll with some mayonnaise and cranberry sauce does make for a pretty great turkey sandwich.

makes 18 rolls

2 envelopes active dry yeast
1/4 cup warm water (110–115 degrees)
2 large eggs, at room temperature
1 cup canned pumpkin puree (not pie filling)
8 tablespoons (1 stick) unsalted butter, at room temperature
1/2 cup sugar

1 tablespoon minced fresh thyme or 1 teaspoon dried
2 teaspoons coarse salt
1/4 teaspoon cayenne pepper
3–4 cups all-purpose flour
Olive oil, for greasing the bowl
2 tablespoons melted butter, for greasing the pans

Sprinkle the yeast over the warm water in a large bowl and stir to dissolve. Using a wooden spoon, beat in the eggs, pumpkin, room-temperature butter, sugar, thyme, salt, and cayenne. Add 3 cups of the flour and beat until smooth, gradually adding more flour as needed to make a soft, sticky, but still manageable dough. Make sure the dough is well mixed. Oil a larger bowl and scrape the dough into it, turning the dough to oil it on all sides. Cover with a kitchen towel and let rise in a warm, draft-free spot until doubled in bulk, about 1 1/2 hours. Punch the dough down, cover tightly with plastic wrap and refrigerate overnight.

Grease two 8-inch cake pans with the melted butter. Punch the dough down again and shape it into 18 round dinner rolls, arranging them in the pans with about ¹/₂-inch space between each. (If the dough is too sticky to handle easily, lightly butter or oil your hands.) Cover the rolls with a kitchen towel and let rise in a warm spot until doubled in bulk, about 30 minutes.

Preheat the oven to 375 degrees. Bake the rolls until browned, 20 to 25 minutes. Serve hot or warm.

cook's notes

- Since the dough is so soft, it needs no kneading. You just stir with a wooden spoon. We've also used a standing mixer with good results.
- To shape these into cloverleaf rolls, butter a 12-muffin pan, tear off tablespoon-size balls, place 3 in each muffin cup, and bake as directed.

SOURCE: *Food & Wine*
COOK: Mary Thomas

bay leaf–scented spoon rolls

MAKING YOUR OWN ROLLS may seem a little over the top, but it's easy — at least these are — and everyone at the table will be overjoyed to see them, especially for holidays. And these rolls are different; they're incredibly moist, crusty on top, and perfumed faintly with a bay leaf that's removed from each roll after it bakes.

The rolls are made with two kinds of flour (cake flour and all-purpose flour) and two kinds of fat (butter and sour cream), which give them a complex taste. The recipe serves a crowd, but you can easily cut it in half.

makes 24 rolls

2 cups warm water
1/2 cup sugar
2 envelopes active dry yeast
4 cups self-rising cake flour
4 cups all-purpose flour
1 teaspoon salt

16 tablespoons (2 sticks) cold unsalted butter, diced
3 cups sour cream
24 bay leaves
4 tablespoons (1/2 stick) melted butter

Butter two standard-size 12-cup muffin pans. Combine the water, sugar, and yeast in a small bowl and let stand until foamy, about 5 minutes.

Whisk together the cake flour, all-purpose flour, and salt in a large bowl. Using a pastry blender or two knives, cut in 16 tablespoons of the cold butter until the mixture resembles small peas. Add the yeast mixture and stir with a wooden spoon until blended. Add the sour cream and stir until combined.

Spoon the dough into the prepared muffin pans and let stand at room temperature for 1 hour.

Preheat the oven to 400 degrees. Spike each roll with a bay leaf and bake for 10 minutes. Lightly brush the tops of the rolls with the melted butter and bake for 15 minutes more, or until golden. Pull out and discard the bay leaves. Serve the rolls warm.

cook's notes

- The bay leaves are a charming idea, but they don't make a serious difference in flavor, so if you'd rather skip buying a new jar of bay leaves, just leave them out.

- You can make the rolls a day ahead and refrigerate them, unbaked, in their pans. Remove them from the refrigerator before baking and let them sit for 2 hours at room temperature in a draft-free place.

- The rolls will keep in an airtight container for 1 day.

SOURCE: *Rosie Magazine*
COOK: Maury Rubin

pumpkin-oat muffins

WE'RE ALWAYS HOPING TO FIND a really great breakfast muffin — one that's moist but not heavy, dense but not a doorstop, sweet but not teeth-achingly so. These pumpkin-oat muffins win on all points and then some.

The recipe comes from Maury Rubin, chef at City Bakery in New York City. Located near Union Square, the popular bakery is known for its superb breakfast pastries.

makes 12 muffins

$3/4$ cup old-fashioned rolled oats, plus more for topping, if desired

$1^3/4$ cups all-purpose flour

$1/2$ cup sugar

$1/4$ cup packed dark brown sugar, sifted to remove any lumps

1 tablespoon baking powder

$1^1/2$ teaspoons pumpkin pie spice

1 teaspoon baking soda

1 teaspoon salt

$1/4$ teaspoon ground cinnamon

1 cup canned pumpkin puree (not pie filling)

$3/4$ cup plain or vanilla whole-milk yogurt

10 pitted prunes, coarsely chopped

$1/2$ cup canola oil

1 large egg

2 tablespoons unsweetened applesauce

Preheat the oven to 350 degrees. Lightly coat the inside of a standard-size 12-cup muffin pan with nonstick spray.

Finely grind the rolled oats in a food processor. Transfer to a large bowl. Add the flour, sugar, brown sugar, baking powder, pie spice, baking soda, salt, and cinnamon and whisk until well blended.

Process the pumpkin puree, yogurt, and prunes in the food processor until the prunes are pureed (specks of the prunes will still be visible). Add the oil, egg, and applesauce and process to combine.

Make a well in the center of the dry ingredients; add the pumpkin mixture to the well. Gradually stir the flour mixture from the sides of the bowl into the pumpkin mixture until just incorporated. Spoon a heaping $1/3$ cup of the batter into each muffin cup. Sprinkle the top with rolled oats, if desired.

Bake for 22 minutes, or until a wooden pick inserted into the center of a muffin comes out clean. Let the muffins cool in the pan on a wire rack for 10 minutes, then turn out the muffins. Serve warm or at room temperature.

cook's notes

- If you're making these muffins to travel, use paper liners in the muffin pan. It makes them easier to transport and easier to clean up.
- Once baked and cooled, the muffins can be frozen in freezer bags for up to 1 month.

SOURCE: R.W. Apple in the *New York Times*
COOK: Bill Granger

coconut bread

BILL'S IS ONE OF THOSE TRUE COMMUNITY BREAKFAST spots that serves great food and that we all wish we had around the corner. Unfortunately, it couldn't be farther away — it's in Sydney, Australia. Word is that the only item that never changes on the handwritten menu is this coconut bread. Happily, we've now got the recipe.

This quick bread is deliciously moist and dense. The coconut flakes in the batter add a lovely island flavor and — highlighted by a bit of cinnamon — they give the bread its distinctive texture. The best way to enjoy this bread is the way they serve it at Bill's: toasted and slathered with butter. A smear of good marmalade or a sprinkle of confectioners' sugar over the butter isn't a bad way to go either.

makes 1 loaf

2 large eggs
1¹/4 cups milk
1 teaspoon pure vanilla extract
2¹/2 cups all-purpose flour, plus more for dusting the pan
2 teaspoons baking powder
2 teaspoons ground cinnamon

5 ounces flaked coconut (about 1¹/2 cups)
1 cup superfine sugar (see note)
6 tablespoons (³/4 stick) unsalted butter, melted
Butter, for serving (optional)
Confectioners' sugar, for serving (optional)

Preheat the oven to 350 degrees. Whisk together the eggs, milk, and vanilla in a small bowl.

Sift together the 2¹/2 cups flour, baking powder, and cinnamon in a medium bowl. Stir in the coconut and superfine sugar. Make a well in the center and pour in the egg mixture. Gradually mix with the dry ingredients until just combined. Add the melted butter and stir until smooth. Do not overmix.

Oil and flour an 8¹/2-x-4¹/2-inch loaf pan. Pour the batter into the pan. Bake until a toothpick inserted into the center comes out clean, 1 to 1¹/4 hours.

Cool in the pan for 5 minutes, then remove the bread from the pan and finish cooling on a rack.

To serve, cut into 8 to 10 thick slices. If desired, toast lightly, spread with butter, and dust lightly with confectioners' sugar.

cook's notes

- ℰ We make this with unsweetened coconut and love the way it tastes. Sweetened coconut flakes would make it too sweet.
- ℰ If you don't have superfine sugar, grind regular granulated sugar in a food processor for a minute or two.

SOURCE: *Good Housekeeping*
COOK: **Silver Rose Resort Winery**

lemon bread

TWO GUESTS AT THE SILVER ROSE RESORT WINERY in Calistoga, California, enjoyed this lovely lemon bread for breakfast while visiting the wine country. They were so smitten that they wrote away for the recipe — and we thank them. Like any good quick bread, the recipe is just that — quick. It's also light, moist, and full of lemony flavor. The addition of walnuts is a nice idea, too.

Slices of this bread spread with sweet butter are delicious for breakfast, and we also think it belongs on a holiday buffet alongside the relishes and side dishes.

makes 1 loaf

1 1/2 cups all-purpose flour
1 teaspoon baking powder
3/4 teaspoon salt
1 cup plus 2 tablespoons sugar
1/2 cup vegetable oil

2 large eggs
1 tablespoon grated lemon zest
1/2 cup whole milk
1/2 cup chopped walnuts
3 tablespoons fresh lemon juice

Preheat the oven to 350 degrees. Grease a 9-x-5-inch metal loaf pan. Combine the flour, baking powder, and salt in a medium bowl.

Using a mixer on high speed, beat 1 cup of the sugar and the oil in a large bowl for 2 minutes, or until well blended. Beat in the eggs and lemon zest. On low speed, blend in the flour mixture until just combined. Add the milk, and then stir in the nuts.

Spoon the batter into the prepared pan. Bake until a toothpick inserted in the center comes out clean, 65 to 70 minutes.

In a small cup, mix together the lemon juice and the remaining 2 tablespoons sugar.

When the bread comes out of the oven, poke holes all over the top of the loaf with a skewer and brush with the lemon mixture. Set the pan on a wire rack and let cool for 10 minutes. Remove the loaf from the pan and cool it completely before slicing and serving.

cook's notes

- Rather than making one large loaf, you can bake this bread in three $5^3/_4$-x-$3^1/_4$-inch metal loaf pans. Expect them to bake in 45 to 50 minutes.
- You can omit the nuts if you like.

SOURCE: *Bon Appétit*
COOK: Patrice Bedrosian, after Julie Lestrange

irish soda bread
with raisins and caraway

PATRICE BEDROSIAN, A *BON APPÉTIT* READER, sent in this recipe in honor of her stepbrother, Jerry O'Leary, a chef who was killed in the attack on the World Trade Center. Jerry's mother always made this skillet bread for her family, and it became comfort food in the aftermath of September 11. We recognized the recipe right away as an old family favorite of our own (although our kids weren't so crazy about the caraway seeds, and we usually left them out).

This isn't an Irish soda bread any Irishman would recognize, but it's very good, jammed with raisins, and incredibly easy to make. If you keep a can of powdered buttermilk in your cupboard, everything here is a staple.

serves 8 to 10

5 cups all-purpose flour
1 cup sugar
1 tablespoon baking powder
1$^1/_2$ teaspoons salt
1 teaspoon baking soda

8 tablespoons (1 stick) unsalted butter, cut into cubes, at room temperature
2$^1/_2$ cups raisins
3 tablespoons caraway seeds
2$^1/_2$ cups buttermilk
1 large egg

Preheat the oven to 350 degrees. Generously butter a heavy ovenproof 10- to 12-inch skillet with 2- to 2$^1/_2$-inch sides. Whisk together the flour, sugar, baking powder, salt, and baking soda in a large bowl. Add the butter and rub it in with your fingertips until coarse crumbs form. Stir in the raisins and caraway seeds. Whisk together the buttermilk and egg in a medium bowl. Add to the flour mixture and stir with a wooden spoon just until well incorporated. The dough will be very sticky.

Transfer the dough to the prepared skillet and smooth the top, mounding it slightly in the center. Using a small sharp knife dipped in flour, cut a 1-inch-deep X in the top of the dough. Bake until a tester inserted in the center comes out clean, about 1 hour and 15 minutes. Cool the bread in the skillet for 10 minutes. Turn out onto a rack and cool completely before cutting and serving.

cook's notes

❧ You can make the bread one day ahead. Wrap it tightly in aluminum foil and store at room temperature.

❧ Fresh baking soda is essential here.

SOURCE: *Cooking Thin with Chef Kathleen*
by Kathleen Daelemans
COOK: Kathleen Daelemans

sweet potato bread
with cranberries, currants, and pecans

THIS IS ONE OF THOSE BREADS that's more like a fruitcake: jammed with little bits of pecans and dried fruit with a base of sweet vegetables.

It's as good with afternoon tea as it is for breakfast, and it's very moist and satisfying. This bread is a good choice if you're on a low-fat diet, though it's not low-calorie.

The sweet potato element can be handled by using canned pumpkin or leftover or microwaved sweet potatoes, and the bread is fast enough that it works for breakfast. It's a perfect choice when you have overnight guests, and it will probably be among the first items to disappear on a holiday buffet.

makes 1 loaf

2 cups all-purpose flour
1¹/₂ teaspoons baking powder
1 teaspoon baking soda
¹/₄ teaspoon salt
1 cup firmly packed light brown sugar
1¹/₂ cups cooked and pureed sweet potatoes, pumpkin, or butternut squash

1 large egg
2 large egg whites
¹/₄ cup vegetable oil
1¹/₂ teaspoons pure vanilla extract
1 cup fresh cranberries
¹/₂ cup dried cranberries
¹/₂ cup dried currants or raisins
¹/₃ cup chopped pecans

Preheat the oven to 350 degrees. Lightly grease and flour a 9-x-5-inch loaf pan. Sift together the flour, baking powder, baking soda, and salt in a large bowl.

In another large bowl, whisk together the brown sugar, sweet potatoes, pumpkin or squash, egg, egg whites, oil, and vanilla extract. Add the dry ingredients to the sweet potato mixture. Stir about five strokes, then add the fresh and dried cranberries, currants, and pecans. Mix until just combined. Do not overmix.

Pour the batter into the prepared pan. Bake until a toothpick inserted in the center comes out clean, 50 to 60 minutes. Cool in the pan for 10 minutes. Turn out the loaf onto a wire rack and cool completely before serving.

cook's note

ℰ Chef Kathleen points out that it's easy to put together this bread in the morning if you do a little prep the night before: measure and sift the dry ingredients, lay out the other ingredients that don't require refrigeration, and get all the tools ready. Putting it all together will take less than 5 minutes.

SOURCE: *Judy Zeidler's International Deli Cookbook*
by Judy Zeidler
COOK: Izzy Cohen

izzy's authentic bagels

BAGEL MAVENS WHO DON'T LIVE IN NEW YORK CITY often bemoan the quality of bagels elsewhere. (And old-time New Yorkers mutter that New York bagels aren't the real thing anymore either: they've become sweeter and fluffier.) If you've never had "real" bagels or you want to duplicate them, here, finally, is an authentic recipe. Izzy Cohen is a retired baker now living in Los Angeles, and his bagels are knockouts.

There are two unusual ingredients here: high-gluten flour and malt. Natural foods stores should stock both, but you can mail-order them if they're unavailable in your area. There's just enough sugar to get the yeast going, and the high-gluten flour assures a really chewy bagel. Making bagels is a lot of fun, and it's a project kids really like.

makes about 15 bagels

- 2 cups cold water
- 1 tablespoon safflower oil
- 2 tablespoons sugar
- 1 tablespoon malt (see note)
- 3/4 teaspoon salt

- 8 cups high-gluten flour (12–13 percent gluten; see note)
- 5 teaspoons active dry yeast
- 1 tablespoon yellow cornmeal

Mix the water, oil, sugar, malt, and salt in the bowl of a heavy-duty electric mixer on medium speed (see note). In another large bowl, mix 6 cups of the flour with the yeast. Gradually add the flour mixture to the water mixture and blend until the dough comes together. Add the remaining 2 cups flour and beat until smooth. (If any flour mixture remains in the bottom of the bowl, add several drops of water to moisten it and beat for 5 minutes more.)

Transfer the dough to a lightly floured board, cover with a kitchen towel, and let rest for 5 minutes. Divide the dough into 15 pieces and cover with the towel while you knead and shape each piece. Knead by folding each piece in half and pushing out any air pockets, then fold in half again and repeat. Shape into a rope about 5 inches long. Join the ends to make a doughnut shape, overlapping them by about 1 inch, and form into a smooth perfect circle. Repeat the process with the remaining pieces of dough.

Sprinkle the cornmeal on the work surface and place the bagels on top. Cover with a towel and let rest for 5 minutes.

Preheat the oven to 425 degrees. Line a baking sheet with parchment. Fill a large heavy pot with water and bring to a rolling boil. Working in batches, drop 4 to 6 bagels (do not crowd) into the boiling water and boil for exactly 10 seconds. The bagels should rise to the top of the water. Transfer with a slotted spoon to a wire rack and drain.

Transfer the bagels to the prepared baking sheet, 2 inches apart. Bake until golden brown, about 10 minutes. Cool on wire racks and serve.

cook's notes

- To order high-gluten flour and malt, call King Arthur's *Baker's Catalogue* (800-827-6836).
- Confession: We once made these bagels without the malt and they were still absolutely delicious.
- You can mix all the ingredients in a large bowl with a wooden spoon. If you're mixing the dough by hand, you may need a little less flour.
- You can top the bagels with chopped sautéed onion and poppy seeds or caraway seeds mixed with a little coarse kosher salt. After boiling and draining the bagels, press the top of each bagel into the seed mixture and bake as directed.
- The bagels aren't quite as good the next day, so freeze them individually and toast just before serving.

SOURCE: *Los Angeles Times*
COOK: Cindy Dorn

rancho bernardo inn's walnut bread

A READER OF THE *LOS ANGELES TIMES* remembered this favorite recipe from fifteen or twenty years ago and asked if it could be resurrected and republished. This initiative counts in our estimation as a major public service. Our hats are off to Gina Zucchero of Thousand Oaks.

If you make this bread once, you'll make it many times, and anyone who tastes it will too, assuming you part with the recipe. It's a quick bread, very easy to make, and full of buttery, toasty nut flavor. It's almost cakey, so don't smother it with jam — a little butter is all it needs, if that.

makes 2 loaves

16 tablespoons (2 sticks) butter, plus more for the pans

2 cups sugar

4 large eggs

4 cups all-purpose flour, plus more for the pans

1/2 teaspoon salt

2 teaspoons baking soda

2 cups sour cream

2 teaspoons pure vanilla extract

1 1/2 cups chopped walnuts

Preheat the oven to 350 degrees. Butter and flour two 9-x-5-inch loaf pans. Cream the 16 tablespoons butter and the sugar in a large bowl until fluffy. Slowly beat in the eggs, one at a time.

Sift together the 4 cups flour, salt, and baking soda into a medium bowl and add to the egg mixture. Blend in the sour cream and vanilla. Stir in the nuts.

Divide the batter between the pans. Bake the loaves until golden, 55 to 60 minutes.

Cool the bread in the pans on a wire rack for 10 minutes, then invert onto the rack and cool completely before slicing and serving.

desserts

desserts

SOURCE: *A la Carte with Lee White*
(WICH-1310 AM, Norwich, Connecticut)
COOK: James O'Shea

lemon posset

WITH JUST THREE INGREDIENTS and perhaps five minutes of your precious time, you can have a dessert that will be the talk of your dinner party. This airy confection, a cross between a pudding and a mousse, is a classic British dessert (albeit transmitted by an Irish chef).

You may be tempted to add lemon zest to the cream, which is fine, but you don't need it because there's plenty of lemon flavor in the juice — and you save the extra step of straining.

serves 6

2 cups heavy cream
3/4 cup sugar
Juice of 2 lemons

Raspberries and confectioners' sugar, for garnish

Bring the cream and sugar to a boil in a medium heavy nonreactive saucepan, stirring constantly.

Reduce the heat to a simmer and stir vigorously for 2 to 3 minutes. Off the heat, whisk in the lemon juice. Pour the cream into small cups or glasses, cool slightly, cover with plastic wrap, and chill until set, about 4 hours. Serve slightly chilled or at room temperature, garnished with raspberries and a dusting of confectioners' sugar.

cook's notes

- The posset looks best presented in cut glass — chill the glasses first so the dessert will set up faster. You can also garnish the posset with blackberries or raspberries (both golden and red), adding a sprig of mint, preferably variegated.
- Lime posset is wonderful, too, and made exactly the same way.
- The posset will keep overnight in the refrigerator. Let it sit for a while at room temperature before serving so that it's not too cold.

SOURCE: Melissa Ceria in the *New York Times*
COOK: Carolina Barbieri

carolina's ricotta berry pudding

THIS INSOUCIANT RECIPE IS THE BRAINCHILD of a transplanted Brit who now lives in Manhattan and throws wonderful off-the-cuff parties. It's a 15-minute bit of work, and it feeds a big crowd. All you need, says Carolina Barbieri, is a big bowl — but an electric mixer helps.

The pudding is creamy, dense but not heavy, and delicately perfumed with orange zest. In the middle and on top are layers of berries — blackberries, raspberries, and strawberries — garnished with chocolate shavings.

serves 14 to 16

2 cups confectioners' sugar
3 cups heavy cream
3 pounds ricotta cheese
1 tablespoon grated orange zest

2 cups strawberries, rinsed and hulled
2 cups raspberries
2 cups blackberries
$1/2$ cup milk chocolate shavings

Combine the confectioners' sugar and cream in the bowl of an electric mixer fitted with the whisk attachment, or beat by hand using a whisk. Add the ricotta gradually, whisking until thick and slightly firm. Add the orange zest and whisk until just blended.

Combine the berries in a large bowl. Put half the ricotta mixture in the bottom of a large serving bowl; top with half the berry mixture and half the chocolate shavings. Add another layer of ricotta and berries, then sprinkle on the remaining chocolate shavings.

Cover lightly with plastic wrap and refrigerate until chilled, about 1 hour. Serve.

cook's notes

- Ricotta is such a major element here that it's worth looking for a really good one, which you're most likely to find at an Italian market. No low-fat ricotta here, please.
- Some variations: use lemon zest instead of orange; use semisweet chocolate instead of milk chocolate.
- At the peak of summer, all three kinds of berries will be available, but just raspberries are fine too.

desserts

SOURCE: *Fresh & Healthy* by Sally James
COOK: Sally James

cardamom-scented orange salad

WHEN YOU CRAVE A LIGHT AND HEALTHY fruit dessert in the winter months, make this. Navel oranges, at their peak in the dead of winter, sit overnight in a light cardamom syrup, taking on a heavenly perfume.

Whether you serve this salad on its own — perhaps accompanied by a little cookie — or with the Honey Yogurt sauce, don't skip the topping of toasted almonds and sliced dates. It adds just the right amount of crunch and sweetness.

serves 4

4 large firm navel
  or Valencia oranges
1 tablespoon orange flower water
  (see note)
1 tablespoon sugar
1 teaspoon cardamom seeds
  or 4–5 cardamom pods, split
  (see note)

6–8 fresh mint leaves
4 dates, pitted and sliced
2 tablespoons flaked almonds,
  toasted
Honey Yogurt
  (recipe follows; optional)

Peel and slice the oranges into $1/4$-inch-thick rounds. Arrange in a layer in a flat-bottomed bowl and sprinkle with the orange flower water, sugar, and cardamom seeds. Cover and refrigerate overnight.

To serve, remove the cardamom seeds and place the orange slices on a serving platter. Spoon over some of the syrup. Scatter with the mint, dates, and almonds. Serve with the Honey Yogurt, if desired.

honey yogurt

1/3 cup plain yogurt

1–2 teaspoons honey, gently
    warmed to soften

Pure vanilla extract

Combine the yogurt, honey, and a few drops of vanilla in a small bowl and mix well.

cook's notes

❧ Orange flower water is available at specialty food markets.

❧ Cardamom pods and seeds can be found in the bulk spice department of most natural-food stores and gourmet markets. The pods are pea-size husks that are easily split open by crushing lightly with your fingers. Once you've retrieved the seeds, discard the pod. Use either whole cardamom pods or seeds; ground cardamom won't do — it clobbers the sweet flavor of the citrus.

tip

If you're unsure about what to do with the rest of the little bottle of orange flower water, here's a great idea from Nigel Slater in his book *Appetite:* drizzle a scant teaspoon over a bowl of vanilla ice cream and top with chopped pistachios.

SOURCE: *Nigella Bites* by Nigella Lawson
COOK: Nigella Lawson

bitter orange ice cream

EVEN IF YOU'VE NEVER DREAMED OF MAKING ice cream and have no ice cream machine, you can make this one. It takes only a few minutes to put together and a few hours to freeze. Not quite ice cream, not quite mousse, this is a cloudlike frozen confection with a velvety texture.

The intensely flavorful Seville orange (bitter orange) is the primary ingredient in British marmalade. It's not yet common in America, but like other once-exotic fruits, you see it more often every year — especially just after Christmas. In the meantime, orange and lime mixed together give a good approximation, and lime all by itself is also great.

serves 6

3 Seville oranges or 1 navel
   orange plus 2 limes
1 cup plus 2 tablespoons
   confectioners' sugar

2¹/₂ cups heavy cream
   Wafer cookies, for serving
   (optional)

If you're using Seville oranges, grate the zest of 2 of them. Squeeze the juice out of all 3 and place it into a large bowl with the zest and sugar. If using the navel orange and limes, grate the zest of the orange and 1 lime. Juice the orange and both limes and add to the zest and sugar as before. Stir to dissolve the sugar, then add the heavy cream.

Whip everything until it holds soft peaks. (A stand mixer is perfect for this job, but a handheld mixer will do.) Turn the mixture into a shallow airtight container with a lid (see note). Cover and freeze until firm, 3 to 5 hours. Remove from the freezer to soften for 15 to 20 minutes (30 to 40 minutes in the refrigerator) before serving. Serve in bowls, in cones, or sandwiched between wafer cookies.

cook's notes

- For the all-lime option, use 4 limes, zesting 2 of them.
- This is the place to use those disposable plastic food-storage containers. Two 25-ounce containers will hold the ice cream perfectly.
- Lawson uses giant pizelle-like wafers, which she refers to as "cookie wafers," for ice cream sandwiches.

SOURCE: Tina Ujlaki in *Food & Wine*
COOK: Peggy Cullen

creamy caramel sauce

HOMEMADE CARAMEL SAUCE makes an instant killer dessert: just serve it with some first-rate vanilla ice cream (or ginger or coffee or chocolate ice cream, for that matter) or over gingerbread and you have something extraordinary. The sauce will take only 15 minutes and is made from a few basic ingredients.

Making caramel can be dicey, but this recipe works perfectly every time. (For a little extra insurance, see note.)

makes about 1¹/₃ cups

1 cup sugar
2 tablespoons water

1 cup heavy cream, scalded
1 teaspoon pure vanilla extract

Bring the sugar and water to a boil in a medium saucepan over high heat. Cook, without stirring, until a cherrywood-colored caramel forms, about 10 minutes. Wash down the sides of the pan as necessary with a wet pastry brush. Remove from the heat and carefully stir in the scalded cream. Let cool slightly, then stir in the vanilla. Serve warm.

cook's notes

- Caramel doesn't like to be agitated, so don't stir it. Instead, once you see the sugar is beginning to turn color, swirl the pan around a little; do that again as it melts and caramelizes, brushing down the sides of the pan as needed with the wet pastry brush. If you have a white enameled cast-iron pan, it will be easy to see the sugar changing color.

- There probably won't be any sauce left over, but if there is, it can have an afterlife as caramel frosting. Cream 8 tablespoons room-temperature unsalted butter with 1 cup sifted confectioners' sugar, then add ¹/₂ cup of the caramel sauce. Beat until light and fluffy.

desserts

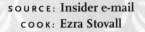

SOURCE: Insider e-mail
COOK: Ezra Stovall

skillet blueberry cobbler

THIS IS ONE OF THOSE WORD-OF-MOUTH RECIPES that made its way from kitchen to kitchen on its own merits. The original comes from the late Ezra Stovall, who lived in the Blue Ridge Mountains of North Carolina. She passed it along to her grandson, Brad, who related it to his wife Daphne, who eventually told our friend Cindy Major. Major lives in Putney, Vermont, and is co-owner of Vermont Shepherd, one of the best cheesemakers in the country.

All you have to do is melt a stick of butter in a cast-iron skillet, add the berries and let them cook a bit, then blob on the batter, and bake. The cobbler comes out with a juicy layer of buttery fruit under a golden, tender biscuit top. Peaches and/or blackberries are also wonderful here.

serves 6 to 8

8 tablespoons (1 stick) butter
4 cups blueberries (see note)
$3/4$ cup plus 2 tablespoons sugar
2 tablespoons water, if needed
1 cup self-rising flour
1 teaspoon baking powder

$1/4$ teaspoon salt
$3/4$ cup milk
Whipped cream or vanilla ice cream, for serving (optional)

Preheat the oven to 400 degrees. Melt the butter in a large cast-iron skillet (10- to 12-inch is good). Add the blueberries and 2 tablespoons of the sugar. Stir gently and cook just until the berries begin to soften. If the mixture seems at all dry, add the water.

Meanwhile, whisk together the flour, the remaining $3/4$ cup sugar, the baking powder, and the salt in a medium bowl. Add the milk and stir to make a thick batter. Spoon the batter onto the fruit. Drag a spatula or spoon through the batter to make streaks of white and blue. Don't mix thoroughly. Bake until a tester inserted in the biscuit top comes out clean and the fruit is bubbling around the edges, about 20 minutes. Serve with whipped cream or ice cream, if desired.

cook's notes

❧ If it's not berry season, you can make this dessert with frozen berries or peaches instead. Let the fruit thaw at room temperature first, so that it doesn't freeze the butter on contact.

❧ If you don't have a cast-iron skillet, any ovenproof dish will work. You can also heat the butter and fruit in a skillet and then scrape them into a baking dish to continue.

❧ The cobbler is best served warm directly from the pan. If you have leftovers or plan to keep it for a while, scrape the cobbler into a nonreactive container.

SOURCE: *Rustico* by Micol Negrin
COOK: Micol Negrin

decadent hazelnut-chocolate pudding

IF YOU LOVE GIANDUJA (pronounced zhahn-*doo*-ya), that great Italian combination of chocolate and hazelnuts (Nutella is the supermarket version), you'll love this dessert. It's very decadent and versatile: if you want to serve it shortly after making it, fine; if you want to serve it the next day, it will happily sit in the fridge.

It might seem as though cocoa would produce a pedestrian dessert, but that's not the case at all.

serves 6

- 1/4 cup hazelnuts
- 1 cup whipping cream
- 2/3 cup plus 1/4 cup sugar
- 1 extra-large egg
- 1 extra-large egg yolk
- 3/4 cup unsweetened cocoa powder, sifted
- 6 butter cookies, crumbled (see note)

Preheat the oven to 375 degrees. Spread out the nuts on an 11-x-17-inch baking sheet and toast for 12 minutes, or until fragrant and golden. Rub the nuts in a kitchen towel to peel them, then chop coarsely.

Using a standing mixer with the whisk attachment (see note), beat the cream until soft peaks form. Add 1/4 cup of the sugar and beat until stiff peaks form. Transfer to a bowl.

Clean the mixer bowl and the whisk. Beat the egg, egg yolk, and remaining 2/3 cup sugar for 5 minutes, or until thick and pale. Beat in the cocoa; the mixture will be very thick. Using a rubber spatula, fold in the hazelnuts, crumbled cookies, and all but 1/2 cup of the whipped cream. Spoon into six 6-ounce ramekins and refrigerate, covered with plastic wrap, for 2 to 24 hours.

To serve, pipe the reserved whipped cream over the ramekins using a pastry bag.

❧ There are plenty of butter-cookie choices at the market. You can buy the imported Danish or Dutch butter cookies that are sold in tins or shortbread cookies such as Nabisco's Lorna Doones.

❧ You can use a hand mixer instead of the standard mixer.

❧ If you don't have a pastry bag, you can improvise with a heavy-duty zip-top plastic bag. Cut off a bottom corner in a sawtooth design, add the whipped cream to the bag, and squeeze out the cream.

❧ If you're serving the puddings the next day, the whipped cream may not survive unless you put it in a small colander over a bowl in the refrigerator, so that any liquid can emerge without swamping it.

desserts

SOURCE: Gang e-mail from *Gourmet* staffers
COOK: Andrew Blake

sticky toffee pudding
with chocolate chips and toffee sauce

THIS GORGEOUSLY WICKED DESSERT had everyone talking this year. Sticky toffee pudding, a luscious, rich cake served warm with a thick toffee sauce, is nothing new to Brits and Aussies, but has only recently begun to make itself known on our shores. This recipe takes tradition one step further, adding chopped bittersweet chocolate.

The technique of soaking the dates in boiling water with baking soda may surprise you. In the brief soak, the dates melt into marvelous sweet, sticky bits that then get stirred into the batter.

This recipe originally came from Sydney, Australia. Somewhere along the line, it was picked up by *Gourmet*'s executive food editor, Zanne Stewart, who sent it to a few people, and then before you could say "sticky toffee pudding," it was the one everyone had to have. Now it's yours.

serves 12 to 14

SAUCE
$1^1/_2$ cups dark brown sugar (see note)
8 tablespoons (1 stick) butter
$^1/_2$ cup heavy cream

PUDDING
6 ounces pitted dates
   (8 ounces unpitted)
$^1/_4$ teaspoon baking soda
$^3/_4$ cup boiling water
6 tablespoons ($^3/_4$ stick) butter,
   at room temperature (see note)

$^1/_2$ teaspoon salt, if using
   unsalted butter
$^3/_4$ cup dark brown sugar (see note)
2 teaspoons pure vanilla extract
2 large eggs, beaten
$1^1/_4$ cups all-purpose flour
2 teaspoons baking powder
7 ounces bittersweet chocolate,
   coarsely chopped
2 teaspoons espresso powder
   (optional)
Crème fraîche, for serving
   (optional)

Preheat the oven to 350 degrees. Butter a 9-inch round cake pan with 2-inch sides and line the bottom with a round of parchment paper.

TO MAKE THE SAUCE

Combine the sugar, butter, and cream in a small saucepan over medium heat. Stir until the sugar has completely dissolved and the sauce is bubbling. Pour half of the sauce into the prepared cake pan, and set aside the rest to serve with the pudding.

TO MAKE THE PUDDING

Put the dates and baking soda in a small bowl, and pour over the boiling water. Set aside.

Cream the butter (add the salt, too, if using unsalted butter), brown sugar, and vanilla together in a large bowl, until white and fluffy. Beat in the eggs a little at a time, sprinkling in 1 tablespoon of the flour when you have added about half the beaten eggs (this helps stop the batter from curdling). Mix in the dates and their soaking water. Sift over the remaining flour and the baking powder and fold them in gently but thoroughly. Stir in the chopped chocolate and espresso powder, if using.

Pour the batter into the cake pan. Bake until the top is golden and firm and the sides of the pudding have shrunk away slightly from the pan, 50 to 60 minutes. Cool on a wire rack for 15 minutes. Run a knife around the edge of the pudding and turn it out onto a serving plate.

Reheat the remaining sauce until bubbling. Spoon the sauce over thick wedges of hot pudding, with a dollop of crème fraîche, if you like.

cook's notes

- For the best toffee flavor, you must use dark brown sugar.
- Use either salted or unsalted butter. Just be sure to include the $\frac{1}{2}$ teaspoon salt if using the latter.
- For individual puddings, use eight 3-inch ramekins. Bake for only about 25 minutes.
- This may be made a day ahead and kept in an airtight container. To serve, cut into wedges, pour some sauce over each slice, and reheat quickly in a hot oven.

SOURCE: *Saveur*
COOK: Marcia Ball

sweet potato bread pudding with praline sauce

WE'RE HUGE FANS OF MARCIA BALL'S hard-rocking, piano-playing Texas blues, and it's no surprise that she's a rip-roaring good cook, too. This sweet potato bread pudding is creamy, custardy, and delicious. It's also pretty, all speckled with bright orange patches of roasted sweet potato. The crowning glory is a warm boozy praline sauce that gets spooned over each serving.

serve 8

PUDDING

8 tablespoons (1 stick) butter

1 loaf soft French or Italian bread, torn into large pieces (see note)

2 medium sweet potatoes (see note)

4 cups milk

4 large eggs

1 tablespoon pure vanilla extract

1 cup sugar

1 teaspoon ground cinnamon

PRALINE SAUCE

16 tablespoons (2 sticks) butter

3/4 cup light brown sugar

1 cup chopped pecans

1/4 cup bourbon

TO MAKE THE PUDDING

Butter a medium (2½- to 3-quart) baking dish with 1 tablespoon of the butter. Arrange the bread in a single layer in the dish and set aside at room temperature to dry out slightly, about 2 hours. Preheat the oven to 400 degrees.

Prick the sweet potatoes in 4 or 5 places with the tines of a fork and bake on a baking sheet until soft, about 1 hour. Set aside until cool enough to handle, then halve lengthwise and scoop out the flesh. If the flesh holds together, break it into large pieces. Tuck the sweet potato pieces between the pieces of bread, mashing them down slightly with a fork.

Beat together the milk, eggs, vanilla, sugar, and cinnamon in a large bowl. Pour over the bread and sweet potatoes and set aside in the refrigerator so the bread can soak up the milk mixture, 2 to 3 hours.

Preheat the oven to 375 degrees. Cut the remaining 7 tablespoons of butter into small pieces and scatter them over the pudding. Bake until the custard is set, 35 to 40 minutes. Set aside to cool for at least 30 minutes before serving warm or at room temperature.

TO MAKE THE PRALINE SAUCE

Melt the butter in a medium heavy saucepan over medium heat. Add the brown sugar and stir with a wooden spoon until the sugar is melted and the mixture begins to boil, about 5 minutes. Remove from the heat and stir in the pecans.

Spoon the warm sauce over the bread pudding and serve.

cook's notes

- Figure on a 12-ounce loaf of bread and about 1½ pounds of sweet potatoes.
- Don't chicken out and take the sweet potatoes from the oven before they are fully cooked. They should be completely soft and beginning to caramelize.

SOURCE: William L. Hamilton in the *New York Times*
COOK: Rick Fox

scotch-a-roos

SCOTCH-A-ROOS ARE A GUSSIED-UP VERSION of Rice Krispies treats, made with peanut butter, milk chocolate, and butterscotch. Don't for a minute think that these are only for kids. Indeed, the *New York Times* style reporter William L. Hamilton invested weeks and considerable expense preparing for the ultimate urbane cocktail party complete with elegant hors d'oeuvres. Everything was going as planned until a late-arriving guest appeared bearing a dish of Scotch-a-Roos, at which point all the guests flocked to devour them, ignoring his carefully prepared cocktail food.

makes about 24

1 cup Karo syrup (see note)

1 cup sugar

1 cup peanut butter

$5^1/2$ cups Rice Krispies cereal

12 ounces milk chocolate chips

6 ounces butterscotch chips

Bring the Karo syrup and sugar to a boil in a large saucepan over low heat. Remove from the heat and add the peanut butter and Rice Krispies. Stir to combine. Spread evenly into a 9-x-12-inch cake pan. Do not press down.

Melt the milk chocolate and butterscotch chips together in a medium saucepan over low heat or in a double boiler. Spread the melted chips over the top and let cool. Cut into squares and serve.

cook's note

℔ We use light Karo syrup and smooth peanut butter.

SOURCE: *Gourmet*
COOK: Alexis Touchet

oatmeal coconut raspberry bars

WE CAN'T REMEMBER ENCOUNTERING raspberry and coconut to-gether before, but they're an inspired combination. These chewy bars are easy to make in the food processor. They're perfect for a picnic or in a lunchbox, make great snacks, and are even good for breakfast.

makes 24 bars

1 1/2 cups sweetened flaked coconut
1 1/4 cups all-purpose flour
3/4 cup packed light brown sugar
1/4 cup sugar
1/2 teaspoon salt

12 tablespoons (1 1/2 sticks) cold unsalted butter, cut into pieces
1 1/2 cups old-fashioned rolled oats
3/4 cup seedless raspberry jam

Preheat the oven to 375 degrees. Butter a 9-x-13-inch metal baking pan. Spread 3/4 cup of the coconut evenly on a baking sheet and toast in the oven, stirring once, until golden, about 8 minutes. Cool.

Combine the flour, brown sugar, sugar, and salt in a food processor. Add the but-ter and process until a dough begins to form. Transfer the dough to a bowl and knead in the oats and toasted coconut until well combined.

Reserve 3/4 cup of the dough, then press the remainder evenly into the bottom of the prepared baking pan. Spread the jam over it. Crumble the reserved dough evenly over the jam, then sprinkle with the remaining 3/4 cup untoasted co-conut.

Bake in the center of the oven until golden, 20 to 25 minutes. Place the pan on a rack and let cool completely. Loosen from the sides of the pan with a sharp knife, then lift out in one piece and transfer to a cutting board. Cut into 24 bars.

cook's note

℞ The bars will keep for 3 days in an airtight container at room temperature.

desserts

SOURCE: Jane Sigal in *Food & Wine*
COOK: Pierre Hermé

chocolate–chocolate chip cookies

WE SEE A LOT OF CHOCOLATE CHIP COOKIE RECIPES each year, but few grab our attention the way this one did. For starters, the cookies get a double dose of chocolate: first from cocoa, then from an impressive amount of best-quality bittersweet chocolate chunks. (Pierre Hermé uses French Valrhona. *Mais oui!*) After the chocolate, the crucial ingredient is the 2¹/₂ teaspoons fleur de sel — that fabulous delicate French sea salt. Surprisingly, the salt doesn't make the cookies taste salty. Instead, it underscores their dark chocolate flavor, making them impossible to stop eating — even if you're not a chocoholic. We know one friend who made these at least once a week for almost two months before she got her fill.

makes about 4¹/₂ dozen cookies

2²/₃ cups all-purpose flour

²/₃ cup unsweetened Dutch-process cocoa powder

2 teaspoons baking soda

11 ounces unsalted butter (2³/₄ sticks), at room temperature

1 cup light brown sugar

¹/₂ cup sugar

2¹/₂ teaspoons fleur de sel

1 teaspoon pure vanilla extract

10 ounces bittersweet chocolate, chopped into ¹/₄-inch pieces (about 2 cups)

Sift together the flour, cocoa, and baking soda in a medium bowl. Cream the butter in a large bowl. Add the brown sugar, sugar, fleur de sel, and vanilla to the butter and beat until combined. Beat in the flour mixture just until blended; the dough will be fairly crumbly but will hold together. Knead in the chopped chocolate until evenly distributed.

Divide the dough in half and transfer to two large sheets of plastic wrap. Shape each piece of dough into a 1¹/₂-inch-wide log and wrap in the plastic. Refrigerate until firm, at least 2 hours.

Preheat the oven to 350 degrees. Line four baking sheets with parchment paper (see note). Using a sharp, thin knife, cut the logs into $^3/_8$-inch-thick slices and arrange them about 1 inch apart on the baking sheets. If the slices crumble, press the dough together to re-form the cookies. Bake the cookies on the middle and lower racks of the oven until puffed and cracked on top, about 17 minutes, rotating the sheets from top to bottom and front to back halfway through baking. Let the cookies cool on the baking sheets for 5 minutes, then transfer them to wire racks to cool completely.

cook's notes

- Fleur de sel, the crème de la crème of salt, is available at specialty and gourmet markets.
- If you use only two baking sheets, be sure to let the sheets cool completely before putting the second batch of cookies on them.
- The cookies can be stored in an airtight container at room temperature for up to 1 week or frozen for up to 2 months.

SOURCE: *Gourmet*
COOK: Melissa Roberts-Matar

pistachio-orange lace cookies

ONE OF OUR ALL-TIME FAVORITE COOKIES is the crunchy, lacy florentine, which shatters at the first bite and is quite difficult to make (and expensive to buy). With its flavor of Grand Marnier, pistachios, and fresh orange, this recipe gives you a similar kind of cookie but one that is far easier to make: it's a straightforward log dough that you cut and bake.

It's also convenient. You can make the dough ahead and even freeze it, so you're ready to serve these impressive cookies at a moment's notice.

They're especially good with tea, Middle Eastern food, and fruit. Because they have a festive quality, they're also great for the holidays.

makes about 3¹/₂ dozen cookies

1¹/₄ cups shelled salted pistachios (not dyed red), about 5¹/₂ ounces

³/₄ cup sugar

6 tablespoons all-purpose flour

5 tablespoons (¹/₄ stick plus 1 tablespoon) unsalted butter, melted and cooled slightly

2 tablespoons Grand Marnier or other orange-flavored liqueur

2 tablespoons fresh orange juice

1 teaspoon finely grated orange zest

Pulse the nuts and sugar together in a food processor until the nuts are finely chopped but not ground. Combine the nut mixture with the remaining ingredients in a medium bowl.

Spread the dough in a 12-inch-long strip on a large sheet of plastic wrap and, starting with a long side, roll up the dough in the plastic. (It will be very soft.) Chill the dough on a baking sheet until firm but still malleable, about 1 hour.

Roll the dough into a 15-x-1-inch log, using the plastic wrap as an aid. Halve the log crosswise and chill the halves, wrapped in plastic, until firm, about 3 hours.

Preheat the oven to 325 degrees. Line two large baking sheets with parchment. Remove the plastic wrap from the log. Cut one log half crosswise into ¹/₈-inch-thick slices with a serrated knife and arrange about 2 inches apart on the prepared baking sheets. Flatten each cookie into a $1^1/2$-inch round with the back of a fork or spoon, dipping the utensil in water and shaking off the excess for each cookie.

Bake on the upper and lower racks of the oven, switching the positions of the baking sheets halfway through baking, until golden, 8 to 10 minutes.

Cool the cookies on the baking sheets for 5 minutes, then transfer with a metal spatula to wire racks to cool completely. Line the cooled baking sheets with clean parchment and repeat with the remaining dough.

cook's notes

- You can chill the log of dough for up to 5 days or freeze it, wrapped in aluminum foil, for 1 month. Thaw frozen dough just to the point that it can be sliced.
- If you have no parchment paper, use foil instead to line the baking sheets.
- The cookies keep, layered between sheets of waxed paper (don't let them overlap), in an airtight container at room temperature for 1 week.

SOURCE: *Cook's Illustrated*
COOK: Dawn Yanagihara

soft and chewy molasses-spice cookies

MAYBE YOUR GRANDMOTHER MADE COOKIES like these. If she did, you're really lucky. In our experience, these are the first cookies to disappear from the cookie platter.

Although they taste homey, they look professional; they could have come straight from the bakery, especially if you make the rum glaze topping, which dresses them up considerably.

makes about 22 cookies

$1/2$ cup plus $1/3$ cup sugar
$2^1/4$ cups unbleached all-purpose flour
1 teaspoon baking soda
$1^1/2$ teaspoons ground cinnamon
$1^1/2$ teaspoons ground ginger
$1/2$ teaspoon ground cloves
$1/4$ teaspoon ground allspice
$1/4$ teaspoon finely ground black pepper
$1/4$ teaspoon salt

12 tablespoons ($1^1/2$ sticks) unsalted butter, at room temperature but still cool
$1/3$ cup packed dark brown sugar
1 large egg yolk
1 teaspoon pure vanilla extract
$1/2$ cup light or dark molasses

GLAZE (OPTIONAL)
1 cup confectioners' sugar
$2^1/2$–3 tablespoons dark rum

Preheat the oven to 375 degrees. Line two baking sheets with parchment paper. Place the $1/2$ cup of sugar in an 8-inch cake pan. This will later be used for dipping the cookies. In a medium bowl, whisk together the flour, baking soda, spices, and salt.

Using a standing mixer fitted with the paddle attachment, beat the butter, the remaining $1/3$ cup sugar, and the brown sugar on medium-high speed until light and fluffy, about 3 minutes. Reduce the speed to medium-low and add the egg yolk and vanilla. Increase the speed to medium and beat until incorporated, about 20 seconds. Reduce the speed to medium-low and add the molasses; beat until fully incorporated, about 20 seconds, scraping the bottom and sides of the bowl once with a rubber spatula. Reduce the speed to the lowest setting; add the flour mixture and beat until just incorporated, about 30 seconds, scraping the bowl down once. Give the dough a final stir with a rubber spatula to ensure that no pockets of flour remain at the bottom. The dough will be soft.

Using a tablespoon measure, scoop out heaping spoonfuls of dough, rolling them between your palms to form 1¹/₂-inch balls. Drop the balls 4 at a time into the cake pan containing the sugar, then toss them in the sugar to coat. Set the balls about 2 inches apart on the prepared baking sheet.

Bake one sheet at a time in the center of the oven until the cookies are browned, still puffy, and the edges have begun to set but the centers are still soft (the cookies will look raw between the cracks and seem underdone), about 11 minutes, rotating the baking sheet halfway through baking. Do not overbake.

Cool the cookies on the baking sheet for 5 minutes, then use a wide metal spatula to transfer them to a wire rack. Cool to room temperature before serving or glazing.

TO MAKE THE GLAZE, IF USING

Return the cookies to the parchment paper on which they were baked. Whisk together the glaze ingredients in a medium bowl until smooth. Dip a spoon into the glaze and drizzle it over the cookies. Transfer the cookies to a wire rack and allow the glaze to dry, 10 to 15 minutes, before serving.

cook's notes

- ℘ You can use a handheld electric mixer instead of a standing mixer.
- ℘ If the dough sticks to your hands when you're shaping the balls, keep a bowl of cold water nearby and dip your hands in occasionally, shaking off the excess.
- ℘ In typical *Cook's Illustrated* style, the test kitchen performed a taste test of the two widely available brands of molasses: Brer Rabbit and Grandma's. Each comes in light and dark varieties. The staff gave Brer Rabbit the edge. We found that Brer Rabbit dark molasses produces a cookie with an attractive deep sepia tone. (Don't use blackstrap molasses.)
- ℘ The cookies will keep in an airtight container or zip-top plastic bag for up to 5 days.

SOURCE: *San Francisco Magazine*
COOK: Liz Prueitt

glazed gingerbread tiles

LIZ PRUEITT AND CHAD ROBERTSON, the husband-and-wife baking duo who earned a reputation as world-class bakers at their Bay Village Bakery in Point Reyes, recently moved into San Francisco's Mission District to open Tartine Bakery. She makes the to-die-for pastries, he makes the amazing bread, and in the mornings it's virtually impossible to find a spare seat in their crowded café.

These bar cookies are thin, moist, a bit chewy, and loaded with flavor. The standard mix of gingerbread spices is punctuated with a bit of black pepper and some cocoa powder. If you have a patterned rolling pin, now is a good time to use it. If not, no matter. Once you brush on the sugary glaze, these beauties look bakery-case good.

makes about 32 cookies

$3^3/_4$ cups all-purpose flour

2 tablespoons cocoa powder

2 tablespoons ground ginger

2 teaspoons ground cloves

2 teaspoons ground cinnamon

1 teaspoon finely ground black pepper

$^1/_4$ teaspoon ground nutmeg

$^3/_4$ teaspoon baking soda

$^1/_2$ teaspoon salt

16 tablespoons (2 sticks) unsalted butter, at room temperature

1 cup sugar

1 large egg

$^1/_2$ cup unsulfured molasses

GLAZE

$1^3/_4$ cups confectioners' sugar, sifted

$^1/_4$ cup cool water

Combine the flour, cocoa, ginger, cloves, cinnamon, pepper, nutmeg, baking soda, and salt in a medium bowl. Using an electric mixer on medium speed, beat the butter in a large bowl until smooth. Add the sugar and beat until fluffy, about 5 minutes. Add the egg and beat until well combined. With the mixer running, pour in the molasses and beat until incorporated. Reduce the speed to low and add the flour mixture, mixing until thoroughly combined. Divide the dough in half, shape into flat squares, and wrap in plastic wrap. Refrigerate until cool but still pliable, about 1 hour.

Preheat the oven to 350 degrees. Line two baking sheets with parchment (see note). Place the dough on the prepared baking sheets and roll it out (with a patterned rolling pin, if you have one) approximately $^1/_3$ inch thick. Bake until the dough is no longer shiny, 8 to 10 minutes. Cool on a wire rack.

TO MAKE THE GLAZE

Whisk together the confectioners' sugar and water in a small bowl until smooth. Using a pastry brush, cover the warm gingerbread squares with the glaze. When cool, cut the cookies into 3-x-4-inch rectangles.

cook's notes

- If you're using rimmed baking sheets, you'll need to roll the dough out on the parchment paper and then transfer it to the baking sheet.
- These cookies keep for several days in an airtight container.

SOURCE: *Paris Sweets* by Dorie Greenspan
COOK: Robert Linxe

grandmother's creamy chocolate cake

THE GRANDMOTHER HERE BELONGS TO ROBERT LINXE, the master chocolatier of La Maison du Chocolat in Paris, but the minute Dorie Greenspan, the Francophile food writer, tasted this sensational chocolate cake, she thought of her own American grandmother and the deeply chocolaty cakes she used to make in a single saucepan with just a few ingredients. This is major comfort food that also manages to be quite sophisticated.

The cake is a sort of cross between a brownie and fudge — dense, not too sweet, incredibly moist, and smooth. It has a single drawback: it's not pretty. So it's best served in bowls, and although *grandmère* probably wouldn't dream of it, we like it *à la mode américaine,* topped with vanilla ice cream.

serves 8

16 tablespoons (2 sticks) unsalted butter, cut into 16 pieces

8 ounces bittersweet chocolate, finely chopped

3/4 cup sugar

4 large eggs, at room temperature

1/4 cup all-purpose flour

Whipped cream, crème fraîche, or vanilla ice cream, for serving (optional)

Preheat the oven to 300 degrees. Butter an 8-inch square baking pan and line it with aluminum foil.

Melt the butter, chocolate, and sugar in a medium heavy saucepan over medium-low heat, stirring almost constantly until well blended. Remove from the heat and let stand for 3 minutes.

One by one, whisk in the eggs. Sift the flour over and stir it in as well. Rap the saucepan on the counter to deflate any air bubbles and pour the batter into the prepared baking pan.

Put the baking pan inside a larger pan and fill the larger pan with enough hot water to come halfway up the sides of the baking pan.

Bake for 35 to 40 minutes, or until the cake is set on top and a knife inserted in the center comes out streaky but not wet. Lift the baking pan out of the water bath and place it on a wire rack to cool to room temperature. Chill the cake for at least 1 hour before unmolding.

When the cake is cold, gently turn it over onto a serving platter, lift off the pan, and carefully remove the foil. The cake is meant to be served upside down, with its sleeker side facing the world. It can be served cold or at room temperature with a scoop of whipped cream, crème fraîche, or ice cream if you like.

cook's notes

- To help the cake cook on the bottom, snap off wooden skewers and layer them on the bottom of the larger pan so the hot water can circulate beneath the baking pan.
- The baking time may be as much as 10 to 15 minutes longer — rely on the knife test to be sure it's done.
- Dorie Greenspan has a great idea for leftovers: cut them into tiny cubes and freeze them. When you're serving vanilla ice cream for dessert (or chocolate or coffee ice cream, we think), soften the ice cream slightly in the microwave, then stir in these little tidbits. They won't actually freeze completely in the freezer, just turn a bit chewy.

SOURCE: *Texas Monthly* Web site
COOK: Sharon Hage

lemon pudding cake

PUDDING CAKE IS THE HAPPY RESULT of a mysterious alchemy. The airy batter (one made with a high proportion of buttermilk to eggs and flour) separates into two layers as it bakes, so that you get a tender cakelike top layer and a silky, tart lemon sauce (pudding) below. The cake is remarkably spongy and light, while the pudding is rich, lemony, and creamy.

There are two options for serving: invert the cakes onto plates so that the pudding sits on top almost as a sauce, or serve the cakes in their ramekins topped with a little sweetened fruit (or fruit sauce) and a puff of whipped cream.

The cakes need to cool for at least 2 hours, and will keep well for a day or two in the refrigerator.

serves 6

3 large eggs, separated
$1/4$ cup plus $2/3$ cup sugar
$1/4$ cup all-purpose flour
1 tablespoon grated lemon zest
7 tablespoons fresh lemon juice (about 2 lemons)
$1/4$ cup melted butter
$1^1/2$ cups buttermilk

Preheat the oven to 325 degrees. Butter and sugar 6 large soufflé cups or ramekins. Beat the egg whites and the $1/4$ cup of sugar in a medium bowl until stiff peaks form. Set aside. Mix together the remaining $2/3$ cup sugar and the flour in a large bowl. Combine the lemon zest, lemon juice, and melted butter in a small bowl. Add this to the flour mixture and stir well. In another medium bowl, combine the egg yolks and buttermilk. Add this to the lemon-flour mixture and stir well. Using a rubber spatula, fold in the beaten egg whites.

Pour the mixture into the prepared soufflé cups or ramekins, filling them only three-fourths full so they don't rise up above the cups. Bake in a water bath until the tops feel slightly firm, about 40 minutes. Do not brown. Let cool to room temperature and then chill for 2 hours or overnight. The pudding cakes can be served in the cups or ramekins with the cake on top, or inverted onto plates so that the pudding layer is on top.

cook's notes

🍋 Seven tablespoons lemon juice is ½ cup minus 1 tablespoon, which may be an easier way to measure. Just dump the leftover tablespoon in a glass of seltzer for a refreshing drink.

🍋 At York Street, her restaurant in East Dallas, chef Sharon Hage makes these cakes with Meyer lemons when they are in season. The cakes aren't as tart, but the perfume is heavenly.

🍋 For a quick garnish, combine the juice of ½ orange with 4 teaspoons sugar and the grated zest of 1 lemon. Add the segments from 2 oranges (blood oranges, if you can find them). Serve the chilled cakes with a dollop of whipped cream and the sweetened orange segments.

tip

The long, thin blade of a boning knife is great for removing the peel from citrus, according to *Cook's Illustrated*. The flexible thin blade carves the peels without taking too much of the fruit.

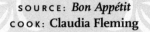

SOURCE: *Bon Appétit*
COOK: Claudia Fleming

maple sugar cake

A GREAT POUND CAKE: now that's something to get excited about. This version comes from Claudia Fleming, the gifted New York City pastry chef who seems to specialize in reviving and improving tired classics. She's replaced the sugar in a sour cream pound cake with maple sugar and topped the whole thing with a lemony glaze, making it as handsome as it is tasty.

Another terrific thing about this cake is that it can be served morning, noon, or night. It's an excellent breakfast treat, good with tea, and just dressy enough for a dinner-party dessert — especially with a little pouf of whipped cream on the side.

Maple sugar is the granulated result of boiling down maple syrup until all the moisture has gone. It is sold at natural food stores and some supermarkets.

makes one 9-inch cake; serves 10 to 12

CAKE
- 2 cups all-purpose flour
- 2 teaspoons baking powder
- 1/2 teaspoon baking soda
- 1/4 teaspoon salt
- 1 1/3 cups sour cream
- 1/4 cup pure maple syrup
- 1/2 cup walnuts, toasted and chopped
- 1/4 cup plus 1 1/3 cups maple sugar
- 1/4 teaspoon ground cinnamon
- 13 tablespoons (1 stick plus 5 tablespoons) butter, cut into pieces, at room temperature
- 2 large eggs
- 2 teaspoons pure vanilla extract

GLAZE
- 1 1/2 cups confectioners' sugar
- 1/2 teaspoon grated lemon zest
- 3 tablespoons sour cream
- 1 tablespoon pure maple syrup
- 1 1/2 teaspoons fresh lemon juice
- 1 teaspoon pure vanilla extract

Whipped cream, for serving (optional)

TO MAKE THE CAKE

Preheat the oven to 350 degrees. Butter a 9-inch bundt pan, then spray it with nonstick spray. Combine the flour, baking powder, baking soda, and salt in a medium bowl. Whisk together the sour cream and maple syrup in another medium bowl. Mix the walnuts, 1/4 cup of the maple sugar, and the cinnamon in a small bowl.

Using an electric mixer, beat the butter and the remaining $1^1/_3$ cups maple sugar in a large bowl until fluffy. Gradually beat in the eggs and vanilla, occasionally stopping to scrape down the sides of the bowl. Add the flour mixture in three additions, alternating with the sour cream mixture in three additions. Transfer two thirds of the batter to the prepared bundt pan. Sprinkle with the walnut mixture. Pour the remaining batter into the pan.

Bake the cake until a tester inserted near the center comes out clean, about 55 minutes. Cool for 20 minutes. Turn out the cake onto a wire rack and cool completely.

TO MAKE THE GLAZE

Whisk together the confectioners' sugar, lemon zest, sour cream, maple syrup, lemon juice, and vanilla extract in a medium bowl. Let stand until thickened, about 30 minutes.

Pour the glaze over the cake. Serve with whipped cream, if desired.

cook's notes

- Maple sugar has a more pronounced flavor than regular granulated sugar. Keep this in mind if you have any left over and improvise other uses for it. It's wonderful sprinkled on hot or cold cereal.
- The cake can be made a day ahead and kept at room temperature.

SOURCE: Jane Dornbusch in the *Boston Herald*
COOK: Cynthia Blain

gingerbread-cider cake

TRADITIONAL DESSERTS REIGNED SUPREME THIS YEAR. Traditional with a twist, that is. This gingerbread cake, the first-prize winner in the *Boston Herald*'s holiday baking contest, is a case in point. The method is wacky, but it works like a charm. A standard gingerbread batter is sprinkled with brown sugar, then a mixture of hot apple cider and melted butter is poured onto the unbaked cake. After baking, the cake comes out airy, moist, tender, and fragrant, with an oozy, caramel-like layer on the bottom.

Like any gingerbread, this is delicious warm from the oven. It's also good at room temperature. Don't forget the ice cream or lightly sweetened whipped cream, if you're so inclined.

serves 10 to 12

2 cups all-purpose flour	1/2 cup sugar
1 1/2 teaspoons baking soda	1 large egg
1 1/4 teaspoons ground ginger	1 cup molasses
1 teaspoon ground cinnamon	1 cup water
1/2 teaspoon salt	3/4 cup packed brown sugar
1/4 teaspoon ground cloves	1 1/2 cup apple cider or juice
1/4 teaspoon ground nutmeg	Vanilla ice cream or sweetened whipped cream, for serving (optional)
8 tablespoons (1 stick) butter, at room temperature, plus 5 1/3 tablespoons butter, melted	

Preheat the oven to 350 degrees. Combine the flour, baking soda, ginger, cinnamon, salt, cloves, and nutmeg in a medium bowl. Set aside.

Beat the stick of butter and sugar in a large mixing bowl on medium speed until creamy, 1 to 2 minutes. Add the egg and continue to beat until well mixed. Reduce the speed to low. With the mixer running, add the flour mixture in three additions, alternating with the molasses and water. Beat after each addition just until mixed.

Pour the batter into an ungreased 9-x-13-inch baking pan. Sprinkle the batter with the brown sugar. Heat the apple cider and melted butter together (you can do this in the microwave rather quickly). Pour the cider mixture carefully over the top of the batter.

Bake until the gingerbread is cracked on top and a toothpick inserted in the center comes out clean, 40 to 55 minutes. Serve warm with ice cream or sweetened whipped cream, if desired.

cook's notes

- Cynthia Blain, who submitted the cake, says her mother used to add finely chopped candied lemon zest to the cake, which sounds like a very good idea to us. Orange zest would be good, too.
- Either light or dark brown sugar is fine.
- Combine the water and molasses to simplify the step of adding them to the batter.

SOURCE: *Williams-Sonoma Taste*
COOK: Emily Luchetti

cornmeal cupcakes with pecan frosting

IT DOESN'T SEEM FAIR THAT CUPCAKES are reserved for kids' birthday parties, so we were especially happy to discover this recipe from the famous San Francisco pastry chef Emily Luchetti. The bit of yellow cornmeal adds a delicious crunch to the buttery pound cake–style batter, and the cream cheese frosting provides the right amount of creaminess, tanginess, and richness.

These cupcakes need a short stint in the refrigerator to firm up the frosting. Just be sure to let them sit at room temperature for a bit before serving to take the chill off.

makes 6 cupcakes

CUPCAKES

- 1 cup all-purpose flour
- $1^1/2$ teaspoons baking powder
- $1/3$ cup yellow cornmeal
- $1/4$ teaspoon salt
- 9 tablespoons (1 stick plus 1 tablespoon) unsalted butter, at room temperature
- $1^1/4$ cups sugar
- 3 large eggs
- $1/2$ cup sour cream

FROSTING

- 6 ounces cream cheese, at room temperature
- 6 tablespoons ($3/4$ stick) unsalted butter, at room temperature
- $1/4$ cup sugar
- $1/2$ teaspoon pure vanilla extract
- 2–3 teaspoons heavy cream
- $1/4$ cup toasted chopped pecans, plus 3 pecan halves, thinly sliced, for garnish

TO MAKE THE CUPCAKES

Preheat the oven to 350 degrees. Spray 6 cupcake molds ($3/4$-cup capacity) with nonstick spray. Sift together the flour and baking powder in a medium bowl. Stir in the cornmeal and salt. Set aside.

In the bowl of a standing mixer fitted with the paddle attachment (see note), cream together the butter and sugar until light. Add the eggs one at a time, beating well after each addition. In three separate additions, add the flour mixture and sour cream alternately, incorporating each before adding the next.

Divide the batter among the prepared cupcake molds. Bake until a wooden skewer inserted into the center comes out clean, 25 to 30 minutes. Remove from the oven; when cool to the touch, unmold and let cool completely on wire racks before frosting.

TO MAKE THE FROSTING

Beat the cream cheese until smooth (the standing mixer works best). Add the butter and sugar and continue beating until smooth. Stir in the vanilla. Add the heavy cream to make the frosting a smooth, spreadable consistency. Stir in the chopped pecans.

Frost the cupcakes and sprinkle the sliced pecans on top. Refrigerate the cupcakes for a couple of hours so the frosting sets up. Then let them sit at room temperature for 30 minutes before serving.

cook's notes

- You can use a handheld electric mixer instead of the standing mixer.
- To toast pecans, place them in a small dry skillet over medium-high heat, stirring, until they are fragrant, about 2 minutes.
- If you want to make the cupcakes a day in advance, wrap them in plastic wrap but don't refrigerate. The frosting can also be made a day ahead, but it should be refrigerated. Let it come to room temperature before spreading it on the cupcakes. They can be served immediately.
- Don't be skimpy with the frosting. A good cupcake has plenty of frosting.

SOURCE: www.bonappetit.com
COOK: Rene Estevez

martin sheen's favorite cheesecake

WE'RE HOOKED ON THE CELEBRITY FOOD portraits that appear at the end of every issue of *Bon Appétit*. In October it was *West Wing*'s Martin Sheen, the man we sometimes forget isn't actually the president. Sheen raved about a pumpkin cheesecake made by his daughter (who plays Leo's assistant on the show) and served by his family every Thanksgiving.

The Boss is right; this is spectacular. Sheen claims you just can't stop eating it, even after a big Thanksgiving dinner. It's a high, firm, mellow cheesecake, gently spiced, and it looks like the product of a fine bakery. That's not too surprising, because Sheen's daughter used to be a pastry chef.

Make the cheesecake a day ahead.

serves 12 to 16

CRUST

9 whole graham crackers
   (about 4 ounces), broken
1/4 cup sugar
1 teaspoon ground cinnamon
4 tablespoons (1/2 stick)
   butter, melted

FILLING

4 8-ounce packages cream cheese,
   at room temperature
1 1/2 cups sugar
3 large eggs
1 15-ounce can pumpkin puree
   (not pie filling)
1 cup heavy cream
2 teaspoons pure vanilla extract
1 teaspoon ground ginger
1/2 teaspoon ground nutmeg
1/2 teaspoon ground allspice
1/4 teaspoon ground cloves

TO MAKE THE CRUST

Preheat the oven to 350 degrees. Wrap a double layer of heavy-duty aluminum foil around the outside of a 10-inch springform pan. Combine the graham crackers, sugar, and cinnamon in a food processor. Process until the graham crackers are very finely ground. Drizzle the melted butter over. Pulse until the crumbs begin to stick together. Press the crumbs over the bottom (not the sides) of the prepared pan.

Bake in the middle of the oven until the crust is slightly golden, about 10 minutes. Transfer to a wire rack and cool while preparing the filling.

TO MAKE THE FILLING

Using an electric mixer, beat the cream cheese and sugar in a large bowl until smooth and fluffy. Beat in the eggs one at a time. Add the pumpkin and the remaining ingredients. Beat just until mixed. Pour the filling into the prepared crust. Place the springform pan in a large roasting pan and add hot water to come halfway up the sides of the springform pan.

TO BAKE AND SERVE

Bake the cheesecake until the filling is slightly puffed and softly set and the top is golden, about $1^1/2$ hours. Transfer the cheesecake to a wire rack to cool. Cover and refrigerate the cake overnight.

Use a knife to cut around the side of the pan to loosen the cheesecake. Release the pan sides, cut the cheesecake into wedges, and serve.

SOURCE: *Atlanta Journal-Constitution*
COOK: The Food Goddess

pumpkin crème brûlée tart

PECANS AND PUMPKIN ARE THE ESSENCE of the holiday table. Here the pecans are used in a crunchy, sweet, cookielike crust, and the pumpkin goes into a rich, creamy custard filling. Then the whole thing is finished with a thin, crackling layer of caramelized sugar. A shallow tart pan rather than a classic pie pan allows for just the right balance of crust, filling, and caramelized sugar topping.

Since this tart can be made a day ahead (the crust can be prepared several days ahead), you'll have one less thing to worry about the day of the feast. All you need to do before serving is caramelize the sugar under the broiler. Or if you've got a blowtorch and some cowboy relative who wants to wield it, let him have at it.

makes one 9¹/₂- to 10-inch tart; serves 8

CRUST

1¹/₄ cups all-purpose flour
³/₄ cups pecans, toasted (see note, page 251) and finely ground
¹/₄ teaspoon ground cinnamon
¹/₄ teaspoon ground nutmeg
8 tablespoons (1 stick) butter, at room temperature
¹/₄ cup sugar
1 large egg yolk

FILLING

7 large egg yolks, at room temperature
³/₄ cup sugar
1³/₄ cups whipping cream
1 cup canned pumpkin puree (not pie filling)
¹/₄ teaspoon ground cinnamon
¹/₄ teaspoon ground allspice
¹/₄ teaspoon ground ginger

¹/₄ cup firmly packed light brown sugar

TO MAKE THE CRUST

Combine the flour, pecans, cinnamon, and nutmeg in a medium bowl. Using an electric mixer, beat the butter and sugar in a large bowl until lightened in color. Add the egg yolk and mix until thoroughly combined. Add the flour mixture and mix just until the dough comes together. Scrape the dough onto plastic wrap and flatten it into a thin disk. Chill until just firm enough to roll out, about 1 hour.

TO MAKE THE FILLING

Meanwhile, whisk together the egg yolks and sugar in a large bowl. Bring the cream to a simmer in a small heavy saucepan. Stirring constantly, gradually whisk the cream into the yolk-sugar mixture. Whisk in the pumpkin, cinnamon, allspice, and ginger. Cool for 1 hour.

TO BAKE AND SERVE

Preheat the oven to 350 degrees. On plastic wrap or a lightly floured surface, roll out the dough ¼ inch thick. Transfer the dough to a 9½- to 10-inch tart pan with a removable bottom, and press the dough into the bottom and up the sides, pinching together any broken pieces. Freeze for 15 minutes. Line the crust with aluminum foil and fill with pie weights or dried beans. Bake until set, 20 to 25 minutes. Remove the foil and weights or beans and bake for 10 minutes more, or until set and light golden.

Pour the filling into the crust and bake for 25 minutes, or until the filling is just set. Transfer to a wire rack and cool. Chill for 2 hours or overnight.

Preheat the broiler. Sprinkle the brown sugar evenly over the top of the filling. Place under the broiler, turning the tart every 20 seconds and watching closely to prevent burning, until the sugar has caramelized. Serve as soon as possible.

cook's notes

- ❧ The dough can just as easily (and successfully) be pressed into the pan with your fingertips instead of being rolled out. We also find that it's simplest to roll out the crust straight away after you've made it. Then line the tart pan with it and chill the crust for about an hour. The chilling will allow the crust to relax and will prevent shrinking, and it's generally easier to roll out a soft dough rather than a hard, chilled one.
- ❧ The sugar topping will stay hard for a short while after caramelizing it, but over time it will soften. Hard or soft, it will always taste good.

tip

Bon Appétit's Thanksgiving issue presented a few good-sounding ways to jazz up a slice of pumpkin pie: rum-flavored whipped cream, mascarpone mixed with ginger preserves, or butter pecan ice cream.

SOURCE: *Baking in America* by Greg Patent
COOK: Greg Patent

chewy butterscotch and pecan cake

OFTEN THE OLDIES REALLY ARE THE GOODIES. This pleasantly chewy sheet cake with a rich butterscotch taste was a Pillsbury Bake-Off contest winner in 1954, and it's just as good today as it was forty years ago. Though it needs no frosting, it's pretty good topped with a scoop of vanilla ice cream or lightly sweetened whipped cream.

serves 12

2 cups (8 ounces) coarsely chopped or broken pecans

1¹/₂ cups sifted all-purpose flour

1 teaspoon baking powder

¹/₄ teaspoon salt

4 large eggs

2 cups packed dark brown sugar

1 teaspoon instant espresso powder

2 tablespoons unsalted butter, cut into a few pieces

2 teaspoons pure vanilla extract

Preheat the oven to 350 degrees. Butter a 9-x-13-inch baking pan and dust with flour. Knock out the excess and set aside. Toast the pecans on a baking sheet in the oven, stirring occasionally, until they smell toasty and just begin to color lightly, about 10 minutes. Set aside to cool.

Resift the flour with the baking powder and the salt into a medium bowl.

Fill the bottom of a large double boiler or a medium saucepan halfway with water and set over high heat. Crack the eggs into the top of the double boiler or a stainless steel bowl off the heat and whisk just to combine the yolks and whites. Gradually whisk in the brown sugar and espresso powder until smooth. Add the butter. When the water is boiling gently, place the egg mixture over the water and stir constantly with a heatproof spatula for about 5 minutes, being sure to scrape the sides, until the mixture feels hot to the touch. Remove from the heat and immediately add the flour mixture. Whisk until smooth. Stir in the vanilla and pecans. Spread the batter evenly into the pan.

Bake in the center of the oven until the cake springs back a little when gently pressed, about 25 minutes. Do not overbake. Cool in the pan on a wire rack. When completely cool, cut into portions and serve.

SOURCE: *Fine Cooking*
COOK: Maryellen Driscoll

banoffee tart
(caramel banana toffee tart)

GET IT? BANANAS + TOFFEE = BANOFFEE (pronounced bah-*naw*-fee). This heavenly dessert was invented in 1972 at the Hungry Monk restaurant in Sussex, England. The Brits have gone bonkers for it and so have we.

The toffee is made by cooking sweetened condensed milk in a water bath for almost 3 hours until it becomes dark, sticky, sweet, and lovely. Then it's only a matter of assembling the tart just before serving.

serves 12

- 1 14-ounce can sweetened condensed milk (preferably Eagle Brand)
- 1 1/3 cups all-purpose flour
- 1/4 cup plus 2 teaspoons sugar
- 1/2 teaspoon salt

- 8 tablespoons (1 stick) unsalted butter, cut into 3/8-inch dice and chilled well
- 2 cups heavy cream
- 1 large egg yolk
- 4 ripe bananas
- 1/4 teaspoon instant coffee granules
- 1/2 teaspoon pure vanilla extract

Fill the base of a double boiler or a medium saucepan halfway with water. Bring to a boil and then reduce the heat to medium (for an active simmer just shy of a boil). Pour the condensed milk into the double boiler's top or into a stainless-steel bowl that fits snugly on top of the saucepan and set it over the simmering water. Every 45 minutes, check the water level in the pan and give the milk a stir. Replenish with more hot water as needed. Once the milk has thickened to the consistency of pudding and has turned a rich, dark caramel color, 2 1/2 to 3 hours, remove from the heat, cool, and cover.

Meanwhile, combine the flour, 1/4 cup of the sugar, and the salt in a food processor. Pulse to combine. Add the butter pieces and gently toss to lightly coat with flour. Blend the butter and flour mixture with about five 1-second pulses or until the mixture is the texture of coarse meal, with some of the butter pieces the size of peas. In a small bowl, whisk together 2¹/₂ tablespoons of the cream and the egg yolk and pour this over the flour mixture. Process continuously until the mixture turns golden and thickens in texture yet is still crumbly, about 10 seconds.

Transfer the mixture to a large bowl and press the mixture together with your hands until it comes together into a ball. Shape the dough into an 8-inch-wide disk and put it in the center of an 8¹/₂- to 9-inch fluted tart pan with a removable bottom. Beginning in the center of the dough and working out toward the edges, use your fingertips to gently press the dough evenly into the bottom and up the pan sides. The edges should be flush with the top edge of the pan. If you find a spot that's especially thick, pinch away some of the dough and use it to bulk up a thin spot. Cover with plastic wrap and freeze for 1 hour.

Preheat the oven to 400 degrees. Line the dough with aluminum foil and cover with pie weights or dried beans. Bake on the lower oven rack for 20 minutes. Carefully lift the foil and weights or beans out of the tart pan, reduce the oven temperature to 375 degrees, and bake until the crust is a deep golden brown, about 15 minutes. Transfer the tart pan to a wire rack to cool to room temperature.

Spread the caramel over the crust using a rubber or offset spatula. If the caramel has cooled and is too firm to spread easily, reheat it over simmering water in the double boiler until loosened but not hot. Slice each banana in half lengthwise and arrange the halves on top of the caramel in a circular pattern. To fit the banana halves snugly in the center of the pan, cut them into smaller lengths.

Put the coffee granules in a small zip-top bag. Press a rolling pin back and forth over the granules to crush them into a powder.

Beat the remaining cream, the vanilla, and the remaining 2 teaspoons sugar in a chilled medium stainless steel bowl with an electric mixer on medium-high speed until it holds soft peaks when the beaters are lifted. (If you overbeat the cream, fold in 1 tablespoon cream to relax it.) Spoon the whipped cream over the bananas and sprinkle with the coffee powder. Remove the pan sides, cut, and serve. The tart can be held for up to 30 minutes in the refrigerator, though it's best not to sprinkle on the coffee powder until just before serving.

cook's notes

- In a pinch, we've substituted a jar of dulce de leche for the toffee in this tart, but the homemade is better.
- The toffee can be made up to 3 days in advance and kept covered tightly in the refrigerator. (If you make it ahead, reheat it just enough to be spreadable when you're ready to make the tart.) The cookielike crust can also be baked a day in advance and kept wrapped at room temperature.
- If you don't have a tart pan with a removable bottom, use a 9-inch springform pan.

SOURCE: California Walnut Commission Web site
COOK: Eric Olson

chocolate-walnut tart

WALL-TO-WALL CHOCOLATE in a toasted walnut crust: this is a serious tart for serious chocolate fiends. The recipe is a contest winner (submitted by a culinary student) from the California Walnut Commission, so walnuts play a starring role. The all-walnut crust comes together with nothing more than bit of sugar syrup and melted butter. The rich filling is a dark chocolate ganache with a touch of orange in the form of Grand Marnier.

Other than turning on the oven to toast the walnuts, making this elegant dessert requires no baking, and the tart keeps refrigerated for a day or two.

makes one 10-inch tart; serves 12

3 cups walnuts, plus 12 walnut halves, for garnish

$^1/_4$ cup sugar

$^1/_4$ cup water

6 tablespoons ($^3/_4$ stick) unsalted butter, melted

$1^1/_2$ cups heavy cream

12 ounces top-quality dark chocolate, finely chopped (see note)

2 tablespoons Grand Marnier

Julienned zest of 2 large oranges, for garnish

Preheat the oven to 350 degrees. Spread the 3 cups walnuts on a baking sheet and toast until fragrant and browning, about 10 minutes. Let cool.

Combine the sugar and water in a small saucepan. Simmer, covered, for 4 minutes to dissolve the sugar. Set aside.

Coarsely chop the toasted walnuts in a food processor. Transfer the chopped walnuts to a medium bowl. Add 2 tablespoons of the sugar syrup and the melted butter. Mix well. Dump the mixture into a 10-inch fluted tart pan with a removable bottom and press into the pan with your fingertips to form a crust. Be sure to press the nut mixture up the sides of the pan. Put the pan in the freezer for about 10 minutes while you make the filling.

Bring the cream to a boil in a small saucepan. Add the chocolate and immediately remove from the heat. Stir until smooth. Stir in the Grand Marnier. Pour the chocolate mixture into the chilled tart shell and refrigerate for 4 hours or overnight.

Combine the remaining sugar syrup and the orange zest in a small nonstick sauté pan. Cook over medium heat until most of the water has evaporated and the zest is translucent, 2 to 3 minutes. Remove from the pan and cool.

Keep the tart chilled until ready to serve. Remove the tart from the pan. To slice, use a knife dipped in hot water and wiped with a towel. Garnish with the reserved walnut halves and the candied orange zest.

cook's notes

- Use the best-quality chocolate that you can find — bittersweet or semisweet, according to your preference.
- Since the crust doesn't get baked, toast the walnuts as dark as you like for the best flavor — don't burn them, but a good toasty flavor is nice here.
- To dress this up even more, dust the reserved walnut halves with confectioners' sugar before adding them as garnish.
- After cooking the candied orange zest, be sure to separate the pieces before they cool. Otherwise you'll get a big clump.

SOURCE: *Icebox Pies* by Lauren Chattman
COOK: Lauren Chattman

gianduja ice cream pie

NUTELLA SPREAD GIVES THIS PIE its dominant chocolate-hazelnut flavor. Simply fold a jar into a bowl of whipped cream, toss in a handful of chopped toasted hazelnuts, and you've got a fantastic "ice cream" pie filling. Now all you need to do is slide it into the refrigerator and wait.

A little dollop of whipped cream on each slice makes a pretty garnish.

makes one 9-inch pie; serves 6 to 8

CRUST

30 Nabisco Famous
     Chocolate Wafers
5 tablespoons ($1/2$ stick plus
     1 tablespoon) unsalted butter,
     melted and slightly cooled
$1/8$ teaspoon salt
$1/2$ teaspoon pure vanilla extract

FILLING

$3/4$ cup hazelnuts, toasted
     and skinned (see note)
$1^1/3$ cups heavy cream, chilled
1 teaspoon pure vanilla extract
1 13-ounce jar Nutella
   Whipped cream, for serving
   (optional)

TO MAKE THE CRUST

Preheat the oven to 350 degrees. Place the wafers in a food processor and process until finely ground. You should have about $1^1/3$ cups crumbs. Combine the crumbs, butter, salt, and vanilla in a medium bowl and stir until the crumbs are moistened. Press the mixture into a 9-inch pie plate and all the way up the sides of the pan, packing tightly with your fingertips so that it is even and compacted.

Bake the crust until crisp, 6 to 8 minutes. Let cool completely before filling. The crust may be wrapped in plastic and frozen for up to 1 month.

Place the skinned hazelnuts in a food processor and chop very finely. Set aside.

Using an electric mixer, whip the cream and vanilla in a large bowl until soft peaks form.

Place the Nutella in a medium bowl and whisk in one fourth of the whipped cream. Gently fold the lightened Nutella mixture into the remaining whipped cream, followed by the chopped hazelnuts.

Scrape the filling into the cooled crust and smooth the top with a rubber spatula. Cover the pie with plastic wrap and refrigerate until the filling is completely set, at least 6 hours and up to 1 day. Serve with whipped cream, if desired.

cook's notes

- For a crunchier, richer chocolate crust, use only 22 wafers and add ¼ cup toasted skinned hazelnuts. Grind these into crumbs together in the food processor. Reduce the butter to 4 tablespoons (½ stick) and add 1 tablespoon sugar.

- To toast and skin hazelnuts, spread them out on an 11-x-17-inch baking sheet and toast for about 10 minutes, stirring occasionally, or until fragrant. Rub the nuts in a kitchen towel to remove their skins.

- The only tricky part of this recipe is folding the cream into the Nutella. When whipping the cream, stop when it is light, airy, and still somewhat supple. If you go for maximum volume, it will be too stiff and remain clumpy. Then give the Nutella a good whisk first to loosen it up some. Finally, don't worry if the end product is not entirely smooth.

SOURCE: Julia Reed in the *New York Times Magazine*
COOK: Mary Cooper

mary cooper's pralines

WE'RE SUCKERS FOR PRALINES — those irresistible sugary confections favored across the South all the way west into Texas — so we were happy to stumble across several versions this year. We tested them all (professional obligation, you know), and these came up the winner. They're nothing but sugar, pecans, evaporated milk, butter, and a whiff of vanilla cooked into a rich, creamy, crumbly, melt-in-your mouth candy.

Make a few batches of pralines around the holidays to have on hand for drop-in guests (they are wonderful with a strong cup of coffee) or to pack in pretty tins and give as gifts. They keep for a week or so, as long as it's not too humid.

makes 2 dozen

1 cup packed dark brown sugar

1 cup sugar

$^1/_2$ cup evaporated milk

1 cup pecan halves or pieces

2 tablespoons butter

$1^1/_2$ teaspoons pure vanilla extract

In a deep, heavy 2-quart saucepan, combine the brown sugar, sugar, and evaporated milk. Cook over medium heat, stirring constantly, until the sugars melt. Continue to cook, stirring frequently to prevent the mixture from boiling over, until a candy thermometer reads 228 degrees. Add the pecans and butter and stir until the butter melts. Continue cooking until the thermometer reads 232 degrees. Remove from the heat and stir in the vanilla. Let cool, stirring occasionally, until the mixture loses some of its gloss (see tip).

Spoon the praline mixture onto parchment paper, forming 24 thin patties. Let cool for at least 30 minutes. Wrap individually in waxed paper squares.

Spoon the praline mixture onto the parchment immediately. If it cools too much and sets up in the pot, it's very difficult to rewarm it enough to spoon it out.

tip

In *Eula Mae's Cajun Kitchen,* Eula Mae Doré gives a few helpful pointers about pralines. She recommends toasting the pecans before adding them. She also explains that after removing the praline mix from the heat, you need to continue to stir until the mixture becomes thick, creamy, and sugary around the edge of the mixture, about 15 minutes. The candy will be a taffy color. Then work very quickly to spoon heaping spoonfuls of the mixture onto the parchment.

SOURCE: **Gillian Duffy** in *New York*
COOK: **Karen Demasco**

peanut brittle

ONE BALMY FALL EVENING we wandered into Manhattan's Craftbar, an informal adjunct to the much more formal Craft. Dessert was very good, but what obsessed us was the peanut brittle that arrived with the coffee. Sweet, slightly salty, buttery, full of roasted peanuts, and with an indescribable airy crunch — this was peanut brittle taken to the stratosphere. We had to find out how to make it.

Just a few weeks later, we opened our *New York* magazine to find the recipe, which Gillian Duffy had managed to get from the pastry chef before we did. The brittle tastes just like the original, and it's a cinch to make. This is a great after-dinner treat with coffee. It also makes a terrific gift. Try it on the buffet during the holidays.

makes about 2 dozen 1-inch chunks

2 cups sugar
8 tablespoons (1 stick) unsalted butter
1/2 cup plus 2 tablespoons water
1/3 cup light corn syrup

1/2 teaspoon baking soda
1 1/2 teaspoons salt
12 ounces whole dry-roasted salted peanuts

Spray a 12-x-16-x-1/2-inch sheet pan lightly with nonstick spray. Combine the sugar, butter, water, and corn syrup in a large saucepan and stir until all the sugar is wet. Cook over high heat, stirring, until the mixture turns medium golden.

Immediately remove from the heat and carefully whisk in the baking soda followed by the salt (take care; the caramel will rise in the pan and bubble). Switch to a wooden or metal spoon and fold in the peanuts. Quickly pour the mixture onto the prepared sheet pan and spread it out using the back of the spoon before it starts to harden. (It may not cover the whole pan.)

Once the brittle is completely cool, break it into bite-size pieces with the back of a knife or other blunt object.

drinks

SOURCE: *With Bold Knife and Fork* by M.F.K. Fisher
COOK: M.F.K. Fisher

age of innocence cup

IF YOU'RE HAVING A VERY LARGE PARTY and need a sophisticated nonalcoholic punch, here's the one for you. It's subtle and not too sweet, has a gorgeous rosy color, and is easy to make. There's a secret ingredient: strong brewed tea. According to Fisher, even tipplers will think there's some alcohol in here because the punch loosens tongues and brightens the eye — that's the tea talking.

Of course, nothing prevents you from adding some brandy and Champagne instead of ginger ale to the mix just before serving. We like vodka in this punch too.

makes about 6 quarts

4 cups freshly brewed strong tea
   (12 tea bags to 1 quart water)
6 cups cranberry juice
4 cups fresh orange juice

2 cups fresh lemon juice
2 cups sugar syrup (2 cups sugar
   boiled briefly with 1 cup water)
4 liters chilled ginger ale

Make the tea by steeping the tea bags in boiling water for 5 minutes. Mix the tea, juices, and sugar syrup and refrigerate in quart jars. For each quart of the tea mixture, use a liter of ginger ale, and pour over a large chunk of ice in a punch bowl. Serve.

cook's notes

- If you're making a full batch, you'll need a truly large bowl to mix the punch. Make half a recipe or even a quarter of a recipe if you don't have a crowd coming.
- The base of the punch will keep for 2 or 3 days in the refrigerator.

SOURCE: Jesse McKinley in the *New York Times*
COOK: Aisha Sharpe

red wine caipirinha

IT TOOK US A LONG TIME TO ACTUALLY TRY THIS RECIPE — after all, what red wine is improved by adding sugar? But now we expect to serve this wonderfully cooling drink at many a summer party.

By comparison, sangria seems like heavily sugared soda. This drink is incredibly simple — no floating fruit and not much alcohol. The sugar disappears, and the main impression you have is tartness, from the lime. Very cool.

serves 1

2 teaspoons sugar
¹/₂ lime, cut into 4 wedges

3 ounces red wine, preferably Rioja, or another medium- to full-bodied red

In a highball glass, muddle the sugar and lime wedges. Fill the glass with ice cubes. Pour the wine into the glass, stir well, and serve.

cook's note

Muddle? If you didn't grow up in the cocktail era, you may not have a muddler — a glass rod for crushing sugar and fruit. The handle of a wooden spoon works fine.

SOURCE: *Saveur*
COOK: *Saveur* staff

tequila salty dog

THE MARGARITA HOLDS THE CROWN as America's most beloved cocktail. We'll drink to that. But sometimes it's good to be a little more adventurous.

Mix some fresh red grapefruit juice with some excellent tequila and you've got a terrifically refreshing, not-sweet drink that's perfect for brunch or a lazy afternoon.

serves 1

1 lime wedge
Coarse salt
1½ ounces tequila (see note)

Squeeze of lime juice
Juice of 1 red grapefruit

Rub the lime wedge around the rim of a tall glass, then dip the rim in coarse salt. Fill the glass one third full of ice. Add the tequila and a squeeze of lime juice, then fill with the grapefruit juice, stir, and serve.

cook's notes

- For mixing, we use Jose Cuervo Tradicional tequila. It's a reposado (the grade below añejo, which is for sipping straight) and reasonably priced.
- Many people consider Texas red grapefruit the best in the country. Grab it if you see it.
- We liked this drink strained of the pulp.

SOURCE: Toby Cecchini in the *New York Times*
COOK: Andrea Cecchini

gin and tonic

TOBY CECCHINI IS A VETERAN BARTENDER who, after fifteen years of tending bar, claims not to have been able to improve on his father's recipe for gin and tonics. There's nothing new in the ingredient list, but there's a lot more lime here than the standard wedge on the edge of the glass. Here, even the spent rinds get sliced up and added to the pitcher. The result is a very pulpy, brightly delicious summer drink.

You'll need a pitcher that can hold at least $2^1/_2$ quarts, and if you have a nice glass one, all the better. This drink is almost as delicious to look at as it is to sip. Other than that, the only thing you need is a breezy porch and nothing on the agenda.

serves 4

5 limes, at room temperature	Cracked ice
16 ounces gin	1 liter tonic water, chilled

Chill four highball glasses in the freezer.

Roll 4 of the limes on the cutting board one by one with the heel of your hand (this brings the aromatic citrus oil to the surface of the skin). Juice the 4 limes. Then slice the used rinds into thin strips.

Combine the gin and sliced lime rinds in a large pitcher and muddle for 2 minutes with a pestle (a blunt-ended rolling pin or a large wooden spoon also works). Add the lime juice and let stand for 5 minutes.

Fill the pitcher halfway with ice. Slowly add the tonic by pouring it, on a slant, down the side of the pitcher. Stir carefully so as not to knock all the fizz out of the tonic. Pour into the chilled glasses. Garnish with lime rounds cut from the remaining lime and serve.

cook's notes

- Look for large, plump limes — and keep them at room temperature so they'll be easier to juice.

- Tanqueray gin is a good choice here, but any good gin will do. We like Bombay, too.

- Cracked ice doesn't become slushy like crushed ice. The quickest way to make cracked ice is to hold a large ice cube in one hand and then thwack it with the back of a spoon.

- If 4 ounces of gin per serving is more than you want to handle, pour smaller drinks. Don't disrupt the proportions of the recipe.

SOURCE: Williams-Sonoma lemon press label
COOK: Unknown

lemon drop

BRIGHTLY COLORED ENAMELED MEXICAN citrus presses are one of our favorite gizmos to give to fellow cooks. The last time we bought one, we noticed this alluring recipe printed on the swing tag. A reconstructed margarita with vodka standing in for the tequila and lemon in place of the lime, it's a trendy bar drink that will get just about any evening off on the right foot. And since it takes nothing more than a few shakes of the cocktail shaker to put together, it's great for a spur-of-the-moment gathering or when you just want to enjoy a quiet drink alone at the end of a long day. Serve it straight up in a sugar-rimmed martini glass and you'll feel oh so chic.

serves 1

1 lemon wedge
Sugar
2 ounces vodka

1 ounce Triple Sec
Juice of $1/2$ lemon
Lemon slice

Rub the rim of a martini glass with the lemon wedge and dip the rim into sugar.

Fill a cocktail shaker two-thirds full of ice cubes. Add the vodka, Triple Sec, and lemon juice. Shake well. Stain into the prepared glass. Garnish with the lemon slice and serve.

cook's notes

- Upgrade this drink, if you like, by substituting Grand Marnier or Cointreau for the Triple Sec.
- If you prefer lemony drinks that make you pucker, skip the sugar around the rim and use only half as much Triple Sec.

SOURCE: *Hot Toddies* by Christopher B. O'Hara
COOK: Christopher B. O'Hara

coquito

EGGNOG MAY BE DE RIGUEUR AROUND THE HOLIDAYS, but who says it has to be boring? Here's a version from Puerto Rico that uses coconut milk in place of cream and rum instead of brandy.

The drink gets its name from coquito nuts, the kernels of a type of tropical palm. Resembling miniature coconuts, coquitos are terribly cute (and starting to appear in specialty markets). Word is they don't have much coconut flavor — but this holiday drink namesake sure does.

serves 8 to 10

8 cups unsweetened coconut milk
3/4 cup sugar
16 large egg yolks
1/4 cup pure vanilla extract

2 cups rum, preferably Captain Morgan's Spiced Rum
Ground cinnamon, for garnish

Heat the coconut milk in a large saucepan until steaming but not boiling. Stir in the sugar until it dissolves. Beat the egg yolks and vanilla in a large bowl until thick and smooth, about 3 minutes. Stir in the rum. Slowly add the yolk mixture to the steaming coconut milk, stirring constantly. Be careful never to let the mixture boil, or it will curdle. When it is completely mixed, remove from the heat and let cool. Place in a sealed container in the refrigerator until cold. Serve well chilled with cinnamon sprinkled on top.

cook's notes

- We've also made this with unspiced rum and liked it very much.
- This nog tastes best well chilled. (Laying a sheet of plastic wrap on the surface as it chills will help prevent a skin from forming.)
- If the nog is at all lumpy or grainy, pour it through a strainer before serving.

credits

Cheese Snips from *Potluck at Midnight Farm,* by Tamara Weiss. Copyright © 2002 by Tamara Weiss. Used by permission of Clarkson Potter Publishers, a division of Random House, Inc.

Garlicky Potato Chips by Lorna Wing. Copyright © 2002 by Lorna Wing. First published in *Party! Food: Essential Guide to Menus, Drinks, and Planning.* Reprinted by permission of Bay/SOMA Publishing.

Curried Chili Cashews by Sally Sampson. Copyright © 2002 by Sally Sampson. First published in *Party Nuts!* Reprinted by permission of Harvard Common Press.

Bourbon Pecans by Regina Schrambling. Copyright © 2002 by the *Los Angeles Times.* Reprinted by permission of the Los Angeles Times Syndicate.

Olive Butter by Brooke Williamson. Copyright © 2002 by Brooke Williamson. First published in *Saveur.* Reprinted by permission of Brooke Williamson.

Chopped Olive Spread from *The Jimtown Store Cookbook: Recipes from Sonoma County's Favorite Country Store,* by Carrie Brown, John Werner, and Michael McLaughlin. Copyright © 2002 by Carrie Brown, John Werner, and Michael McLaughlin. Re-

printed by permission of HarperCollins Publishers, Inc.

Salsa-Baked Goat Cheese by Rick Bayless. Copyright © 2002 by Rick Bayless. First published in *El Mundo de Frontera* newsletter. Reprinted by permission of Rick Bayless.

Crabby Cheese Puffs Copyright © 2002 by About.com. First published on www .about.com.

BLB's Mini BLTs by Bonnie Lee Black. Copyright © 2002 by Jeffrey Steingarten. Reprinted by permission of Jeffrey Steingarten.

Smoked Salmon Rolls with Arugula, Mascarpone, Chives, and Capers from *In the Hands of a Chef,* by Jody Adams and Ken Rivard. Copyright © 2002 by Jody Adams and Ken Rivard. Reprinted by permission of HarperCollins Publishers, Inc., William Morrow.

Antipasto Roasted Red Peppers with Anchovies and Bread Crumbs from *Patsy's Cookbook,* by Sal J. Scognamillo. Copyright © 2002 by J.F.S. Enterprises, LLC. Used by permission of Clarkson Potter Publishers, a division of Random House, Inc.

Tip for Ktpiti (Spicy Feta and Red Pepper Dip) from *Modern Greek,* by Andy Harris, photographs by William Meppem. Copyright © 2002. Used with permission of Chronicle Books LLC. Visit www.chroniclebooks.com.

Italian Leek Tart (Porrata) by Cesare Casella. Copyright © 2002 by Cesare Casella. First published in the James Beard House newsletter. Reprinted by permission of Cesare Casella.

Seared Scallops with Crème Fraîche and Caviar by Cynthia Callahan. Copyright © 2002 by Bellwether Farms. First published on a Bellwether Farms crème fraîche package. Reprinted by permission of Bellwether Farms.

Escarole and Little Meatball Soup (Minestra) from *The Sopranos Family Cookbook*, by Allen Rucker and Michele Scicolone. Copyright © 2002 by Warner Books, Inc. Reprinted by permission of Warner Books, Inc.

Garlic Soup with Ham and Sage Butter from *Between Bites*, by James Villas. Copyright © 2002 by James Villas. Used by permission of John Wiley & Sons, Inc.

Elwood's Ham Chowder by Elwood and Donald Barickman. Copyright © 2002 by Elwood and Donald Barickman. First published on page 258 of the November 2002 issue of *Martha Stewart Living*. Reprinted by permission of Donald Barickman.

Pumpkin Chowder by Cheryl Slocum. Copyright © 2002 by *Country Living*. First published in *Country Living*. Reprinted by permission of *Country Living*.

Lentil and Swiss Chard Soup by Tasha Prysi. Copyright © 2002 by Tasha Prysi. First published in *Food & Wine*. Reprinted by permission of Tasha Prysi.

Broccoli-Leek Soup with Lemon-Chive Cream by Diane Rossen Worthington. Copyright © 2002 by Diane Rossen Worthington. First published in *Food & Wine*. Reprinted by permission of Diane Rossen Worthington.

Quick Asian Noodle Soup with Lemongrass and Mushrooms from *Appetite*, by Nigel Slater. Copyright © 2000 by Nigel Slater. Photographs by Jonathan Lovekin. Used by permission of Clarkson Potter Publishers, a division of Random House, Inc.

Tortilla Soup with Chicken and Avocado by Martha Holmberg. Copyright © 2002 by Martha Holmberg. First published in *Fine Cooking*. Reprinted by permission of Martha Holmberg.

Tip for Cheater's Chicken Stock from *Michael Chiarello's Casual Cooking*, by Michael Chiarello with Janet Fletcher, photographs by Deborah Jones. Copyright © 2002 by NapaStyle, Inc. Used with permission of Chronicle Books LLC. Visit www.chroniclebooks.com.

French Bread and Shallot Soup Reprinted with permission from *When French Women Cook*, by Madeleine Kamman. Copyright © 2002 by Madeleine Kamman, Ten Speed Press, Berkeley, Calif. Available from your local bookseller, by calling Ten Speed Press at 800-841-2665, or by visiting us on-line at www.tenspeed.com.

Cream of Grilled Tomato Soup by Eric Villegas. Copyright © 2002 by Eric Villegas. First published on the Restaurant Villegas Web site, www.restaurantvillegas.com. Reprinted by permission of Eric Villegas.

Tomato-Bread Soup (Pappa al Pomodoro) by Matt Colgan. Copyright © 2002 by the *San Francisco Chronicle*. Reproduced with permission of the *San Francisco Chronicle*, in trade book format, via the Copyright Clearance Center.

Blender Gazpacho from *My Kitchen in Spain:*

225 Authentic Regional Recipes, by Janet Mendel. Copyright © 2002 by Janet Mendel. Reprinted by permission of HarperCollins Publishers, Inc.

Lime-Cucumber Soup with a Kick by Patricia Solley. Copyright © 2002 by Patricia Solley. First published in the *Washington Post.* Reprinted by permission of Patricia Solley.

The Wedge from *Desperation Entertaining,* by Beverly Mills and Alicia Ross. Copyright © 2002 by Beverly Mills and Alicia Ross. Used by permission of Workman Publishing Company, Inc., New York. All rights reserved.

Grilled Onion Salad by Vincent Scotto. Copyright © 2002 by Vincent Scotto. First published in the *New York Times Magazine.* Reprinted by permission of Vincent Scotto.

St. John's Parsley and Onion Salad by Fergus Henderson. Copyright © 2002 by Jeremiah Tower. First published in *Jeremiah Tower Cooks,* published by Stewart, Tabori & Chang. Reprinted by permission of IMG Literary.

Salade Russe by Michael Wild. Copyright © 2002 by Michael Wild. First published in the *San Francisco Chronicle.* Reprinted by permission of Michael Wild.

Tip for Cucumber Salad with Cream Sauce Reprinted with permission from *The French Menu Cookbook,* by Richard Olney. Copyright © 2002 by Richard Olney, Ten Speed Press, Berkeley, Calif. Available from your local bookseller, by calling Ten Speed Press at 800-841-2665, or by visiting us on-line at www.tenspeed.com.

Raspberry, Avocado, and Watercress Platter Reprinted with permission from *Complete Vegetarian Cookbook,* by Charmaine Solomon. Copyright © 2002 by Charmaine Solomon, Ten Speed Press, Berkeley, Calif. Available from your local bookseller, by calling Ten Speed Press at 800-841-2665, or by visiting us on-line at www.tenspeed.com.

Moroccan Carrot Salad with Cumin by Simy Danana, from *Saffron Shores,* by Joyce Goldstein, photographs by Leigh Beisch. Copyright © 2002. Used with permission of Chronicle Books LLC. Visit www.chroniclebooks.com.

Shepherd's Salad with Bulgarian Feta by David Rosengarten. Copyright © 2002 by David Rosengarten. First published in *The Rosengarten Report.* Reprinted by permission of David Rosengarten.

Green Bean Salad with Olives, Goat Cheese, and Basil Vinaigrette by Tara Duggan. Copyright © 2002 by the *San Francisco Chronicle.* Reproduced with permission of the *San Francisco Chronicle,* in trade book format, via the Copyright Clearance Center.

Tip for Goat Cheese Balls by Daniel Boulud. Copyright © 2002 by Daniel Boulud. First published in *Chef Daniel Boulud: Cooking in New York City,* Assouline Publishing, Inc.

Zucchini, Corn, and Tomato Salad by Gina Marie Miraglia. Copyright © 2002 by Condé Nast Publications, Inc. First published in *Gourmet.* Reprinted by permission of *Gourmet.*

Zucchini Salad with Lemon and Mint by John Ash. Copyright © 2002 by *Delicious Living.* First published in *Delicious Living.* Reprinted by permission of Penton Media.

Italian-Style Tuna Salad with Green Beans, Potatoes, and Red Onion by David Pasternack.

Baked Pasta with Sausage and Tomato Pesto from *Seriously Simple,* by Diane Rossen Worthington, photographs by Noel Barnhurst. Copyright © 2002. Used with permission of Chronicle Books LLC. Visit www.chroniclebooks.com.

Southwest King Ranch Casserole from *The Whole Foods Market Cookbook,* by Steve Petusevsky and Whole Foods Market Team Members. Copyright © 2002 by Whole Foods Market Services, Inc. Used by permission of Clarkson Potter Publishers, a division of Random House, Inc.

Spicy Baked Rice by Claudia M. Caruana. Copyright © 2002 by Claudia M. Caruana. First published in *Chile Pepper.* Reprinted by permission of Claudia M. Caruana.

Scrambled Eggs, Long-Cooked Broccoli, and Feta Cheese Sandwich from *Nancy Silverton's Sandwich Book,* by Nancy Silverton with Teri Gelber. Copyright © 2002 by Nancy Silverton, photographs copyright © 2002 by Amy Neunsinger. Used by permission of Alfred A. Knopf, a division of Random House, Inc.

Convent Chicken Reprinted with permission from *The Convent Cook,* by Maria Tisdall. Copyright © 2002 by Maria Tisdall, Ten Speed Press, Berkeley, Calif. Available from your local bookseller, by calling Ten Speed Press at 800-841-2665, or by visiting us on-line at www.tenspeed.com.

Braised Chicken with Prunes by Amanda Hesser. Copyright © 2002 by the New York Times Company. First published in the *New York Times.* Reprinted with permission.

Roasted Turkey with Herbs by Bobby Flay. Copyright © 2002 by Bobby Flay. First published in *Newsweek.* Reprinted by permission of Bobby Flay.

Tip for Leftover Turkey Salad by Judy Rodgers. Copyright © 2002 by Judy Rodgers. First broadcast on *NPR News.* Reprinted by permission of Judy Rodgers.

Lady Bird Johnson's Barbecue Sauce by Lady Bird Johnson. From *Legends of Texas Barbecue Cookbook,* by Robb Walsh. Copyright © 2002. Used with permission of Chronicle Books LLC. Visit www.chroniclebooks.com.

Oven-Roasted Ribs by Pam Anderson. Copyright © 2002 by Pam Anderson. First published in *CookSmart.* Reprinted by permission of Houghton Mifflin Company.

Pork Chops Milanese with Arugula and Cherry Tomatoes from *The Babbo Cookbook,* by Mario Batali. Copyright © 2002 by Mario Batali, photographs copyright © 2002 by Christopher Hirsheimer. Used by permission of Clarkson Potter Publishers, a division of Random House, Inc.

Roasted Fresh Ham with Salsa Verde by Ben and Karen Barker. From *The Pleasures of Slow Food,* by Corby Kummer. Copyright © 2002. Used with permission of Chronicle Books LLC. Visit www.chroniclebooks.com.

Best-Ever Grilled Asian Beef Reprinted with permission from *Fast Entrées,* by Hugh Carpenter and Teri Sandison. Copyright © 2002 by Hugh Carpenter and Teri Sandison, Ten Speed Press, Berkeley, Calif. Available from your local bookseller, by calling Ten Speed Press at 800-841-2665, or by visiting us on-line at www.tenspeed.com.

Porcini-Crusted Filet Mignon with Wilted Arugula from *Welcome to My Kitchen,* by Tom Valenti and Andrew Friedman. Copyright © 2002 by Tom Valenti and Andrew Friedman. Reprinted by permission of HarperCollins Publishers, Inc.

Chili for a Crowd (first published as Chile Con

Carne and Lumpy Guacamole) by Martha Stewart Living Omnimedia, Inc. Copyright © 2002 by Martha Stewart Living Omnimedia, Inc. Published on page 124 of the January 2002 issue of *Martha Stewart Living*. Reprinted by permission of Martha Stewart Living Omnimedia, Inc.

Pomegranate-Braised Brisket with Onion Confit from *The Gefilte Variations,* by Jayne Cohen. Copyright © 2000 by Jayne Cohen. Reprinted with the permission of Scribner, an imprint of Simon & Schuster Adult Publishing Group.

Apulian Lamb and Fennel Stew Copyright © 2002 by Clifford A. Wright. First published in *Real Stew*. Reprinted by permission of Harvard Common Press.

Rosemary-Scallion–Crusted Rack of Lamb from *Sara Moulton Cooks at Home,* by Sara Moulton; photography by Elizabeth Watt, recipes developed with Charles Pierce; wine advice by Michael Green. Copyright © 2002 by Sara Moulton. Used by permission of Broadway Books, a division of Random House, Inc.

Sautéed Shrimp with Chipotle Chiles by Zarela Martínez. Copyright © 2002 by Zarela Martínez. First published in *Zarela's Veracruz*. Reprinted by permission of Houghton Mifflin Company.

Chili Shrimp and Coconut Rice by Kay Chun. Copyright © 2002 by *Real Simple*. First published in *Real Simple*. Reprinted by permission.

Grilled Garlic-and-Pepper Shrimp with Kumquats from *Asian Grilling by Su-Mei Yu.* Copyright © 2002 by Su-Mei Yu. Reprinted by permission of HarperCollins, Inc., William Morrow.

Grilled Shrimp with Prosciutto, Rosemary, and Garlic by Maurizio Paparo. Copyright © 2002 by Maurizio Paparo. First published

on www.oregonlive.com. Reprinted by permission of Maurizio Paparo.

Smoky Shrimp and Halibut Stew by Bruce Aidells. Copyright © 2002 by Bruce Aidells. First published in *Bon Appétit*. Reprinted by permission of Bruce Aidells.

Scrambled Eggs with Scallops and Bacon by Jason Epstein. Copyright © 2002 by Jason Epstein. First published in the *New York Times Magazine*. Reprinted by permission of Jason Epstein.

Mussels with Smoky Bacon, Lime, and Cilantro by Michael Romano. Copyright © 2002 by Michael Romano. First published in *Food & Wine*. Reprinted by permission of Michael Romano.

Pan-Fried Fresh Salmon Cakes by the editors of *Cook's Illustrated*. Copyright © 2002 by Boston Common Press. First published in *American Classics*. Reprinted by permission of Boston Common Press.

Caramel-Braised Cod by Kim Landi. Copyright © 2002 by Kim Landi. First published in *Fine Cooking*. Reprinted by permission of Kim Landi.

Green Beans with Lemon and Mint from *Lemon Zest,* by Lori Longbotham. Copyright © 2002 by Lori Longbotham. Used by permission of Broadway Books, a division of Random House, Inc.

Zucchini with Cilantro and Cream by Helene Wagner-Popoff. Copyright © 2002 by Condé Nast Publications, Inc. Originally published in *Bon Appétit*. Reprinted by permission.

Chard with Ginger by Niloufer Ichaporia King. Copyright © 2002 by Niloufer Ichaporia King. First published in a cooking class handout for The Gardener, Healdsburg, Calif. Reprinted by permission of Niloufer Ichaporia King.

Greens with Garlicky Toasted Bread Crumbs (Pancotto) by Faith Willinger after Bernardino Lombardo. Copyright © 2002 by Faith Willinger. First published on www.faithwillinger.com. Reprinted by permission of Faith Willinger.

Fennel-Roasted Vegetables from *Michael Chiarello's Casual Cooking,* by Michael Chiarello with Janet Fletcher, photographs by Deborah Jones. Copyright © 2002 by NapaStyle, Inc. Used with permission of Chronicle Books LLC. Visit www.chroniclebooks.com.

Brussels Sprouts Puree by Julia Reed. Copyright © 2002 by Julia Reed. First published in the *New York Times Magazine.* Reprinted by permission of the Wylie Agency for Julia Reed.

Spiced Braised Red Cabbage by Marcus Samuelsson. Copyright © 2002 by Marcus Samuelsson. First published in the Aquavit newsletter. Reprinted by permission of Marcus Samuelsson.

Turnip Flapjacks by Kerri Conan. Copyright © 2002 by Weldon Owen Publishing. First published in *Savoring America: Recipes and Reflections on American Cooking* (Williams-Sonoma, The Savoring Series). Reprinted by permission of Weldon Owen Publishing.

Tip for Turnip Fries by the staff of *Saveur,* after Deborah Madison. Copyright © 2002 by *Saveur.* First published in *Saveur.* Reprinted by permission.

Garlicky Smashed Potatoes and Greens from *Make It Italian,* by Nancy Verde Barr. Copyright © 2002 by Nancy Verde Barr. Used by permission of Alfred A. Knopf, a division of Random House, Inc.

Greek-Style Potatoes with Olives and Feta by Adam Reid and Meg Suzuki. Copyright © 2002 by Boston Common Press.

First published in *Cook's Illustrated.* Reprinted by permission of Boston Common Press.

Sweet Potatoes with Ginger and Apple Cider by Rozanne Gold. Copyright © 2002 by Rozanne Gold. First published in *Bon Appétit.* Reprinted by permission of Rozanne Gold.

Roasted Portobello and Potato Gratin by Eric Ripert. Copyright © 2002 by Eric Ripert. First published in the *New York Times.* Reprinted by permission of Eric Ripert.

Corn Pudding with Basil and Cheddar from *Barefoot Contessa Family Style,* by Ina Garten. Copyright © 2002 by Ina Garten, photographs copyright © 2002 by Maura McEvoy. Used by permission of Clarkson Potter Publishers, a division of Random House, Inc.

Quick, Soft, Sexy Grits by Jan Birnbaum. Copyright © 2002 by Jan Birnbaum. First published in *Food & Wine.* Reprinted by permission of Jan Birnbaum.

Orange-Raisin Couscous with Almonds and Parsley from *Let the Flames Begin: Tips, Techniques, and Recipes for Real Live Fire Cooking,* by Chris Schlesinger and John Willoughby. Copyright © 2002 by Chris Schlesinger and John Willoughby. Used by permission of W. W. Norton & Company, Inc.

Texas Rice by Abby Mandel. Copyright © 2002 by the *Los Angeles Times.* Reprinted by permission of the Los Angeles Times Syndicate.

Minted Fried Rice from *Martin Yan's Chinatown Cooking,* by Martin Yan. Copyright © 2002 by Martin Yan. Reprinted by permission of HarperCollins Publishers, Inc., William Morrow.

Apricot and Pistachio Baked Rice by Katy Massam. Copyright © 2002 by Condé Nast

Publications, Inc. First published in *Gourmet*. Reprinted by permission of *Gourmet*.

Cumin-Scented Barley by Karen MacNeil. Copyright © 2002 by Karen MacNeil. First published in the *New York Times Magazine*. Reprinted by permission of Karen MacNeil.

Instant Black Beans by Angela Pontual. Copyright © 2002 by Angela Pontual. First published in the *New York Times*. Reprinted by permission of Angela Pontual.

New Orleans Red Beans by Frank Brigtsen. Copyright © 2002 by Frank Brigtsen. First published in *Food & Wine*. Reprinted by permission of Frank Brigtsen.

Giant Popover with Wild Mushrooms from *Local Flavors: Cooking and Eating from America's Farmers' Markets*, by Deborah Madison. Copyright © 2002 by Deborah Madison. Used by permission of Broadway Books, a division of Random House, Inc.

Bread Stuffing with Fennel and Swiss Chard by Suzanne Goin. Copyright © 2002 by Suzanne Goin. First published in the *Los Angeles Times*. Reprinted by permission of Suzanne Goin.

Kumquat and Cranberry Compote by Lori W. Powell. Copyright © 2002 by Condé Nast Publications, Inc. First published in *Gourmet*. Reprinted by permission of *Gourmet*.

Buttermilk and Cream Biscuits by Debbie Putnam. From *Everything Tastes Better with Bacon*, by Sara Perry, photographs by Sheri Giblin, © 2002. Used with permission of Chronicle Books LLC. Visit www.chroniclebooks.com.

Slow-Rising Pumpkin-Thyme Dinner Rolls by Regina Schrambling. Copyright © 2002 by the *Los Angeles Times*. Reprinted by permission of the Los Angeles Times Syndicate.

Bay Leaf–Scented Spoon Rolls by Mary Thomas. Copyright © 2002 by Mary Thomas. First published in *Food & Wine*. Reprinted by permission of Mary Thomas.

Pumpkin-Oat Muffins by Maury Rubin. Copyright © 2002 by Maury Rubin. First published in *Rosie Magazine*. Reprinted by permission of Maury Rubin.

Coconut Bread by Bill Granger. Copyright © 2002 by Bill Granger. First published in *Sydney Food*, Murdoch Books. Reprinted by permission of Bill Granger.

Lemon Bread Copyright © 2002 by Silver Rose Resort Winery. First published in *Good Housekeeping*. Reprinted by permission of Silver Rose Resort Winery.

Irish Soda Bread with Raisins and Caraway by Patrice Bedrosian, after Julie Lestrange. Copyright © 2002 by Condé Nast Publications, Inc. Originally published in *Bon Appétit*. Reprinted by permission of Condé Nast Publications, Inc. and Patrice Bedrosian.

Sweet Potato Bread with Cranberries, Currants, and Pecans by Kathleen Daelemans. Copyright © 2002 by Kathleen Daelemans. First published in *Cooking Thin with Chef Kathleen*. Reprinted by permission of Houghton Mifflin Company.

Izzy's Authentic Bagels by Izzy Cohen. Copyright © 2002 by Izzy Cohen. First published in *Judy Zeidler's International Deli Cookbook*, by Judy Zeidler. Reprinted by permission of Judy Zeidler.

Rancho Bernardo Inn's Walnut Bread by Cindy Dorn. Copyright © 2002 by the *Los Angeles Times*. Reprinted by permission of the Los Angeles Times Syndicate.

Lemon Posset by James O'Shea. Copyright ©

2002 by James O'Shea. Reprinted by permission.

Carolina's Ricotta Berry Pudding by Carolina Barbieri. Copyright © 2002 by Carolina Barbieri. First published in the *New York Times*. Reprinted by permission of Carolina Barbieri.

Cardamom-Scented Orange Salad and Honey Yogurt from *Fresh & Healthy*, by Sally James. Copyright © 2002 by Sally James. Reprinted by permission of Media 21 Publishing.

Bitter Orange Ice Cream from *Nigella Bites*, by Nigella Lawson. Copyright © 2002. Reprinted by permission of Hyperion.

Creamy Caramel Sauce by Peggy Cullen. Copyright © 2002 by Peggy Cullen. First published in *Food & Wine*. Reprinted by permission of Peggy Cullen.

Decadent Hazelnut-Chocolate Pudding from *Rustico*, by Micol Negrin. Copyright © 2002 by Micol Negrin. Used by permission of Clarkson Potter Publishers, a division of Random House, Inc.

Sticky Toffee Pudding with Chocolate Chips and Toffee Sauce by Andrew Blake. Copyright © 2002 by Andrew Blake.

Sweet Potato Bread Pudding with Praline Sauce by Marcia Ball. Copyright © 2002 by Marcia Ball. First published in *Saveur*. Reprinted by permission of Marcia Ball.

Scotch-a-Roos by Rick Fox. Copyright © 2002 by Rick Fox. First published in the *New York Times*. Reprinted by permission of Rick Fox.

Oatmeal Coconut Raspberry Bars by Alexis Touchet. Copyright © 2002 by Condé Nast Publications, Inc. First published in *Gourmet*. Reprinted by permission of *Gourmet*.

Chocolate–Chocolate Chip Cookies by Pierre Hermé. Copyright © 2002 by Pierre Hermé. First published in *Food & Wine*. Reprinted by permission of Pierre Hermé.

Pistachio-Orange Lace Cookies by Melissa Roberts-Matar. Copyright © 2002 by Condé Nast Publications. All rights reserved. Originally published in *Gourmet*. Reprinted by permission.

Soft and Chewy Molasses-Spice Cookies by Dawn Yanagihara. Copyright © 2002 by Boston Common Press. First published in *Cook's Illustrated*. Reprinted by permission of Boston Common Press.

Glazed Gingerbread Tiles by Liz Prueitt. Copyright © 2002 by Liz Prueitt. First published in *San Francisco Magazine*. Reprinted by permission of Liz Prueitt.

Grandmother's Creamy Chocolate Cake by Robert Linxe. From *Paris Sweets: Great Desserts from the City's Best Pastry Shops*, by Dorie Greenspan, illustrations by Florine Asch. Copyright © 2002 by Dorie Greenspan. Used by permission of Broadway Books, a division of Random House, Inc.

Lemon Pudding Cake by Sharon Hage. Copyright © 2002 by Sharon Hage. First published on the *Texas Monthly* Web site. Reprinted by permission of Sharon Hage.

Maple Sugar Cake by Claudia Fleming. Copyright © 2002 by Claudia Fleming. First published in *Bon Appétit*. Reprinted by permission of Claudia Fleming.

Gingerbread-Cider Cake by Cynthia Blain. Copyright © 2002 by Cynthia Blain. First published in the *Boston Herald*. Reprinted by permission of Cynthia Blain.

Cornmeal Cupcakes with Pecan Frosting by Emily Luchetti. Copyright © 2002 by Emily Luchetti. First published in

index

index